THE ART OF
READING PEOPLE

First published in 2016 by:
Disquiet Dog Publishing
51 Bruce Avenue
Worthing
West Sussex
BN11 5LA
United Kingdom
www.disquietdog.com
info@disquietdog.com

Ordering Information:

Quantity sales. Special discounts are available on quantity purchases by corporations, associations, and others. For details, contact the publisher at the address above.

Designations used by companies to distinguish their products are often claimed as trademarks. All brand names, product names and trademarks used in this book are the property of their respective owners, adn the sue of such trademarks does not imply any affiliation with or endorsement of this book by such owners. Although every reasonable precaution has been taken in the preparation of this book, the publisher and author assume no responsibility for errors or omissions. Neither is any liability assumed for damages resulting from the use of information contained herein. If professional advice or other expert assistance is required, the services of a competent professional should be sought.

British Library Cataloguing in Publications Data

A CIP catalogue record for this book is available from the British Library

ISBN 978-0-9935111-0-3

Printed and bound in the United Kingdom by TJ International Ltd, Padstow, Cornwall

THE ART OF
READING PEOPLE

JOHN CREMER

Jovial · Lunar · venus · MARS · SATURN · Mercury

Gain instant insight into the hardware of human beings

Disquiet Dog
PUBLISHING

To James Westly, friend, mentor and teacher of presence, for opening the door.

Contents

How to Read This Book 11

Prologue 13

Introduction 17

CHAPTER 1:   The Mind...20

CHAPTER 2:   The Heart...22

CHAPTER 3:   The System...24

CHAPTER 4:   The Concept of Types.........................26

CHAPTER 5:   The Template.......................................29

                           Core attributes 29

                           Relationship to rules..............................30

                           Behaviour at social events......................31

                           Ideal or typical occupations...................31

                           Famous and historic examples 32

                           Personal stories....................................32

                           Types, race and culture..........................33

CHAPTER 6:   The Types 34

                           The Circle of Types 34

                           Mars...39

                           Jovial 61

                           Lunar 81

                           Venus 99

Mercury 119

Saturn 139

CHAPTER 7:   Combined Types...157

Mars-Jovial...158

Jovial-Lunar 163

Lunar-Venus 169

Venus-Mercury 174

Mercury-Saturn 179

Saturn-Mars...185

CHAPTER 8:   Solar 195

CHAPTER 9:   The Chemistry between types 214

I'm a Mars: how do I get on with…?...216

I'm a Jovial: how do I get on with…?...220

I'm a Lunar: how do I get on with…?...224

I'm a Venus: how do I get on with…?...229

I'm a Saturn: how do I get on with…?...234

CHAPTER 10:   Frequently Asked Questions...244

CHAPTER 11:   Reports from Early Adopters..251

CHAPTER 12:   In Conclusion 259

References...261

Illustrations...261

How to Read This Book

To gain maximum value from this material requires a specific discipline which is rarely practised these days – that is the suspension of both disbelief and belief. Take nothing here on trust and at the same time don't automatically reject these ideas because they are unusual. Try to spend a bit of time on a mental tightrope between those two positions and verify everything for yourself. It may be well worth the effort.

There are essentially two streams to this book – the fast stream and the deep stream – feel free to choose the one that most suits your style.

The fast stream

If you simply want to cut to the chase and start using this system immediately, this is the stream for you. Here is the bare minimum amount of information that you need to get you going. It is even laid out as soundbites.

- There are six basic models of human vehicle aka types.

- By observing physical characteristics we can figure out a person's type.

- When we know someone's type we know something about their 'hardware'.

- 'Hardware' is deeply embedded in us it and influences our preferred speed of operation, our innate likes and dislikes and also which types we tend to get along with.

- We all have a default setting in our hardware which influences how we react when we are under stress.

- This default is our greatest strength when used wisely and our greatest weakness when it takes possession of us.

- When we know our own type we can make more conscious choices about our actions.

- Our conscious choices result in increased happiness and success.

- This system is ancient, but you probably don't care about that.

Have you read the above? Then take a massive short cut and skip the Introduction and the first five chapters. Then, at the beginning of each chapter on the types, jump straight ahead to 'Physicality'.

You can also skip everything in italics! These are just relevant quotes and personal stories.

Have fun.

The deep stream

This is for those who like to take a calmer approach and explore at a more leisurely pace. This book is laid out to provide context and background for the system and plenty of historical and current examples of types. There is a methodical assembly of the structure and its various permutations and interactions. You will also find interviews and personal stories to add flesh to the bones of the structure.

It is hoped you will find an embarrassment of riches which will increase your desire to learn more and apply the insights that you gather in your everyday life. So take the time to savour this unusual feast of provocative yet practical ideas. Make notes, discuss, reflect, research and feel free to offer your own discoveries and connections by emailing me here: john@readingpeople.biz.

Make sure you get your money's worth. I probably know what type you are.

Prologue

Scottsdale, Arizona, USA 1987: I am sitting outside a café with a remarkable man named James Westly. Earlier that day he had given a presentation to a small gathering about how to recognise different types of people by observing their physical characteristics. This information had resonated deep within me. Since the age of six, I had been keenly aware of my need to understand humanity and our role on planet Earth. This quest had alternately slumbered and awakened throughout my life, like an itch that I just could not scratch. I had been drawn to read and explore all manner of esoteric teachings and had attended numerous intensive personal development trainings. These experiences had provided glimpses of the possibility of living a more purposeful life, but the changes they brought had always been short lived and temporary. The system James had laid out on a flip chart in his living room was still abstract and brand new to me. I had not yet begun to realise the depth and potency that the system held and the potential it offered to help me to understand myself and other people. Nonetheless, I sensed I had come into contact with something of real meaning and lasting value.

As we sat together outside the cafe after his presentation, I felt James recognise that something beyond idle curiosity was at work within me. He began to take the learning one crucial step further. He said, almost casually, "Look at that man over there; what is his type?"

I saw a stocky middle-aged fellow with thinning reddish hair, sunburned skin, beer belly, bandy legs and piercing blue eyes striding along purposefully with a stance and demeanour not unlike a bulldog.

I pondered, recalled the presentation and replied, "Well, red hair, robust build, ruddy complexion and blue eyes all suggest a Mars type." James nodded sagely and probed further, "Which side of Mars is he?"

I could see that our 'specimen' was carrying a bit of weight around his belly. He was sweating in the Arizona heat and he was balding. "Well, he's not bony, so I would say Jovial." James allowed the flicker of a smile to cross his face. "Yes, he's a Mars-Jovial type, bull's-eye!"

At that moment the system came alive: an intriguing diagram on a flip chart with historical and mythological references was now embodied in a living breathing example before me. The scales fell from my eyes and I began to scan everyone around me as if I was seeing them for the first time. The only frame of reference I have since found for this seminal experience is the moment in the movie *The Matrix* when Morpheus says to Neo, "Welcome to the real world." I attended every single presentation of the system over the following seven years, each time learning a little more and finding ways to deepen my understanding of people using this extraordinary tool. I tracked every branch and source of the system that I could uncover and began to find correlations throughout historical and contemporary events. The seed had been planted and was taking root.

Bath, Somerset, England 2006: I am standing in front of a dozen chief executives in a board room. On a flip chart beside me is the diagram of the system. To say that I feel nervous would be an understatement – I am about to present this highly unusual material to a group of business leaders for the first time and the presentations that they typically see are focused on hard skills – bottom-line topics with clear real-world business applications. My inner critic is making me acutely aware that my presentation is not even at the 'soft skills' end of their frame of reference – my content is off the end of their scale and can only be filed under the heading 'downright bizarre!'

Fortunately, I have learned to manage my rather unpleasant inner critic. This was by way of a personal meltdown which caused simultaneous collapse in my physical, mental and financial circuits. I had returned to my native England and begun a new life which had one simple rule – I would only do what I truly loved to do. This led me to teaching and performing improvisation, founding an improvised comedy troupe and from there I blundered into teaching improvisation skills to business leaders. Once I had become established in my new career, I was asked if I had any material other than improvisation which would benefit CEOs, to which I recklessly replied "Well, actually there is this system…"

I took a deep breath and launched into the talk, remembering all I had learned from James, while leaning heavily on my improvisation training to keep the group engaged. There came a pivotal moment when I had described one of the types and then asked the group, "Who knows one of these types in their own life?" A delegate raised his hand and gave a pitch perfect description of one of his employees whom he had found difficult to communicate with. Everything lined up, from the physical characteristics, to the professional role he played and the way he reacted to stress. Several heads began to nod vigorously. He was clearly not alone in encountering this type. I was able to assure the delegate that, once he found his own type, we could explore the habitual misunderstandings that arise naturally between his own and his employee's types and find ways to create new avenues of communication. One of the solid benefits of applying this system is the means to depersonalise conflict by becoming aware of the types of the players involved. The situation shifts from "I don't get on with them" to "My type and their type tend to grate on each other." This gives us an invitation to move beyond making the other person wrong to a more objective position, where it is easier to find accord.

The session went so well that it was recommended to the whole network of CEO groups and I continued to refine the delivery and applications. The early version used newspaper cuttings to show famous examples of types and a diagram on rolled up flip chart, which I lugged around the country in a cardboard tube in a spirit of determined Luddism. The roots were now solid and the branches were spreading and leafing out.

Philadelphia, Pennsylvania, USA 2013: I have just come off stage after presenting a distilled 90-minute version of the system to 1,200 top financial advisors from around the world. The presentation was translated simultaneously into twelve languages. After describing each type, I had asked for audience volunteers to come onto the stage to be 'specimens' for the audience to view. There was much laughter and engagement and I was gratified to receive a standing ovation at the end. The diagram and imagery was projected onto giant screens – no more newspaper cuttings! By this time I have presented the system to a range of major clients, from banks to telecoms companies, high-ranking police officers, software designers and even the UN.

With the advent of internet access, the sort of obscure historical references to this system that could previously only be followed by trekking to Syria to view a temple frieze, or sneaking into the bedchambers at the Vatican to see a fresco, are now only a click away. I have been fortunate to engage with designers and artists who have pointed me towards rich sources of imagery and historical references that would otherwise have eluded me. People from every walk of life and profession have shared their stories with me on audio and video to deepen the learning for others. Business leaders and CEOs have told me tales of applying this system within their organisations to enrich their client relationships and support their teams in deepening rapport and collaboration. Therapists and teachers have told me the value of understanding the type of their clients and students in order to serve them better. This learning is now coming to fruition.

Meanwhile, back in Philadelphia, an intense fellow called Gary from New York has approached me at coffee break with a certain glint in his eye. I recognize this look. He tells me that he has been attending this annual conference for fifteen years and this is the first time that a presentation has resonated so deeply within him. Gary is overflowing with questions and is intrigued and curious. He wants to know more about his own type and the sources of the material, but most of all he wants to see if he can actually use it himself. I take a look around the room and say, "Look at that woman over there; what's her type?"

Introduction

We humans have been observing each other closely for many thousands of years and we have been highly motivated to do so. For the survival of individuals and of our species, it has been quite simply a matter of life and death to assess other people. Those who could read people more accurately and rapidly than others had a distinct advantage.

According to anthropologists, Homo sapiens has existed in its current form for more than 100,000 years. For over 90 per cent of this period we lived in small bands, typically in groups of a few dozen members of several extended families. When encountering another group of humans, the first concern would have been simply to calculate the relative numbers in each group as a matter of physical survival. At a purely physical level, being outnumbered is a red flag! The second concern would have been to sense the mood of the other group – were they friend or foe? Were they approachable or menacing? The third step would be to see what sort of people they were and to explore whether it would be possible to trade or share with them and, if so, how best to engage them.

One theory of the remarkable numerical expansion of the human species is that it was largely driven by our ability to collaborate – to pass on to other people effective strategies for survival and reproductive success – which was facilitated by our ability to distinguish between different kinds of people and then communicate with them in different ways. Despite the common perception that prehistoric life was, to borrow Thomas Hobbes' phrase, "nasty, brutish and short", archaeological studies and observations of the few remaining hunter-gatherer cultures strongly indicate that it took our distant ancestors around four hours' work a day to obtain a varied and wholesome diet and acquire the means of physical survival. The rest of their time could be spent in observation and exploration of the cosmos and the natural world. They would have had plenty of time to observe each other, with very few distractions. A person from 100,000 years ago would have pretty much the same intellectual and emotional abilities as you or I, and they inevitably sought to understand themselves and each other more deeply. The insights they gained were passed on to their own and other groups through ritual, song, art and storytelling. Before the use of the written word, this knowledge would be refined, adapted and embellished as it was transmitted.

With the development of agriculture, people settled in larger communities and organised more complex institutions. Throughout history, the store of human knowledge has continually evolved. Looking back we see definite peaks in the expression of this accumulated wisdom. As we do this, we may be baffled and even humbled by the achievements and motivations of the ancient Egyptians, Persians and Sumerians or the builders of the Gothic cathedrals.

Much of this accumulated wisdom has been hidden before us, in plain sight, for our whole lives. We are each, in more ways than we can understand, the products of our culture, of the time and circumstances of our life up to this moment. Our modern Western culture is a largely materialistic and scientific-based value system, in which technology is venerated and any sense of connection to the unseen or unproven is seen as a quaint relic of our uninformed 'primitive' past. It is easy to believe our own modern myths and to see ourselves as standing at the peak of human achievement. In doing so, we run the risk of cutting ourselves adrift from the profound knowledge that has been gathered, often at great cost, by those who have gone before us. From our technologically-advanced viewpoint, it is tempting to see our ancestors as somehow naïve or less informed. Yet, when we enquire more deeply, it is discomforting to observe that, while we can instantly access vast quantities of information, we often find it difficult to evaluate the quality of this knowledge. We seem to know 'the price of everything and the value of nothing'.

There are great possibilities in recognising that ancient peoples used different symbols to express concepts which can deeply affect and benefit our lives in the present moment. Universal truths are not affected by the passage of time; gravity acts today exactly as it did in Babylon in 4000BC. A modern businessman desires the latest Aston Martin with exactly the same passion as a Roman senator desired the finest chariot. The external trappings change; human nature and objective truth remain the same. In our era of globalisation and instant communication, we need our ancient wisdom more than ever. It is vital for us to understand ourselves and other cultures both quickly and at a deep level in order to be able to interact effectively.

The intention of this book is twofold. One aim is to provide you with an opportunity to see human beings differently for long enough to benefit from the concepts collected here. This is best achieved by neither blindly accepting nor reflexively rejecting these ideas out of hand. The second aim is to promote compassion and understanding for ourselves and others by recognising that certain fundamental parts of our nature are practically beyond our control. This concept is deeply offensive to some people, who see it as deterministic and limiting. Paradoxically, it is often by recognising our fixed tendencies that we gain access to more options. By catching a glimpse of our unconscious patterns we can become more awake. A sense of humour is tremendously helpful in this process: the less seriously we take ourselves, the more flexible and resilient we become. Habitual non-productive patterns of behaviour dissolve quite readily when exposed to the vibration of laughter.

So this book is an invitation to open the mind and heart. Let us examine each in turn.

CHAPTER 1: The Mind

If you are reading this book in English, it is highly likely that, no matter what your native culture, much of your thinking has a Western European structure. There is an insidious curse upon most modern thought, which is the veneration of duality: the act of dividing almost everything into pairs of opposites, such as Yes or No, Good or Bad, True or False, Democrat or Republican. This way of thinking is useful to a young child who is learning to navigate life's basic choices, but unfortunately it has become a large part of the foundation for our mental structure as adults. By falling into this trap, we may lose the ability to see the bigger or more subtle picture. It is as if some part of our mind feels threatened by a new concept until it can safely stuff it into an 'either this or that' file. The nefarious activities of these binary pairings contaminate and infantilise much of what passes for debate or discussion in our media. It is useful to be aware of this tendency when approaching the material in this book, as there may well be a mental programme running within you which is constantly asking, "Is this stuff true or false?"

> *It is the mark of an educated mind to be able to entertain a thought without subscribing to it.* Aristotle

In other words, can we resist the urge to rush to judgement and prematurely categorise new information? Ancient sages sought synthesis – finding connections in which elements of the cosmos reflect each other. In this system of Reading People, we seek to open our minds to connections that on the surface appear deeply illogical yet, with examination, have a curious resonance. By avoiding duality and sitting with the discomfort of not having black-and-white answers to some of the questions that arise from this material, something new can arise in our world view.

When approaching new knowledge, it is useful to avoid another pitfall of modern thinking, one created by a specific mental insecurity that has its roots in modern education. This is the fear we have around being caught red-handed without an answer. During our school days, when our teacher asked a question, we were expected to produce the correct answer immediately by rummaging around in an inner mental filing cabinet stuffed with facts. If we could do this quickly, we were rewarded; if not, we were shamed or punished.

So when we encounter new information, our drive towards binary divisions runs around trying to stuff it into an existing file without entertaining the possibility that it might not fit in any of our current files. In the Bible, this was referred to as pouring new wine into old bottles; contaminating new thought by filing it with old thought. For most people, this system of Reading People is brand new. Of course, there are many psychometric systems for understanding and assessing people, so despite our best efforts, the urge to stick this information in with something that we already know may prove overwhelming. If you are familiar with any other system of types, please be aware of this tendency within yourself!

CHAPTER 2: The Heart

We are drawn to understand our fellow humans and yet are constantly baffled in the process. Our enormous creative potential is continually squandered in wasteful pursuits at both personal and global levels. Through a lack of self-knowledge, we imagine ourselves to be simultaneously both greater and lesser than we truly are: greater, in that we believe that we act rationally from noble impulses, and lesser, in our blindness to our true qualities. We claim the glitter of second-hand dualistic beliefs as having true value and so never seek the real gold within. It is no wonder that we so often fail to understand other people. It is far easier to ascribe to others the shortcomings that we deny within ourselves. Having labelled those we don't comprehend as 'them', we withhold from them the compassion and understanding that we ourselves desire and perhaps, on occasion, demand.

Common to all faiths is the Golden Rule: treat others as you wish to be treated. The elegant simplicity of this idea resonates in all sensible human beings.

Upon examining ourselves and observing our own behaviour towards others, certain questions arise:

- How can I treat people as I would wish to be treated?
- At a more refined level – how can I treat people as *they* wish to be treated?
- How do I stop myself reacting to people in habitual ways?
- How do I employ the finer qualities within myself when reacting with other people?
- How do I evoke the finer qualities of others?

By taking on board the concepts of this system, we can come to understand some of the subliminal forces influencing human behaviour. By seeing our own engrained patterns and recognising how challenging it is to change them, we become more tolerant of other people's engrained patterns and take their actions less personally. Applying the knowledge of Reading People at home, professionally and internationally promotes harmony and respect and supports each of us in making our unique contributions to humanity.

A Sufi tale

You are in a boat on a river.

An empty boat floats downstream and bumps into your boat.

You carefully take this boat to the shore and tie it up safely,

So that the owner can find it and reclaim it.

Later, another boat, occupied, bumps into your boat.

You curse the occupier and call him names for his carelessness.

CHAPTER 3: The System

Central to the system of Reading People is this concept: the human body is a vehicle and each of us is operating our own vehicle, one of several models, in our journey through life on Earth. It is also possible to recognise different human models as distinctly as the different models of car that pass in traffic. There are six basic models and each one of us inhabits a vehicle that is a combination of two of these. Each model of vehicle is referred to as a type and has recognisable characteristics common to all vehicles of the same type. Once we know the type of our own vehicle, we become aware of ways to flourish in harmony with its capabilities. To know another's type means we can engage with that person more effectively. To judge or try to change one's type is pointless – we cannot change our own vehicle any more than a car can change its own tyre!

Simply allowing the information to be received as non-judgementally as possible brings a deeper sense of one's type. This changes the relationship between one's Self and the vehicle.

It helps at this point to begin to separate 'hardware' from 'software'.

One way to view this material is that our type is the 'hardware' that we inhabit from birth and which cannot be changed any more than we can change the colour of our eyes. In theory, our hardware has a genetic basis and deeply influences how we experience the world and other people. It influences our speed of operation, our relationship to rules and regulations, our level of comfort when in the public eye, our innate likes and dislikes, level of trust of other types and many other embedded factors.

For example, I am primarily a Mars type, the warrior, which means I find it challenging to remain calm when technology will not do my bidding. No amount of meditation, deep breathing or therapy has changed my impulsive desire to kick my laptop across the room when it misbehaves. In fact, I have actually destroyed three laser printers which refused to do my bidding!

Our 'software' is our life experience, culture, education and attitudes. This we can develop and evolve through training, life experience and the choices we make. If we are on a path of personal development, we seek to adapt our software to mitigate some of the less-ideal automatic reactions of our type and give more airtime to the more useful qualities of our hardware.

We will always be expressing the software through the hardware. If we are in a situation or occupation which is fundamentally unsuited to our type, then this awareness can identify the source of the discomfort and be a powerful stimulus for us to make beneficial changes. Conversely, if our occupation is in harmony with our type, we can more easily resist outside pressure that would seek to have us conform to someone else's agenda.

Once, as I presented to a small group, participants were quickly able to identify their own types. One woman, Lisa, had accurately identified herself as a combination of two types (Lunar-Venus, described later) and was keen to identify the ideal occupation for that particular blend. I told her she would be perfectly suited to a stable position connected with admin in the healthcare profession, at which point she burst into tears and began sobbing convulsively. As the group was open and supportive, we gently enquired what this information had triggered. Lisa had been a manager in a healthcare office for 15 years; she absolutely loved her job, feeling valued and appreciated and with no wish to do anything else. However, her family had been pushing her for many years to be more ambitious and to 'make something more of herself'. We enquired further and established that her family members were of a completely different type (Mercurial) that would be uncomfortable sitting behind a desk for more than ten minutes! Once Lisa saw that they were trying to help her by advocating she do what their type would do, she was able to see their pressure as well-intentioned, albeit misguided. More importantly, she realised that her chosen role was totally aligned with her own type and released the sense of guilt and failure that had been pushed upon her. Lisa was then more freely able to be who she actually was and not try to act like another type.

The body is a device to calculate the astronomy of the spirit. Rumi

CHAPTER 4: The Concept of Types

The concept of personality types is not new: it goes right back to the very beginning of human thinking, and it seems as if almost every generation comes up with their own variation, from Jung's notion of 'introvert' and 'extrovert' to the Myers-Briggs categories so beloved of Human Resources departments. The difference here is that we are taking the whole person into account – their 'hardware' as well as their 'software', so to speak. In this section we will be focusing on the hardware that is our type (and looking at some historical hardware definitions).

The Emerald Tablet of Hermes Trismegistus states, "That which is above is like that which is below". This refers to the principle that the microcosm reflects the macrocosm. The atom is a model of the Solar System; the human lung structure reflects trees, leaf skeletons and river deltas and so on.

When previous civilisations looked at a night sky free from noise, light pollution and air pollution, they were able to perceive the quality of influence of each planet. They saw this influence reflected in humanity and they left us clues to this ancient knowledge in the form of their mythology. The Babylonians named the seven days of the week after the visible bodies of the Solar System; in French and Spanish, this remains to some extent unaltered.

The Sumerians were the earliest culture we know of that connected the names of the planets with their gods and goddesses and attributed psychological traits to them. These correlations were continued and refined by the ancient Greeks and then the Romans. Our current language carries traces of this knowledge in the definitions of words that follow the planetary attributes. Medieval alchemists produced drawings showing the temperaments and costumes of the planetary types and their typical occupations.

Thus each of the six types is named simultaneously after a deity and a visible planet of the Solar System and there are some remarkable parallels between the planets and their associated deities.

Bringing together further strands, each type has recognisable, unchanging physical characteristics that have been observed for millennia. This concept is one of the most challenging and controversial elements of the system and one which can provoke strong reactions when first encountered. The idea that looking at someone's body shape, hair colour, complexion and eye colour indicates their type is a controversial one, which is discussed in greater detail in the chapter on frequently-asked questions.

A relatively-recent and slightly-obscure reference to these ideas is found in *The Laws of Scientific Hand Reading,* by William G. Benham, an American who devoted his life to the study of palmistry after meeting an old gypsy woman who initiated him into the secret of recognising types. Benham refers to the types as 'mount types', but uses the same descriptions of planetary deities. The book was published in 1900, so it requires a little effort to read his Victorian prose:

> *The fact that there are well-defined specimens of all these types on the streets of our cities to-day, that they can be easily recognised, and that eighty-five per cent of these typical people are at their best in the same occupations, all have the same faults, the same virtues, like the same kind of surroundings, live, think, and act after the same plan in everything they do, proves that the original method in creating humanity has not been changed, but that the laws of creation are in operation to-day just as they were in the beginning. If we can feel sure that there are, as I say, seven types of people, each of which has distinctly separate qualities and if we can know what these qualities are, it must be a fact that, when we learn to distinguish these seven types from each other as we meet them, we shall at once know their characteristics, what people of their type have done through ages past and what the outcome of their life is likely to be, judged by those of the same type who have gone before.*
>
> *There is another fact about these types: they look alike, and in my future treatment of the subject I shall give you mental illustrations of their appearance. Thus knowing each type well, what they look like, how they reason, live, think, work, play, treat their fellows, or marry, as well as their natural occupations and peculiarities, you can, when you meet one of a certain type, dissect him with ease, knowing him better than he knows himself.*

Another angle of approach to the system of Reading People is found in *The Glands Regulating Personality*, by endocrinologist Louis Berman. In his book, published in 1922, Berman proposes that one gland is dominant in an individual and that the influence of the dominant gland shapes the physical body and psychological outlook of each person. Berman's work dovetails neatly with Benham's 'mount types' and also with the traits that mythology associates with the gods and goddesses. He writes:

> *When observing types it is vital to focus on physical characteristics above all other indicators. Most people's type can be determined with relative speed and ease by simply looking for a few visible cues.*

We will be referring to William G. Benham and Louis Berman M.D. throughout this book.

CHAPTER 5: The Template

It's not always easy to grasp all the different elements that go into making up a person's type. In order to make this whole approach to reading people as clear and systematic as possible, I have developed a template covering the seven most significant aspects through which a type will manifest itself. Each of these aspects of a type is explained below, and then, in the following chapters, each type is described in terms of its different aspects. As you read through, it will quickly become clear how these different elements relate to you and to people you know.

Core attribute

Each of the six basic types has a specific core attribute. This is a term referring to the kingpin around which much of our perception and experience of life revolves. Our core attribute can be viewed as simultaneously our greatest weakness and our greatest strength: a double-edged sword which cuts both ways. Each type is geared to react in certain habitual ways; when we are alert, we can use the energy of our core attribute for a purpose, like an engine that drives us forward. It is a dynamic asset and a fine tool. When our activity is consciously aligned with our core attribute, we perform well and no other type can do what we are doing so effortlessly and clearly. We experience the exhilaration of 'flow' or being 'in the zone'. With awareness, it is possible to have a degree of choice in deciding where and when to make best use of this attribute.

When someone judges their core attribute and decides to change it, almost inevitably the means they choose to do this will be a reflection of their core attribute. For example, one core attribute is dominance: the desire to direct others and position oneself above them. A dominant type will try to control and eradicate their inner dominance – using the technique of dominance! A destructive type will attempt to forcefully uproot and destroy their destructive impulses. Our core attribute is fundamental to our type and cannot be changed. Through objectivity and observation we may change our relationship to our core attribute, but we cannot make it go away, and certainly not by using the very same tool as a weapon.

Our core attribute may be obvious to ourselves and others or it may require some diligent enquiry to observe it in action. Some people are raised in an environment where expression of their core attribute is discouraged or even punished, so they learn to disguise or suppress it (in Lisa's story, above, her Persistence and Selflessness were judged by her family using their core attribute of Power). However, the energy of one's core attribute will erupt when triggered by stress or circumstance. When this occurs, our attribute is a primal energy force which can use us as a puppet for its own end. We may feel 'right' and powerful when this happens, but in reality we are acting unconsciously and often in ways that are destructive to ourselves and our relationships.

When we are gripped by the full force of our core attribute it is a form of possession: we cannot be reasoned with and any attempt by others to oppose or mitigate the effects simply adds fuel to the fire. We all 'lose it' from time to time and when our attribute takes over the show we lose perspective and relativity, acting in ways that are disturbing to our everyday self. At its worst, the core attribute is the wellspring of obsession, crimes of passion, self-neglect, deception, heartlessness, violence and addiction

In a movie, when an actor of a specific type plays a role that matches that type and acts out the attribute of that type, there is a congruity which resonates within the audience. At a visceral level we say to ourselves "Yes that type would do that."

Relationship to rules

In our interactions in work, society and our family, there are overt and also unspoken rules influencing our actions. Each type has a tendency to react automatically to authority and structure. This will be strongly influenced by some aspect of the core attribute. A lack of awareness of this dynamic can cost us dearly in our professional and personal relationships, without us ever taking responsibility for our part in the drama. If we simply react the same way to authority and make it about 'them', we never look at our own role in the situation. Raising our awareness of our knee-jerk reactions gives us the possibility to make different choices. To diminish the amount of judgement we have towards other people and the roles they play is never easy, but is a price that is worth paying once we are tired of repeatedly banging our heads against the same wall. We will probably never come to love the rules, but we can begin to avoid unnecessary and pointless suffering.

Behaviour at social events

Each type tends to have different responses to social occasions and varying levels of comfort in group interactions. To see this without judgement allows us to develop strategies to suit our type. We can determine where and when we are likely to flourish with others and also avoid forcing ourselves into awkward and unproductive scenarios. We can see where social activity is an escape from self-enquiry and, conversely, how isolation can cost us the joy of relating to others.

Everything in our lives comes from or through other people and in many ways the quality of our life is directly influenced by the quality of our relationships. There is much value in understanding how our type best relates to those around us.

Ideal or typical occupations

In an age when we seem to spend increasing amounts of our time at work, being in a position for which we are unsuited is an invitation to misery. Certain types are naturally at ease in certain professional roles; they enjoy these roles and find expression for the positive elements of their core attribute.

Work for those who are aligned with their core attribute is invigorating and satisfying and they can't wait to get going in the morning. When the type matches the job, it is like a piece of a jigsaw puzzle fitting perfectly into place. In his superb book *Good to Great*, Jim Collins calls this alignment of talent and role "being on the right seat on the bus". Awareness of this alignment is one of many practical applications of Reading People. Organisations are far more effective when type aligns with role. Otherwise people waste time and energy trying to change themselves in ways that are stressful and non-productive. When our job role does not match our type, we experience dissatisfaction, stagnation and frustration.

Levels of employee engagement have been measured repeatedly and found to be at historic lows. People may show up to work physically in order to pay the bills, but their hearts and even their minds are not in it. The role they play professionally evokes the unhealthy elements of their core attribute and their colleagues, clients and organisations pay the price.

We will examine the ideal occupations for each type. Often people will have naturally gravitated towards these jobs, but societal or family expectations may have discouraged them from pursuing a career for which they are best suited. It is my fervent hope that at least one reader will benefit from this book by discovering their type, find their dream occupation listed in that chapter and then wave this very book in the face of their family as they jump ship and follow their destiny!

If this happens to be you, dear reader, please email me here: john@readingpeople.biz.

Famous and historic examples

It is useful to have recognisable examples to build a picture of each type. This gives an immediate visual image and also a sense of the traits of the type. The life stories of historical figures illustrate how strong an influence type has in terms of guiding choices to the point where some people can be considered iconic pictures of their type. Some of these 'larger than life' examples give us further insight into the extreme negative and positive effects of each type's core attribute.

Personal stories

I have conducted interviews with people from various walks of life who are clear examples of types and captured in their own words how it is to be a certain type. Each chapter includes several personal stories which deepen and enrich the learning.

Types, race and culture

It seems pretty clear that the six types are not evenly distributed around the globe; if that were the case then each type would make up approximately one sixth of the population of each country or area. Simple observation shows us that certain types are disproportionately represented in certain areas and indeed are drawn towards specific countries and even cities. Recognising the predominant type of a culture can facilitate clear communication and deeper understanding and respect. Just as we can study the default position of an individual of a certain type, so we can also study the default position of a culture. In each chapter on types there is thus an exploration of the location where we observe that type to be 'clustered' and numerically dominant. For some people this is a charged topic, which is explored in more depth in the chapter about frequently-asked questions; this concept is fundamental to the system, so cannot be omitted or glossed over. It also makes travelling a lot more fun!

Let us now view the structure of this multi-layered gem of knowledge:

CHAPTER 6: The Types

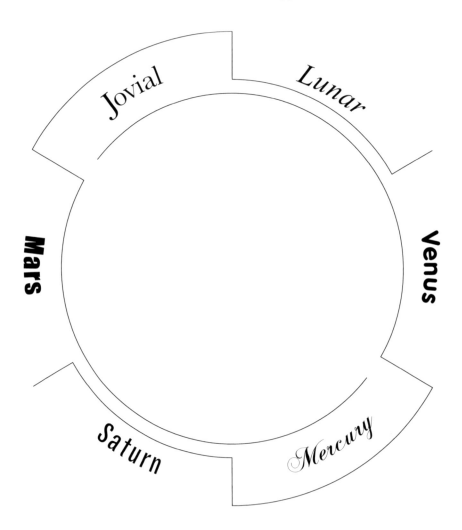

The Circle of Types

The circle traditionally represents the larger whole – literally 'all encompassing'.

In this instance, the circle represents the whole of humanity.

We plot six points on the circumference equidistant from each other.

One way to visualise this is as a clock face with a type at every other hour.

At each of the six points, we place the visible planets of our solar system. So, starting at the top and viewing clockwise, the Moon is placed at 1 o'clock, Venus at 3, Mercury at 5, Saturn at 7, Mars at 9 and Jupiter at 11.

This structure provides a framework for understanding the human experience; schematically, the specific vehicle each of us is operating can be found represented at a point on this circle of types or planetary archetypes.

We typically see people as a combination of two types, such as Lunar-Venus, Venus-Mercury, Mercury-Saturn, Saturn-Mars, Mars-Jovial or Jovial-Lunar. Combinations are only possible between two points adjacent on the circle, so we don't find Mars-Lunar or Saturn-Venus.

Occasionally, someone appears to be located right on the point, seeming to embody the characteristics of only one type, in which case they are considered to be a pure type: Lunar, Venus, Mercury, Saturn, Mars or Jovial.

The Sun is at the centre and exerts an additional influence to some people's overall type; this brings a whole extra layer of understanding which will be explored in a later chapter.

Using this structure, it becomes possible, with practice, to calibrate exactly where a person is found on the circle, to discover what this means to the individual and to explore how they relate to other types. In the course of writing this book, I have interviewed people who are clear examples of types and their words are included as case studies in order to give experiential depth to the chapters.

Let us now examine each of the planetary types in turn. While we do so, think about yourself, and about those you know, and see where you, and they, fit in. You might find it helpful to have a mirror to hand, since your physical appearance is a critical indicator of your type, and you may well be astounded to see the extent to which the person you know so well from the inside is revealed so clearly on the outside.

MARS *nullo genitus patre, sed Iunone parente,* 3 *Asper, atrox, durus, prælia & arma sequor.*

Mars

In mythology, Mars is the Roman god of war; He was the most prominent of the military gods worshipped by the Roman legions. His festivals were held in March, the month named for him and which opened the season for military campaigns, and in October, when military campaigns were traditionally shelved for the winter.

In the English language, we find this definition:

Martial-adjective

1. Inclined or disposed to war; warlike: the ancient Romans were a martial people.
2. Of, suitable for, or associated with war or the armed forces: martial music.
3. Characteristic of or befitting a warrior: a martial stride.

In astronomy, Mars is the fourth planet from the Sun and is often described as the 'Red Planet', as the iron oxide prevalent on its surface gives it a reddish appearance. Mars is a terrestrial planet with a thin atmosphere, having surface features reminiscent both of the impact craters of the Moon and the volcanoes, valleys, deserts and polar ice caps of Earth. The rotational period and seasonal cycles of Mars are similar to those of Earth. Mars is the site of Olympus Mons, the highest known mountain within the Solar System and of Valles Marineris, the largest canyon. The biggest storms in the Solar System erupt periodically on Mars, darkening the surface for months, so Mars is a planet of extremes.

The astronomical symbol for Mars is a stylised version of the sword and shield of the god of war.

Physicality

Men who are predominantly or overwhelmingly Mars tend to be on the short side and robust. They have a bullet-shaped or rounded head, wide face, square jaw, thick neck, broad muscular shoulders, barrel chest, short stubby fingers with strong wide hands, a small mouth with thin lips, small ears and bandy legs. When a Mars man enters a room, it may look as if he just

THE ART OF READING PEOPLE

dismounted from a horse! The hands often hang with the palms facing backwards, as if he is ready to go for his gun.

If a Mars is of Caucasian extraction then his eyes will be blue and piercing and he may well fix you with a penetrating gaze. His hair will be red or ruddy (in childhood the hairline of a Mars boy typically runs in a straight line across the forehead); his skin will have freckles and a lack of melanin which means he will resemble cooked bacon after exposure to an excess of sunlight.

In the work of Louis Berman, the Mars type corresponds to the adrenal type:

> *The skin is one of the chief clues to the adrenal personality... Skin pigment bears a direct relation to the reaction of the organism to light, especially ultraviolet rays, to the radiation of heat and hence to the fundamental productions and consumptions of energy by the cells. So the gland of energy for emergencies writes its signature always all over the skin.*

William Benham focuses on extreme examples of the Mars type, which he calls Martians:

> *In gaining the material for this chapter I have taken the most pronounced Martians... and from these cases, several thousand in number, I have tabulated what I believe to be an accurate and trustworthy system of handling this type... The Martian is of medium height, very strongly built, muscular looking, carries himself erect, shoulders back and has the appearance of one ever ready to defend himself... the hair is short, stiff sometimes curly and of an auburn or red colour... the legs are short but stout and muscular, the bones are big and strong, the feet are broad and the instep inclined to be flat, making the subject walk in a proud and determined manner... The Martian by his very appearance shows his true character, full of fight, either aggressively or in self-defence, mentally or physically, a strong robust constitution and one ardent in all things.*

Famous examples include Wayne Rooney, George W Bush and Henry VIII – who certainly gave full rein to his destructive Mars energies in beheading two of his wives and destroying the monastic tradition. Martials have a habit of dramatically sweeping away whatever displeases them!

It can require closer observation to identify a Mars man of African descent, due to the obvious differences in pigmentation. His hair will have a reddish tinge and his eyes will be on the pale side, sometimes green. His face will be broad and his body robust and compact, with a forward-leaning gait. There may be discernible freckles and some dryness to his skin. It is the author's observation that albino people of African descent are almost invariably Mars types. The gene that determines red hair is recessive, meaning it must be carried by both parents to show up in the child, so it may be that genetic science will find connections between type and genetic inheritance.

Famous examples include Mike Tyson, Nelson Mandela and Martin Luther King. In these examples, we see the best of Mars in a determination to fight for justice against the odds and also the worst of Mars in the biting off of an opponent's ear during a boxing match.

Mars types are comparatively rare amongst Asian people. Physical cues are a more square face than is typical, male pattern baldness, pale or greenish eyes, a robust and compact physique with ruddy skin and reddish hair.

We need to go back in history a bit for some well-known examples: Genghis Khan and Attila the Hun, who certainly took the warrior ideal to extremes.

Next, let's observe Mars women. A Mars woman will tend to be robust, compact and built for action; her face is square, ears small and close to her head. Her lips are thin and may well almost disappear when she concentrates. Her skin will emanate a healthy glow, especially after exercise. Her shoulders are square, her hair fair, red or reddish; her breasts are small and her demeanour may well be slightly tomboyish or androgynous. Historically, patriarchal cultures have been uncomfortable with the energy of Mars women, feeling threatened by their tendency to be independent and to stand up for themselves. Mars women do not fit the mould of submissive homemaker and soft mother that insecure men try to force them into!

Louis Berman is not overly subtle here in his description of Mars women:

> Among women, the adrenal type is always masculinoid. If physically feminine... she will at least show the qualities of a psychic virilism. A generation ago [he writes in 1922] such a woman had to repress her inherent trends and instincts in the face of public opinion and law, and so suffered from a feeling of inferiority. Nowadays, many of these

women are striding forward and will attain a good many of the masculine heights. An adrenal type will probably be the first woman president of the United States.

Famous examples include Hilary Clinton, Venus and Serena Williams, Emily Watson, Kate Adie and Angela Merkel. Kate Adie is none too popular with camera operators due to her desire to be filming her reports right on the front line during armed conflicts. Mars people are drawn to where the action is unfolding.

Mars traits

The following is a composite description of traits which would be found in those who are predominantly Mars, in other words, situated within a few degrees of the Mars point on the circle.

In some ways this is a cartoonish sketch, designed to spotlight features and to give you the means to observe clear examples of this type. It is useful to observe extreme examples of types and Mars people are generally quite easy to spot. With an abundance of adrenaline and testosterone coursing through their veins, a Mars type is built for action and movement. When travelling, they want to go directly from A to B and do so in a hurry; they are not widely famed for their patience. Obstacles on their path are to be removed, climbed over or flattened; to a Mars, altering one's course is seen as sign of weakness and weakness is not in their repertoire.

A Martial is invigorated by having a clear target or purpose and gets frustrated by delays or detours. They respond well to sharply-defined goals and measurable rewards, which must be delivered promptly when targets are met. It is unwise to move the goalposts when employing a Martial; they will deliver the goods as agreed and expect you to keep your end of the bargain. If you do not reward them promptly and fairly, a confrontation is on the cards and you become their next target!

At a fairground we can find Martials gathered around the trial of strength machine, vigorously swinging a huge mallet and cheering loudly when the chunk of metal shoots up the rail and rings the bell at the top. They expect the processes of professional life to be equally clear cut and linear.

In their speech, a Mars will be refreshingly blunt and direct. If you want the straight, unvarnished truth, ask a Martial friend or colleague for feedback and then brace yourself firmly for the result: they are highly likely to embody a drive known as 'automatic honesty', which is a compulsion to tell the bald truth when it may actually be wise to be diplomatic. The cartoon character Popeye with his catchphrase "I am what I am!" captures this characteristic quite neatly.

The Mars relationship to forthright honesty is neatly captured in the following story.

Bronwen is a highly successful organisational development consultant with over twenty years of experience working with senior leadership teams in oil companies, engineering firms and professional services. She is an archetypal Mars, with blonde hair and piercing eyes that reflect her Celtic heritage. Bronwen talks about her style of working:

> The teams I work with are predominantly male, so I have to demonstrate my expertise. I have to be assertive and direct and it is helpful to be jolly and jokey to get under their defences. I feel honoured to be able to build trust with people, help them to develop and to overcome obstacles and as a consequence make a difference to the business and to their colleagues. When working with people in the realm of change there is inevitably tension and resistance in the room and I feel this internally: I get hot and feel a knot in my stomach. I have learned to recognise this sensation and use the energy to address what is happening in the room, either with humour or by direct confrontation. While I do this in a professional manner there are some groups of engineers that I just shout at.

When I expressed surprise at this, Bronwen enlightened me:

> I know they shout at each other, so it is not unheard of. The last time I did this with a very senior group they sat up and took notice and have remembered it ever since – so they got the message, which is what matters, and they take what I'm saying more seriously! I find it energising to struggle on a project with a client; it means something is happening – we are getting somewhere. My clients describe me as highly professional, creative and energetic and say that I definitely shoot from the hip. I get certainly get results.

I asked Bronwen how her Mars energy shows up in her personal life:

> *I get very frustrated at systems and objects that don't work, this drives me absolutely bananas. The last thing I wrecked was my laser printer; I pummelled it to death because it stopped working after I had warned it. Before that it was a pressure washer which I bounced on some concrete as hard as I could, then I kicked it and jumped on it because it wouldn't work! My friends appreciate my direct honesty though it's a real double-edged sword; one friend told me, "your bluntness is one of the things I value most about you but I find it very uncomfortable." I'm loving and giving in a friendship so people are able to cope with the honesty. People say I name things that other people are afraid to name.*

I asked Bronwen if she meant that she is willing to be the one who points out the 'elephant in the room' and she replied, in impeccable Mars style, *"Yes – and the piles of elephant poo too!"*

In fairness, a Martial will generally be willing to receive forthright feedback in return and will be grateful if you give it to them straight. They would prefer you to go toe to toe with them and attack everything they hold dear, rather than meekly agree with them in order to keep the peace. A Martial will test a relationship by taking a strong adversarial position to see if the other party will hold their ground and disagree head on. As odd as this appears to other types, this is part of the process of forging a friendship with a Mars: they do not want you to agree with them, in fact if you try to soften your position they will become more extreme and unreasonable. What they are doing is seeing if you are willing to take a stand and fight; they may well be vehemently opposed to your beliefs while deeply respecting the strength with which you defend them.

One relationship which went through this process was that between Martin McGuiness and Ian Paisley in Northern Ireland. Here are two Martials (Martin McGuiness being almost pure Mars), who stood diametrically opposed from both the religious and political perspectives. Martin McGuiness is a Catholic Republican committed to a united Ireland and having historical ties to the IRA, while Ian Paisley was a conservative Protestant committed to keeping Northern Ireland part of the United Kingdom. There is a long history of violent bloodshed between those they represented, but through political power-sharing circumstances the two were compelled to cooperate with each other, despite both of them holding views conducive to mutual hatred. The outside world was astonished to see a genuine friendship forming between them. This lasting friendship is impossible to understand from a superficial viewpoint, but easy to dissect from the perspective of this system. Here were two equally strong-willed Martials, refusing to budge an inch from their deeply-held convictions and thereby coming to respect and admire each other.

The moral of this story is that if you disagree with a Mars let them know: they may go red in the face and come out swinging verbally; they will test all your defences, and do their best to shift you away from your position, but if you look them in the eye and stand your ground, you have earned their respect. If you back down or show a lack of will then the attack will be relentless; they will move in for the kill and not give up until you surrender.

Mars is the god of war, so Martials enjoy a good argument; it gets their juices flowing and their senses alert, you can see their eyes brighten and their nostrils flare when the atmosphere gets contentious. They use any weapon at their disposal once battle lines are drawn and have no time for half measures. A verbal tussle is a fight to the finish and when it is over the Martial feels satisfied, regardless of whether they have won or lost. What is important to them is that they have found out who is who and where everyone stands – the cards are on the table in plain view.

During childhood, Martials tend to enjoy a bit of rough and tumble – scrapes and grazes are frequent, but they seem to simply bounce and keep going when they fall over. Physical sports are a healthy outlet for their boundless energy, which leads them to stick with games to the bitter end. You can observe palpable disappointment when the final whistle blows and the match ends; Mars just wants to keep going!

It is possible to determine type at an early age, as we see in the following story.

Marcus is two years old, but even at this early age, from his appearance and behaviour it is obvious that he is 95 per cent Mars. His mother Rachel talks about the unique challenges and excitements of raising a Mars child:

His physical strength and level of determination are quite extraordinary. For instance, at toddler gym most children hang on the monkey bars for five seconds or less, then drop off or give up, but Marcus will hang on for up to 90 seconds, and he will not let go until he has to – all the while pulling exaggerated 'exertion faces' for onlookers. He loves it when people gather round and time him! When he eventually falls off he wants to do it again and again. When he falls over and hurts himself he cries briefly and seeks comfort, then is up and at it again, as if the pain gives him even more adrenaline. He recently fell in a pond, screamed in terror when fished out, ran to me for a quick hug, got dried and changed and went straight back to the same spot and resumed throwing stones in the pond. He seems compelled to test his boundaries and overcome them. His best friend has a toy rabbit which he knows is hers and will bring her if she is sad or has left it somewhere. If she leaves it on the floor and another child picks it up, he will immediately take it from them. In fact, if any child is holding a similar rabbit of their own, that will also be forcibly removed and taken to her. He's like a miniature policeman, diligently enforcing the right of ownership of the rabbit. We have been asked to leave the local library on several occasions when he has decided to sweep shelves full of books onto the floor faster than I can pick them up. Several of my friends (who are very fond of Marcus but have less energetic babies themselves) have told me that they have reconsidered the timing of having a second child after watching some of my epic struggles with him and realising what they could be in for next time.

Martial girls are often athletic and tomboyish and enjoy competing with the boys, often giving as good as they get and feeling disgruntled that they can't be picked for the boys' rugby team. It can be deeply harmful for parents and teachers to impose a cultural image of soft, passive femininity upon a Martial girl and expect her to conform to an agenda that is fundamentally different from her nature. A Martial female is simply not wired to be a 'nice little girl'.

Martial children are alert for any injustice that is shown towards them by adults. They will go bright red in the face and shout "It's not fair!" the quickest, loudest and longest of all types. It is important to provide an outlet for their direct energy. As children, my niece and nephew would thoroughly enjoy a trip to the local junkyard where they could throw rocks at dumped cars. This is a highly inexpensive and effective form of therapy for Mars children! All children need to go through the process of socialization. With a Martial, there's a delicate balance between curbing their mechanical honesty and giving the message that it is not OK to tell lies: they are prone to thinking in black and white, so the message "You must tell the truth – but not all the time" is a little too ambivalent for them. Martials are compelled to tell the truth and to suppress this urge is sometimes akin to pressing down on a coiled spring.

Here's a true story: my Martial younger brother was picking his nose on a crowded bus. When my mother quietly told him to stop, he announced in a very loud voice, which is common to Mars children: "When I get home I am going to hide under the bed and pick my nose all I want!"

Subtlety and subterfuge do not come naturally to young Martials; they prefer direct confrontation. The boy who pointed out the nakedness of the Emperor in Hans Christian Andersen's story 'The Emperor's New Clothes' is a sure bet to be of this type.

An adult Martial who has grown up in a Mars culture and has not had his or her nature suppressed by outside influences will have a great many, if not all, of the following traits.

They will subscribe to the 'work hard, play hard' ethos and may unwind by raucous drinking bouts, which they expect or demand that their team or colleagues join them in or face being called 'soft'. If they are the last one standing at the bar, it is a badge of honour that they wear with pride.

A holiday for a Mars is often like a military campaign, with targets, dates and strategy; there will be little time for aimless relaxation. Other types do not find a holiday led by a Mars to be restful; in fact, there may be even more frantic activity than usual.

Self-reliance and independence are to be venerated, respected and demonstrated. A Martial will find difficulty in uttering the following sentences: "I need some help" or "I can't do this by myself."

Turning the other cheek is not a prominent tactic in their repertoire either. In the world view of a Mars, no one can perform a task as quickly or efficiently as they can and by the time they have explained how to do it to someone they may as well have done it by themselves.

Extreme sports and high-risk activities are their method of unwinding, as they have a high threshold of pain endurance and relish the charge they get from testing their strength against obstacles.

At weekends, we find gatherings of Martials engaged in the following pursuits: skydiving, rock climbing, mountain biking, rugby, soccer, hurling, football, home brewing, hedge laying, felling trees, big game fishing, hang gliding, wrestling, hunting, paintball, surfing (especially if the waves are big enough to be life threatening), spelunking, stock car racing, Morris dancing (trust me, never make fun of a Morris dancer), mountain rescue or re-enacting historical battles; in short, anything that is arduous and potentially dangerous. If you go to a gym and notice people sweating more profusely than other people, grunting loudly, grimacing and producing crashing sounds with the weights, then you know the type involved.

It is unlikely Martials will be engaged in the following: badminton, embroidery, macramé, painting delicate watercolours, ballet, ping-pong, practicing Bach choral motets or playing the piccolo.

A social gathering of Martials is interesting to observe as they are quite proud of any suffering they have survived and part of their bonding process is to display and compare their physical scars and recount the ordeal that imprinted the scars on their body. Basically, at some level, most Martials like to suffer. A deeper bonding ritual for them is the sharing of emotional wounds, such as messy divorces and professional skulduggery. There is a scene in the film *Jaws* where the three central male characters get drunk and enact this ritual, moving from physical scars to a broken heart.

Loyalty to team, family, company and/or country is of high importance. Once a Mars is on your side they will stick with you through thick and thin and expect the same. It is extremely unwise to betray or manipulate a Mars; their response on discovering duplicity in someone they trust is often swift and extreme. The adrenal charge is doubled by the fact that they berate themselves for being foolish and trusting the betrayer in the first place.

The excitement of facing challenges and the value of loyalty is evident in this personal story: Frank is a serial entrepreneur who derives great satisfaction from the re-development and professional upkeep of unusual high-end properties. He has a proven track record in many diverse start-ups and in turning around companies that are struggling. He is a walking embodiment of Mars: stocky, blue-eyed, robust and hearty. Here, Frank clearly expresses many elements of the Mars world view in business:

I hugely enjoy the turn-around phase of a business. I love to come in as the hero and solve a tricky situation. I love the adrenaline that a difficult situation naturally produces and, for me, the higher the stakes are, the better it is. Once the urgency is over and there is an effective strategy in place, I tend to get bored because the day-to-day running of a business holds no interest for me – I move on to the next challenge.

A big part of what inspires me in a start-up is the ability to be able to define its essence – the values and ethics of the business – and make sure that these are embedded in the brand. This means that the appointment of any subsequent candidates into the business will require them to fit the bill – in other words, to be aligned with the values and ethics of the business. If that essence is clearly expressed to all existing employees, any prospective candidate who doesn't fit should be easy to spot. I'm a big fan of the 'F.I.F.O' approach and I'm especially adept at the 'F.O' bit!

Here is Frank on his relationship to honesty when coaching his clients on strategy:

I am brutally honest and always tell my coaching clients, "If you don't want scary answers, then don't ask scary questions." They can get angry and upset at what I say, but at the end of the day, they come to know that I don't have an axe to grind or a selfish agenda and, frankly, that I simply tell it like it is. If they want to shoot the messenger, that's fine, too! Sometimes I will say something totally outrageous just to see how they react. If they fight back, I steer the conflict into an incisive, productive and highly contextual, honest conversation. If they agree with me, well, then I would suggest I have enabled them to say something they are not comfortable with expressing.

I break down barriers and start conversations, however difficult, and inject a change in energy to achieve change. With any problem, conflict or difficult situation, there are three options: to change, accept or remove the irritant. I know how to get to the core of the issue, to get it discussed, and to effect the change that's needed. Even if that change is just one of acceptance – the fact that the conversation has happened creates the state of acceptance. Then everyone can get on to the next thing. And quickly, too – before I get bored!

Frank has an extraordinary take on the crossing points of honesty and loyalty:

If someone steals a tin of paint or a piece of wood from one of my sites, then they are instantly dismissed, and with no exceptions, because they are insulting me. I take it very personally. If someone steals a big, expensive piece of equipment, I will want to have a conversation with them.

When I expressed surprise at this seeming-dichotomy, Frank went on to enlighten me:

If someone steals something that expensive, then they probably have big problems in their life. It is an act of desperation, therefore, and I would want to help them if I can. The person who steals a tin of paint has decided they are not one of us – they are not aligned with the values and ethics that we hold to our hearts – whereas someone who is in trouble can definitely still be one of us. I will be there for them through thick and thin – because that's what loyalty is.

Office politics can be a treacherous minefield for Martials, as playing a double game does not come naturally to them and there is an unspoken expectation that everyone is acting the same way as they are. The adult equivalent of a Mars child blowing up with the childhood energy of "It's not fair!" can be rather explosive. Michael Douglas captured this rage in the movie *Falling Down,* when he finally snapped under the pressures of modern life and went on a rage-fuelled spree. His dad, Kirk Douglas, was also Mars, which is why he played such a great part in the movie *The Vikings.* The word 'berserk', meaning 'injuriously, maniacally, or furiously violent or out of control', is an Old Norse term for the state that Vikings would go into when fighting. Michael Douglas went berserk in Los Angeles in *Falling Down.*

Due to their automatic honesty, Martials do not make adept liars in the public eye. They may be able to maintain a muscular mask of their facial features, but their ears go bright crimson, the novelist Jeffrey Archer being a case study of this phenomenon. His facial expressions during his various trials were painful to observe as a grim reflection of his inner turmoil.

Their systems are charged with adrenaline, causing the continual need to move and express. They embody an abundance of lusty passionate sexual energy, which builds up inside them, and they can become irritable and unpleasant if they do not have sex regularly. One of the conflicts within some Mars males is having a need to discharge this excess energy while having a partner who is not so highly driven: the battle between lust and loyalty can become an internal wrestling match. With a dash of alcohol in the mix, things can get a little bumpy!

Words and concepts which inspire a Mars include project, target, struggle, battle, hard slog, challenge, campaign, step up to the plate, last stand, against the odds, and almost any language or imagery with a military connotation.

Words which insult a Mars include soft, lazy, dishonest, weak, wishy-washy, co-dependent and needy.

Other types judge Mars types as being hot-headed, tactless, bull in a china shop, blunt and crude. Most Martials would agree, but not care that much! They see themselves as strong, solid, dependable, brave, hard-working, hands-on, salt-of-the-earth people. The speech that begins "Once more into the breach, dear friends… " from Shakespeare's *Henry V* is stirring poetry to the ears of a Mars.

Martials view the other types as being lazy, soft, prissy, slow, airy-fairy and over sensitive. Their humour is earthy and bawdy and they dearly love to attack any excessive displays of political correctness. They have a strong affinity for siding with the underdog and are drawn to fighting for causes, especially those connected to righting perceived injustices. They will put their life on the line to protect the powerless and disenfranchised from exploitation.

Martials tend to be on the front line at demonstrations and revolutions and are found in abundance in the military, where having a clear target focuses their energy and frees them to act forcefully without doubt or questions. They often divide people into good guys or bad guys and the only option available is to be 'with us or against us'. George W Bush brought this simplistic outlook to the foreign policy of the USA. In personal development work, Martials exercise ruthless self-enquiry and are quite willing to give unsolicited direct feedback to others.

Core attribute

The core attribute of the Mars type is Destruction. This is a compulsion to move forcefully against obstacles or adversity without wavering or surrender.

At the healthy, functional end of the spectrum, this attribute fuels a willingness to go all the way, with total honesty and a deep determination to discover and align with the truth in all situations. Mars wields the sword of truth: there is no time for half measures, small print or hypocrisy, and now is the moment in which to act. There is a refreshing immediacy and clarity at work here, sweeping away the old and stagnant and making room for the new. Consistent, purposeful and trustworthy, the warrior fights fairly for a higher cause, be it the security and welfare of friends and family or success in the workplace or on the sports field.

William Benham writes:

> *Under all circumstances he is cool, collected, calm, does not lose his head, is equal to emergencies and does not get discouraged if things go against him. He does not give up fighting even when the chances seem slim and when knocked down he rises again seemingly unaware of the possibility of defeat. This power of resistance, this faculty for never giving up, often makes the Martian successful over all obstacles.*

Alexander the Great demonstrated this attribute: he was shown the Gordian knot and was told that whoever could untie it would rule the world; all that had tried had failed, so he simply drew his sword and cut it in two, neatly capturing this spirit of fierce courage and direct action. On a smaller scale, when a Martial is driving and sees a tin can in the road, they can rarely resist changing course slightly to flatten the can – it gives them a wee thrill.

At the unhealthy, dysfunctional end of the spectrum, the attribute of

Destruction takes over, the Martial loses perspective and lacks compassion for themselves and others. When gripped by destruction, Mars can be totally reckless and out of control, destroying relationships, careers and friendships for no purpose beyond the raw thrill of the moment. Belligerent and aggressive, they crash through the world sending others fleeing for safety. Any hint of weakness or appeasement evokes further attack, as if the awareness of the vulnerability of others has become a trigger for bullying rather than for protection. Idi Amin was totally possessed by this attribute, as was Germany during both World Wars.

White supremacist movements worldwide seek to inflame destruction via racism and intolerance amongst disenfranchised Martials. On a smaller scale, a Mars CEO can have tunnel vision and be more focused on destroying the competition than on creating a successful company. In Martials who were repressed or suppressed during childhood, this fury can turn inwards and they become self-destructive through drugs, alcohol, affairs, over-eating, reckless driving or other high-risk behaviours. Alcoholism and violence are a volatile combination for this type; a disproportionately high percentage of violent criminals are Martials, and the term 'crime of passion' is shorthand for an uncontrolled outburst of destruction.

Relationship to rules

Martials respond well to clear boundaries and fairness. If the rules are just, they are happy to obey them and frequently play the role of law enforcer. It feels instinctively right to them to protect the weak from the strong, to keep the good guys safe from the bad guys. On police cars in the USA we see the motto 'To protect and serve' and they are always ready to take down the bad guys. John Wayne as a US Marshall is an iconic Martial lawman. The courage of Mars comes into play when they put their lives on the line to enforce the law for the benefit of society. They can be seen as the immune system of a country or organisation, maintaining solid borders and keeping out hostile invaders. Nightclub bouncers and security guards embody this trait effortlessly. If the system that they are defending becomes corrupt or unfair, Mars will be active at the turning point in a revolution. They will defend the state out of a sense of loyalty, but will swiftly turn their destructive impulses upon their government as soon as they realise that they have been duped or manipulated into being on the wrong side. The fall of Nicolae Ceauşescu in Romania was an example of this dynamic in action: his strongly-loyal security team turned on him and took direct action. Whether they are defending or attacking a system, you can be sure a Martial will be doing so with passionate vigour and an unshakeable sense of being in the right. An example of this would be Martin Luther sparking the Reformation by nailing his Ninety-Five theses to the door of All Saint's Church in Wittenberg – pretty direct action against what he saw as the corruption in the Papacy.

Social situations

At public events, Martials tend to fall into two camps, according to whether formative influences have habituated them towards fight or flight. Fight-oriented Martials will head straight to the bar and from there to the liveliest spot in the room, where they will elbow their way to the centre of the action and wade into discussion without waiting to process the situation too deeply. If there is contentious discussion, they will soon join in and, with their adrenalin flowing, eyes gleaming and sleeves rolled up, they will aim squarely for the jugular vein of their opponent. If they are physically attracted to someone in the room, their favourite tactic is an immediate frontal approach, followed by dogged pursuit of their quarry; in the mind of a Martial, romantic wooing and poetic subtlety are for softer types.

They may well test the limits of social norms with their risqué humour and loud provocative comments and they enjoy acting hurt and bewildered when people take offence. At a business networking event, business opportunities are approached head on and leads diligently followed.

Flight-oriented Martials will be quieter and more hesitant, scanning for possible threats and potential sources of embarrassment. These Martials blush easily and are acutely self-conscious, feeling that others are appraising them as negatively as they habitually judge themselves. Alcohol can become a crutch to cope with social anxiety and they seek the calmer corners of the room, looking for someone safe to latch onto. Any disturbance will send them scurrying towards the exit; they would much rather back down than fight, but if pushed into a corner woe betide anyone who has misread their quietness for weakness. A flight-oriented Mars does not erupt very often, but when they do it is wise to seek cover!

Professional environments

Martials flourish in a working environment where the following factors are present:

- Firm boundaries

- Sharply defined roles – even to the point of 'us and them'

- Clear targets

- Hierarchy

- Hands-on chain of command

- Orders and procedures

- Urgency

- A just reward system

- Fairness

- Loyalty

- Action

- Corporate structure

- Protection of vulnerable people.

The following occupations are filled with Martials: police, military, coast guard, paramedics, mining, fire fighters, debt collection (Martin Luther King's 'I have a dream' speech calls the US government to account for promises made and not kept), border patrol, demolition, construction, stunt actors, geologists, oil rigs, mining, ranching, lumberjacks, blacksmiths, investigative reporters, sports referees, PE teachers (the one in the film *Kes* being a fine example), union leaders, mechanics, test pilots, nightclub bouncers and direct sales.

Famous examples: These include Rupert Grint, Emma Stone, Paul O'Connell, Kenneth Branagh (his performance as *Henry V* is a distillation of Martial intensity and focus), Ewan McGregor (especially as Renton in the movie *Trainspotting*; in his personal life he undertakes long dangerous motorbike journeys 'for fun'), Ade Edmondson (Viv in *The Young Ones*), Steve McQueen (Mars actors often play the good guy fighting against the odds), James Cagney, Nick Nolte and Anthony Hopkins.

The vast majority of celebrity chefs are Martials: Heston Blumenthal, Jamie Oliver, Julia Child, Gordon Ramsey, Anthony Worrall Thompson, Rick Bayless, Aldo Zilli and Mario Batali. They love the noise, heat, sense of urgency, shouting obscenities, deadlines, sharp objects and alcohol!

Other notable Martials are Dame Judy Dench, Imelda Staunton (her performance in the movie *Vera Drake* capturing Martial integrity), Juliet Stevenson, Ernest Shackleton, Dr Dre, Meg Whitman, Martin Luther, Katherine Tate, Philip Seymour Hoffman (destruction manifesting as self-destruction in his personal life), Emily Watson, Ginger Rogers, Pamela Reed, Damian Lewis, Geri Halliwell, Annie Lennox, Glenda Jackson, Ludwig Van Beethoven, Idi Amin, Mike Tyson and Vincent Van Gogh.

Then there are Sir Alan Sugar (think of the relish with which he says "*You are fired!*"), Richard Branson, who loves his dangerous sports, Daniel Craig, the Klingons, Vladimir Lenin, Wayne Rooney, Yosemite Sam, Ed Balls, JFK, Kate Adie, Pablo Picasso, Margaret Thatcher, Sun Tzu – author of *The Art of War*, Deborah Meaden (the fiercest dragon in the den, but she has a soft spot for the underdog), Mr T, Chris Evert, Boris Becker, Prince Harry (he just loves the military) and Johnny Rotten.

Martial animals include the bulldog, piranha, Tasmanian devil, Rottweiler, lion, sea bass, giant trevally, hawk and ginger tom cat.

Predominantly Martial countries and cultures include Ireland, Scotland, Wales, Germany, Turkey, the Huns, the Mongol hordes, the Zulus, Xhosa and the Serbs.

Countries where Martials are in the majority may feel like a rumbling volcano that could erupt at any moment. The attribute of destruction is like a vibration that resonates and spreads once it reaches a certain pitch, as a single crystal dropped into a saturated solution causes instant crystallisation.

True story: I once found myself in central Belfast at dusk on Saint Patrick's Day. Much alcohol had flowed and the raucous air of celebration began to shift towards a sense of menace and tension. I remembered the words that Claudius Ptolemy wrote around 200 AD: "The inhabitants of Britain and Germany have a greater familiarity with Mars and are accordingly wilder, bolder and more ferocious" and I decided that now was the ideal time for this lone Englishman to head back to his hotel!

We love Martials for their honesty, resilience, straight talking, independence, strength, directness, protectiveness, assertiveness, courage, efficiency, vitality, nerve, dynamism, enterprise, pioneering, recklessness, sense of duty, devotion, fairness, initiative, grit, pushing of boundaries and crude jokes

How sluggish and vague the world would be without Mars the God of War to embolden and challenge us all.

IVPITER.
Ioann. Stradan. inuen.
Ioann. Collaert sculp.
Phls Galle excudit.

Saturno genitore satus, diuûm atq; hominum Rex,   IVPITER, ardenti fulmina vibro manu.

Jovial

In mythology, Jupiter or Jove was the king of the gods and the god of sky and thunder. He was venerated in ancient Roman religion; the largest temple in Rome was that of Jupiter Optimus Maximus where he received the spoils of victory. In their courts of law, people called upon Jove to witness the oath, which led to the common expression 'By Jove!'

In the English language we use the adjective 'Jovial' to mean

1. Endowed with or characterised by a hearty, joyous humour or a spirit of good-fellowship: 'a wonderfully jovial host.'

2. Of or pertaining to the god Jove, or Jupiter. Synonyms: merry, jolly, convivial, gay, joyful, mirthful. Jovial, jocose and jocund agree in referring to someone who is in a good humour.

   Jovial suggests a hearty, joyous humour: 'a jovial person'.

   Jocose refers to that which causes laughter; it suggests someone who is playful and given to jesting: with jocose and comical airs.

   Jocular means humorous, facetious, mirthful, and waggish: jocular enough to keep up the spirits of all around him.

   Jocund, now a literary word, suggests a cheerful, light-hearted, and sprightly gaiety.

In astronomy, Jupiter is the fifth planet from the Sun and the largest within the Solar System. Jupiter is classified as a gas giant, having two and a half times the mass of all the other planets in our Solar System combined. Jupiter is primarily composed of hydrogen with a quarter of its mass being helium. Because of its rapid rotation, Jupiter possesses a slight but noticeable bulge around the equator (Jovial types may also possess a bulge around their middle from rich food!). The outer atmosphere is visibly segregated into several bands, resulting in turbulence and storms along their interacting boundaries. There are at least 63 moons and Ganymede, the largest of these, has a diameter greater than that of the planet Mercury. The planet Jupiter has long been associated with happiness and good fortune. The astronomical symbol for Jupiter is believed to be either a stylised version of the letter Z for Zeus (Jove's Greek counterpart) or a depiction of a throne.

In endocrinology, the Jovial type corresponds to the posterior pituitary type, as described by Louis Berman. This gland regulates the release of oxytocin, sometimes referred to as the love hormone, due to its role in bonding and childbirth, and also vasopressin, which is believed to influence social behaviour and pair bonding.

Physicality

Jovials are one of the two planetary types, the other being Venus, that are labelled by our youth and diet-obsessed Western culture as 'overweight'. The broad brush definitions of overweight people are 'apple shaped' or 'pear shaped', and recent discoveries in genetic science have indeed found genes which determine whether fatty tissue is stored on the upper or lower body. From this perspective, Jovials are apple shaped and tend to carry weight on the upper body. Venus people are pear shaped, tending to carry weight on the lower body.

The archetypal Jovial male will have a pinkish complexion with fine fair hair, which is likely to have started to recede at a relatively young age (the vast majority of bald men are Jovials). He will carry weight on the chest and abdomen and may have spindly legs. The face is full, even jowly and if, as is often the case with Jovials, they indulge a taste for the finer things in life, they will acquire double, triple or quadruple chins as the years go by. Hugging a Jovial male friend can bring to mind an image of a well-stuffed, comfortable leather couch! Another feature of this type is that young Jovial men may look and feel older than their chronological age, so they seem quite adult as teenagers and so on. The actor and comedian John Goodman is clear example; a more current male Jovial in the public eye is James Corden, who was feted for his debut on US television and immediately advised to lose weight!

An archetypal pure Jovial woman will be Rubenesque with a fleshy face, fair hair, large breasts, deep chest, full waist, narrow hips, and slender legs; their voice and laugh is often rich and resonant. Kathy Bates, the movie actress, fits the bill nicely. Jovial women enjoy wearing bright colours and rich, flowing fabrics and will definitely relish attracting attention upon entering a social gathering with a confident and radiant bearing.

Caucasian Jovial women will have pale or pinkish skin. African and African-American Jovial women seem to be far less affected by Western cultural messages about what size women 'should' be and positively emanate a lustrous glow, a hearty regal aura and ready laughter. Aretha Franklin springs readily to mind here.

Asian Jovials include Mao Zedong and Imelda Marcos – with her 6,000 pairs of shoes as an indicator of the Jovial flair for excess.

William Benham:

> *The Jovial is a large man inclined to be fleshy, his flesh is solid… his eyes are large and expressive, pupils are clear and dilate under the play of the emotions… the expression is mild and almost melting, bespeaking honesty and a kindly spirit. The cheeks are well rounded so the cheek bones are not to be seen. The walk is stately and dignified… the Jupiterian perspires freely, especially from the top of the head; this often leads to baldness early in life. The hair is brown, running into chestnut; in women of this type it grows long, is abundant and fine in quality, inclining to be curly. The chest is well developed and his large lungs are bellows from which is forced a rich, musical voice, just the voice to give commands or to speak to and influence a multitude.*

Jovial traits

Jovials have a regal, grandparental feel; they love to have people around them in a jolly, harmonious environment. Simply being in the presence of a Jovial can change one's mood to a more positive outlook and they know intuitively how to use their tact and charm to good effect. Other types often see them as lucky because their generosity of spirit attracts loyal benefactors and contacts. They instinctively cast themselves in leading roles in social and personal situations.

Just as the planet Jupiter radiates heat, so Jovials enjoy radiating their personal warmth to their large circles of friends. Jovials move freely between different groups, which may be quite diverse, so they may be deeply involved in an esoteric spiritual quest one moment, then networking with high powered business leaders and then working to support a charity.

Shakespeare could well have written "All the world's a stage, and all the men and women merely players; they have their exits and their entrances, and one man in his time plays many parts" with a Jovial in mind.

Jovials are harmonisers, preferring to see the similarities and connections amongst people rather than the differences; they are also keen on congratulating themselves on how well they carry this off. In observing a Jovial working a room or holding court it is hard to escape the feeling that a part of themselves is watching and appraising and adjusting their performance as it unfolds. They carry this act off with such grace and tact that we make allowances for the sense that they are acting one of their many roles. It's easy to expect a knowing wink in our direction as if they are letting us in on the game and saying to us "I know you can see that this is a performance but aren't I doing it well?" We can only agree and feel fortunate to be let in on the act. A Jovial enters a room in grand style, ideally with an entourage following them, and they get noticed with sweeping gestures and the resonant tone of their voice.

I was once presenting this system to a group of business owners on a retreat. I had arrived at the conference venue, but had no idea where the meeting was being held. Having previously met the chairman and knowing Richard to be a confirmed Jovial, I knew all I had to do was wait and listen. Sure enough, within a few moments I heard familiar laughter booming down a corridor from some distance away and knew exactly where to head.

Jovials love to coach, guide and mentor and see the success of their protégés as a glowing reflection of, and living tribute to, their own qualities. Jovials are lively raconteurs and most of their stories are about themselves and their talents and successes. They enjoy spending money and are not very good at budgeting, believing that they should simply buy what they want regardless of their bank balance. It is impossible to convince a Jovial that there is any truth in the adage 'less is more' – they know that more is more and that is exactly what they want and feel they richly deserve. It is hugely amusing to go shopping with a Jovial as the internal process of Jovial purchasing logic always follows these simple steps:

1. The Jovial sees an item that they like

2. The fact that they like the item means they deserve to own it

3. Therefore the item must be bought immediately

4. Cost of item is irrelevant

5. The bank balance is a trivial matter for lesser mortals to stress over

6. The Jovial presents a credit card to buy the item

7. If credit card is refused, they present another card; this step is repeated (see step 5 above) until a card is accepted and the item is purchased.

It follows that a Jovial will sometimes maintain an external image of abundance and success by employing some highly-creative uses of credit and loans.

I worked in an old people's home in the mid-1980s. Most of our residents had dementia of varying degrees and would not leave the premises. One well-spoken and highly-cultured Jovial lady resident in her mid-seventies was quite eccentric and called herself 'Lady V…'. One day, a huge van from the local high-end department store pulled up outside to deliver an exquisite suite of furniture. It turned out that 'Lady V…' had gone shopping, taken a shine to the suite, opened an account and arranged delivery. We had to explain that she lived in a small shared room, had nowhere to put the furniture and no money with which to pay for it. Jovial desire, gravitas and charm had obviously been at work here!

Kenneth Grahame's rambunctious Toad of Toad Hall is a Jovial icon and his passionate *cri de coeur*, "But I must have it, I must!" echoes in the heart of every Jovial, adult or child, rich or poor. When they get what they want, they glow with pleasure for a short time, until the next bauble come into view. King George IV of England was a classic Jovial who practically bankrupted the British treasury to build the Royal Pavilion in Brighton. Indian and Chinese art and architecture were in vogue at the time and in typical Jovial style he wanted both. The result is a building with an Indian exterior and a Chinese interior; the decor in every room is completely overblown and George IV would host dinners that had 36 courses.

The twin Jovial loves of learning and quality are embedded in Mike's story: Mike is without question a Jovial, he is large in every way and he radiates warmth and an infectious love of learning. He is a serial business owner who has dedicated the later part of his career to bringing his experience of chief executive peer learning groups to directors of charities. Here Mike talks about how he sees the importance of giving back:

> *Having had the benefit of running many businesses I felt compelled to bring the lessons I had learned to charities in order to help them be more commercially successful. Most private sector business owners have at least one eye on the bottom line, whereas charities can be overly focused on the cause they serve, to the detriment of running the business as a business. I want to help leaders of charities avoid the mistakes I made and feel I can have more impact in two months working with charities than in a year working with private sector CEOs. While I feel it is important to pass on the benefits of my wisdom and experience I am totally clear that I do this primarily for myself. My apparent altruism is actually selfish – I feel good doing it.*

Mike spent time in the wine trade and was picked to attend the Champagne Academy. As a result he hosts tasting events and finds great joy in educating people about champagne:

> *Champagne is about quality, tradition, celebration and achieving the absolute best. Champagne producers work within strict guidelines and are always seeking continual improvement, which I see as a great example for us all and the way I like to see businesses run. I love non-vintage champagne because it requires great artistry to produce exceptional champagne from ordinary grapes – it is a labour of love. Sharing my love of champagne is another way I can give back.*

Mike also shares his Jovial love of fun and could be speaking on behalf of all Jovials here:

> *My purpose in life is to have fun doing the things that are important to me. Some people don't understand this; it is selfish but I want to enjoy what I do. Everything I do is must be enjoyable or I find a way to make it so. Laughter and humour are some of the best values in the world in my book.*

Most Jovials have a wide range of interests and tastes and their home environments can be totally cluttered with the accoutrements of their eclectic pursuits. Jovials delight in giving gifts to those close to them, and the bigger and more noticeable the gift, the better. There is something truly endearing in seeing the anticipation on the face of a Jovial as a friend unwraps a gift they have given them. It is vital to show gratitude and appreciation at this point and for some time afterwards too: Jovials are warm-hearted and cheerful, but one of the few things they find unforgiveable is ingratitude. At some level, while brushing it off with an apparent aura of indifference, the Jovial will be fully aware of the sincerity of the 'thank you' and the frequency of repeats. Jovials are unthinkingly generous to their friends, while almost unconsciously keeping track of the gifts they have given. They may well become demanding when they want something in return. It is easy to misjudge their seemingly casual open-handed beneficence: beneath the easy going surface is a shrewd and intricate accounting process. When the Jovial decides it is time to call in a favour, it may come from out of the blue, but a rapid and positive response is expected or even demanded. From the Jovial's side of the deal, they are simply asking a friend, whom they have helped many times in the past, to now help them out – 'now' being the crucial word here! From the other side of the deal, it can feel as if a large, invisible bill has accumulated for items on which prices were never discussed and that has now been presented for immediate payment.

Jovials can be masters of diplomacy, having a sixth sense for other people's emotional needs and an ability to broker and negotiate delicately-balanced deals and agreements. They strive for harmony and find discord between friends or family members to be a source of almost physical internal pain. If their efforts to soothe and heal a situation break down, they are unlikely to stick around for the more contentious episodes, preferring to withdraw rather than expose themselves to a hostile environment. An arena where insults and recriminations are flying thick and fast through the air will send them running for cover instantly, where they will wait until the storm dies down to see what can be mended. Jovials can perform miracles working behind the scenes as go-betweens when they care about both warring parties; they tell each side exactly what they need to hear and draw them ever closer to reconciliation. A good example of this is Hans Blix, the Jovial Swedish diplomat and UN weapons inspector, who worked tirelessly under extreme conditions to try to head off the Iraq War.

The flip side of this sixth sense for other people's emotional needs is that a Jovial can be an absolute master of the undercurrents of office politics, skilfully dividing and conquering by making several different parties each feel that they are the Jovial's sole confidants. They then eke out insider information in an intricate dance of manipulation. When confronted, their eyes widen with feigned innocence and a wounded expression of bewilderment that anyone could even hint at suspecting that they were doing anything other than acting in the best interests of all concerned. They will even have a few handy emotional buttons to subtly push and thereby unsettle their accuser.

Jovials have another truly remarkable talent, which is a method of making people feel privileged to be asked to do something for them, as if they have been specially chosen above all others for the task. There are items in shops in England that bear the 'Royal Seal of Approval', with a fancy crest on the packaging and the words 'By Appointment to Her Majesty the Queen'. Manufacturers compete for this seal as no doubt it boosts sales and credibility. A Jovial can ask someone to pick up their dry cleaning for them in such a manner that it is as if they have been selected to be the 'Collector and Deliverer of Royal Dry Cleaning.'

Next time you are out shopping with a Jovial you may want to notice how smoothly a request to 'hold this for a moment' slides into you carrying their purchases for them for the rest of the day!

The mind of a Jovial is expansive and open to learning. Coupled with their enthusiastic hearts, this gives them a passion for exploring and understanding science, arts and culture. It is common to see Jovials at the opera with their eyes closed, deeply enraptured by the music, and one suspects that in their mind's eye is a picture of themselves on the stage, regally attired and belting out arias to feverish applause. A Jovial may have difficulty channelling their excitement for new knowledge into accomplishment; they find the vivid fantasy of being a virtuoso musician far more engaging than the tedious hours of practice that are required.

Louis Berman writes unflatteringly of Jovials or, as he calls them, men of the posterior pituitary type:

> *The post pituitary type is short, rounded and stout, they have heads that seem too large for their bodies and they acquire an abdominal paunch early. They exhibit the feminine tendency to periodicity of function, their moods, activities, efficiency are cyclic, reminding one of the menstrual variations of the female. This rhythmicity saturates their personalities, so that poetry and music almost morbidly appeal to them. A number of the great poets and musicians are to be classified as of the feminine pituitary species.*

Because they have a natural affinity and talent for learning, there may well be a gap between the level of ability that they believe they have and the actual reality. Anyone pointing this out is likely to be on the receiving end of some bluster and huffiness. Jupiter is, after all, the god of sky and thunder and, when crossed beyond the point of tolerance, Jovials are prone to erupt with loud stinging barbs and rumbling expressions of disdain. The initial outburst tends to blow over quickly, but a Jovial who feels hurt is apt to hold a grudge for a long time. It may take much soothing and placating of their wounded pride to bring them back to the reconciliation and harmony that they secretly wish for. Once the conflict is healed and in the past, then the Jovial will be the first party to make jokes about it, even about the very issue which set them off in the beginning. If the wounds are too deep and the other party does not take the appropriate steps to resolve the situation, then they incur the worse possible punishment – banishment from the Royal Court. From the Jovial perspective, as the king or queen of their circle, the wrongdoer must be ejected to the outer darkness, where they will wither far from the radiance of the Jovial until they see the error of their ways. The only way to re-enter the Royal Court is through a determined and prolonged campaign of flattery. This is the Achilles heel of every Jovial; they are like putty in the hands of anyone who knows how to flatter them. A good salesman will know this intuitively and we can observe this process when a Jovial is buttered up in an exclusive boutique and leaves with armfuls of designer clothes and a dented credit card.

Words which inspire a Jovial include party, collaboration, splash out, well respected, big impact, finest quality, exclusive, invitation only and selected.

Words which insult or demotivate them include unimaginative, bog standard, run of the mill, stingy, petty, nitty-gritty, pedantic and provincial.

The other types judge Jovials as being pompous, self-indulgent, arrogant, snooty, touchy, self-deluded, over-sensitive drama queens.

Jovials judge other types as being tight fisted, narrow minded, timid, pedantic, overly literal riff-raff.

Jovials naturally see themselves as being gallant, courteous, gifted, dignified, generous, cultured, patrons of the arts, Renaissance men and women, who are natural leaders and who really belong in the 18th Century.

They are at their very happiest when celebrating success with friends and admirers, toasting, spinning yarns, telling tasteful jokes and making the walls reverberate with raucous laughter.

Their worst experiences are during times of financial constraint and a loss of social prestige: a Jovial on a diet is not pleasant company!

The Renaissance was a Jovial period in history – an explosion of interest and vast amounts of money spent on rediscovering and interpreting ancient arts and literature, scientific discovery, alchemical experiments and musical composition. The royal courts of Europe would compete to outdo each other in ostentatious displays of grandeur and sophistication.

Core attribute

The core attribute of a Jovial is Vanity. This is an acute awareness of one's own talents and abilities and one's position in social structures.

At the healthy, functional end of the spectrum, this attribute enlivens and empowers a Jovial with the innate belief that they are uniquely special, capable and accomplished. At its best, Jovial vanity is an accurate sense of high self-esteem and self-worth. This asset gives Jovials the confidence to explore new horizons and share the treasures of their experience with their retinue, to make a valuable and relevant contribution to society. Pure, positive Jovial Vanity has an endearing and infectious quality.

I once watched a 5-year-old Jovial get on a bus. As his mother paid the driver it was as if his retainer was dealing with the trivial details. He meanwhile strode down the bus like a little prince; he found two empty seats and sat in one of them as if he was taking his rightful place on a throne.

If you have a Jovial child, avoid using phrases such as 'don't show off', 'don't get too big for your boots' and other such advice, which is typically used to supress the spirit of young Jovials. Allow them to be raconteurs and storytellers and please bite your tongue when they exaggerate their achievements. They will find their own boundaries and sense of objectivity using their innate emotional intelligence, which is far more valuable than any set of societal rules. If they overstep the mark in self-promotion, a private light-hearted word will bring them into balance far more effectively than a public rebuke. In our materialistic and image-obsessed culture, it is rare that a child suffers from an excess of self-esteem; typically, the reverse is true. With a Jovial child, in terms of an accurate appraisal of self-worth, the path to moderation will be via excess!

The radiance of vanity attracts people and warms their hearts; you can observe people's posture change after a few minutes around a contented Jovial.

William Benham:

> They are aware of the influence they exert and it naturally makes them vain. This vanity knows the power of the rich musical voice in swaying men, and they like to hear the sound of this voice as well as to see it shape the views of others. Leadership is always uppermost in their minds. With all his vanity, the Jupiterian is warm hearted. He has a fellow-feeling for humanity that exhibits itself in practical ways. A word of comfort from so strong a person to one in distress does a world of good, and the kindly spirit he shows to all who appeal to him binds closer the following he attracts. Nor is his kindness confined to words, for he gives as well, and is generous and charitable. These Jupiterian beneficences are dispensed in a manly, open hearted way that makes the recipient feel that the donor is glad to give.

At the unhealthy, dysfunctional end of the spectrum, the attribute of vanity brings an arrogant self-delusion about the degree of their abilities and a defensiveness which seeks to maintain this inflated self-image. This feeds a weakness for boasting and a deep craving for any form of flattery. They can become manipulative and vindictive, surrounding themselves with 'yes men' and being spiteful to those who are less than totally fawning. They embody the traits of the archetypal tyrant king, queen or dictator.

We all move constantly along the spectrum of our core attribute, depending on mood, circumstance and level of self-awareness. It seems that Jovials can move relatively quickly and frequently from one end of this spectrum to the other. In the arts, we might see a Jovial director basking in the glory of a successful opening night, then stamping her foot and becoming enraged by one line in a review, and then overjoyed when a friend tells her some negative gossip about the critic who wrote the review and so on and so on. Their emotional pendulum swings can be quite dramatic and bewildering to those around them and bring to mind the king who has the bearer of bad news beheaded and lavishly rewards the bearer of good news.

This attribute can make the Jovial prone to excess in all areas of their lives: at one end believing they deserve to have everything they want right now because they are special; at the other end needing to compensate for feeling so deflated and unappreciated. This leads them to compulsive spending, overeating and alcoholism. We are each a combination of two types and the Mars-Jovial combination is especially prone to alcoholism: Mars likes to drink and Jovial likes a lot of everything. Therefore many Mars-Jovials like to drink a lot!

Relationship to rules

Jovials appreciate rules that promote harmony, decorum and the circulation of abundant wealth. They are tuned in to social convention and good manners and like people to act nicely towards each other. They act against violations of these social rules by withdrawing from the riffraff and by excluding persistent wrongdoers from their circle of friends. Aggressive rebels are met with sharply-barbed put downs that remind them firmly of their place in the grand scheme.

Jovials find deep offence with any restrictions upon their spending, generation of profits or celebration of good fortune. They see these sorts of petty rules as something thought up by small-minded jobsworths specifically to spoil their fun, and they feel these rules should only apply to the 'little people' They see themselves as above these minor rules, and any attempt by an ordinary person to enforce these rules is met with the classic Jovial retort, "Don't you know who I am?"

Social situations

At a social event, Jovial will be graciously playing the role of host (regardless of whether or not it is their party!), greeting people as they arrive, making introductions and generally orchestrating the proceedings. They like to make a grand, sweeping entrance, commence holding court loudly and all too often drink and eat to excess. They make superb raconteurs and no one seems to mind that most of their anecdotes have themselves as the central character. You often see them surrounded by a cheerful circle, perspiring freely, glass in hand and laughing until tears course down their quivering cheeks. When they are on form, they truly are the life and soul of a party. Jovials will often make it their mission to single out a shy social misfit, cheer them up and cajole them into the swing of things – involuntarily if necessary!

They love big parties and like to announce their exits loudly with many hugs and air kisses, ideally accompanied by a large, adoring entourage. At networking events, they get a huge thrill from facilitating mutually-beneficial introductions and basking in the glow of gratitude and approval.

Professional environments

Jovials flourish in a working environment where the following factors are present:

- An incoming stream of people
- Fun
- An air of anticipation
- Laughter

- Creativity

- Warmth

- The finer things in life

- Artistic expression

- Flow of money

- Bustle

- Drama

- Intrigue

They are found in all areas of the arts, making superb orchestra conductors and patrons, classical musicians, film and theatre promoters, directors and producers. They are strongly drawn to the realm of comedy, which gives a natural outlet to their good nature and often surprising sense of humour, as demonstrated in Donald's story, below.

Donald is a Jovial in his late 50s who writes comedy scripts for TV, radio and film. We talked about his finely-tuned Jovial instinct for successfully writing humorous pieces:

> *I don't write with the audience in mind; I simply write what I find funny. Not everyone in the audience will love it, but it usually works. There is a tension inside me when I see a sketch that I have written performed before a live audience for the first time and I wonder if the jokes will work. It is like a dialogue where a pattern is established which repeats and then builds to a punchline. When the audience starts laughing I feel elated, as if there is a communication established and my ideas are validated. My material is often quirky and when it gets a laugh I love it that someone thinks like me. If I know there are more peaks to come in the sketch I can sense the audience anticipating them and it feels like lighting a firework and waiting for it to go off. After the event, when the adrenalin dies down, I can reflect on the experience and really savour the success.*

Donald talked about his boyhood love of humour:

> *I listened constantly to radio comedy as a child; I loved the Goons.*

Having always made my friends laugh at school, I formed a comedy theatre company in my early 20s and we loved performing our own material. My career as a comedy writer came about because I had the confidence to send sketches to the BBC and I just assumed that they would immediately include them in a top-rated topical show. My first sketch to be performed on TV was rewritten by other people before filming and I was indignant when it went out on air – but I was happy to be paid half of my weekly wage for a three-minute sketch. I then called the BBC, told them I was in the area and blithely wandered in with no awareness of how difficult it was to get material accepted. Things just kept rolling along from there.

As a result of his successful career Donald has been able to embrace a Jovial love of the finer things in life:

The world of cinema and TV is quite rarefied and can be indulgent. At first, I had to learn to enjoy good food and wine; now it is second nature to me. I love to entertain guests, collect paintings and be a host and raconteur.

I could not resist asking Donald about the idea of budgeting, which typically produces a rueful look and a wistful smirk in a Jovial. I was not disappointed:

I'm not good at budgeting. I constantly underestimate my living expenses. I live well and I don't worry about it. My weakness around money is that I spend it on the interesting things, like fine art, but I resent spending it on boring things, like new tyres for my car or the mortgage. For me, something like car tyres are a waste of money because you have to have them – what most other people see as luxuries, I see as essential and vice versa. I just trust that the money will come in and it always does. [Donald actually touched wood at this point!]

Donald went on to capture the 'I must have it, I must!' philosophy:

Sometimes I just don't know why I buy things; for example the cover on my iPad cost more than the iPad and I rarely even use it, because it's not the definitive iPad. I have the definitive cover, but not the definitive iPad! I made a living as an antiques dealer for a year but I had to give up because I didn't want to sell anything I had bought because I loved it all too much to get rid of it.

We also find Jovials happily engaged as publicans, linguists, diplomats, old-style high-street shopkeepers – especially jolly butchers, fund raisers for large charities, financiers, high-end antique dealers, middle managers, team leaders, auctioneers, preachers, carnival barkers, town criers, restaurant hosts, teachers and chefs.

Jovials are remarkably successful at relationship-based sales, as we see in Jane's story:

Jane is a Jovial type who is highly successful in the field of medical equipment sales. She is warm, friendly and especially talented in relationship-based sales. She shared her insight into the process of building robust business relationships with me:

It takes time to build trust. In every job I've had, I have never been successful in the first year; I observe, learn my clients' practice and get to know them personally. I go into their environment and understand how they work and what they need. You don't go round to someone's house for the first time and start moving the furniture around! I never win awards in my first year in a job, though I tend to do very well long term – I have won 17 national and 2 international awards in 27 years. I get a buzz from a big sale, but the most satisfying feeling is when a consultant rings me up and asks for my advice and brings me in on a case. It means my expertise and the relationship are both sound, and when the outcome is successful, things could not be much better.

Jane and her husband have visited over 60 countries and here she shares her Jovial love of culture and variety:

In my work I often stay in 5-star hotels, so when I travel for fun I seek out a wide range of experiences: I am much more flexible on where we stay as long as I have a nice bed, a shower and a bar. I like learning new things and I have a large appetite for life and adventure, so I try to stuff as much experience in as possible. For me, life is not a rehearsal and I am definitely on stage. On a recent hiking trip to Patagonia I was helped down a glacier by my tall dark handsome Argentinian guide and couldn't stop giggling; the next day I was hiking 150 miles away and woman came up to me and told me that she recognised me from the glacier by my laugh!

Jane encapsulates the Jovial view of the purpose of wealth:

My philosophy on money is to avoid being totally reckless but at the same time there is nothing I won't do because of cost. If I want the experience, I spend the money After all, you can't take it with you – there are no pockets in shrouds.

Famous examples: Ceelo Green, Adele, Rembrandt van Rijn (he died penniless but owned warehouses filled with exotic items from around the world), Falstaff (a pitch-perfect character study of a Jovial), Babe Ruth, Gert Frobe (who played the Jovial villain Auric Goldfinger in the James Bond film), Shelley Winters, Chris Farley, Oprah Winfrey, Tommy Cooper, Dawn French, Richard Griffiths (his portrayal of Uncle Monty in the film *Withnail and I* is a pristine example of an actor playing his own type to perfection), Winnie the Pooh, Chris Farley, Jabba the Hutt, Baloo the bear from *The Jungle Book*, William 'the refrigerator' Perry, Santa Claus (he always knows who has been good and who hasn't, and if you are not on his list you don't get a present), Louis Armstrong, Pantomime Dames (especially Widow Twankey), the Modern Major General from Gilbert and Sullivan, Hyacinth Bucket, King Edward VII, Robbie Coltrane, Porky Pig, George Melly, Christopher Biggins, Harry Secombe, Billy Bunter, John Candy, Roscoe 'Fatty' Arbuckle, Susan Boyle, Rush Limbaugh, Louis XIV of France and Hermann Goering.

Jovial animals include whales, elephants, walruses, pigs, bumblebees, orang-utans and St Bernard dogs.

Countries and cultures that are predominantly Jovial include New Orleans, Poland, Hungary, Bavaria (the Oktoberfest is a Jovial ritual event) and the Czech Republic – in short, any Eastern European country that willingly tolerates the Polka.

Countries where Jovials are in the majority have an easy going, welcoming feel with an undercurrent of tension around making social faux pas. It can be difficult to refuse excessive hospitality politely without ruffling some feathers. Consequently it is only too easy to gain weight when visiting a Jovial country!

We love Jovials for their warmth, generosity, radiance, dignity, grandeur, regal nature, enthusiasm, openness, poise, splendour, confidence, theatricality, extravagance, brilliance, wit, savoir faire, large presence, impulsiveness, wisdom, eloquence, humanitarianism, flamboyance and booming laughter.

How dull and narrow this world would be without Jove, King of the Gods to arouse and inspire us.

LVNA.
Ioan. Stradan. inu.
Ioann. Collaert sculp.
Phls Galle excudit.

7

Filia LVNA Iouis, roséi soror ignea Phoebi,   Clarâ nocturnas luce abigo tenebras

Lunar

In mythology, Diana was the Roman moon goddess, huntress, jealous guardian of privacy and ruler of the night. She was also an emblem of chastity and was the equivalent of Artemis, the Greek goddess of the hunt, wild animals, wilderness, childbirth, virginity and young girls. Artemis later came to be identified with Selene. Typically these goddesses are depicted in painting and sculpture with bow and arrows, stags, hounds at their feet and a crescent moon above the head.

In English, the word Lunar is an adjective meaning:

1. Of or pertaining to the moon: the lunar orbit.

2. Measured by the moon's revolutions: a lunar month.

3. Resembling the moon: round or crescent-shaped.

4. Of or pertaining to silver.

The word lunar is also the root of words like lunatic and lunacy, meaning moon struck or obsessed.

Astronomically, the Moon is Earth's only natural satellite. It is the largest satellite in the Solar System relative to the size of its host planet, being a quarter the diameter of Earth. It stays in synchronous rotation with Earth, which means it always shows us the same face, hence the phrase 'dark side of the moon', meaning the side that we never see from Earth. It is the brightest object in the sky after the Sun, although the surface is actually dark. Its prominence in the sky and regular cycle of phases has meant that, since ancient times, the Moon has had an important cultural influence on our language, calendar, art and mythology.

The Moon is sometimes regarded poetically as the child of the Earth: according to one school of thought, when the Earth was molten rock, the Moon was torn off and solidified to become our satellite. The Moon's gravitational influence produces the ocean tides and the minute lengthening of the day. The Moon's current orbital distance, about thirty times the diameter of the Earth, causes it to be the same size in the sky as the Sun, which means that the Moon covers the Sun precisely during a total solar eclipse.

The astronomical symbol for the Moon is the crescent, found on the headdresses of Diana and Selene.

In endocrinology, the Lunar type corresponds to the pancreas, which produces digestive hormones regulating the release of available energy. It acts as a brake on the adrenals and is connected to the lymphatic system.

Physicality

Lunar men are not of an athletic build. Their hair is usually mousey and fine; their skin is pale or yellowish in colour, and the face round, with a weak or receding chin. Some Lunar men are tall and thin, with a fragile constitution. There may be greyish bags or colouring under the eyes, which are often pale, with a look of timidity to them. The chest is often small or even sunken; their shoulders rounded or sloped and there is little body hair. The voice tends to be quiet and thin and there may be a slightly effeminate feel to them. Lunar men are not likely to be amongst those who were picked first for the rugby team! Paul Kagame, the president of Rwanda, is a Lunar man who brought calm to his nation in the wake of genocide. Bill Gates and Steve Jobs used their Lunar persistence as a path to success, as did Jack Ma, the founder of Alibaba.

Lunar women usually have small breasts, not much of a waist and narrow hips; their hands and feet are small and delicate. They may well have a 'china-doll' appearance, which makes them exquisitely beautiful and graceful, though this is a cool, untouchable beauty – think Christina Ricci. Their hair is often fine and very straight, typically brown, but occasionally blonde, and there can be a definite 'moonish' look to their face, with a chin that is weak or occasionally pointed. Again, there is often very little body hair. Some predominantly Lunar adults look as if their bodies had stopped developing partway through puberty, so they do not acquire large masculine muscles or rounded feminine curves. Jennifer Lawrence and Taylor Swift are Lunar women as was Rosa Parks.

Lunar traits

Mars can be seen as the masculine warrior in this system, Jovial as the warm grandparent and Lunar as the delicate child; again, the Moon is seen as the child of the Earth. Lunars are the type that is most frequently misunderstood by the other types. The Moon is a satellite, not a planet in its own right, and Lunars seem slightly removed from the general cut and thrust of social interaction. They tend to process sensory input rather slowly and methodically and would prefer to give no response rather than a rushed or ill-considered one. When observing a Lunar friend, one gets the impression that they are carefully digesting emotional stimuli, as opposed to being affected by them and simply reacting spontaneously. Lunars have a rich and intricate emotional life and care deeply about people and principles; they are simply not overly demonstrative and consider it extremely bad form to lose one's cool, especially in public view. This aura of emotional reserve can frustrate the more direct or demonstrative types to the point where they become determined to provoke a reaction. Watching an impatient Mars interact with a Lunar is akin to watching a child poking a snail to try to get it to move faster – it doesn't work!

Lunars respect other people by giving them space and time and prefer the same consideration in return. As a reserved, polite type, they are far more often intruded upon than they are seen intruding on others. Lunars need to go at their own pace and in their own space; they actively avoid the spotlight, feeling exposed and awkward when people are watching them. When a Lunar enters a meeting that has already started their discomfort is acute and palpable; they will creep silently to the nearest available seat, barely breathing and avoiding eye contact. They do not like to be seen violating protocol and losing face in front of their peers. Hearty back-slapping Jovial attempts to jolly a Lunar along or drag them into centre stage at lively events are excruciating for all parties involved.

Their attention is automatically drawn to details, especially to what is missing or inaccurate. In fact, their attention to detail is supreme amongst the types, to the point where it can appear obsessive to others. Lunars notice the tiny stain on a carpet or the picture that is hanging very slightly askew and it bothers them: they want things to be put right and are well aware that most other types don't even notice these details, let alone care about them. While Mars bulldozes straight ahead and Jovials expect the little people to deal with the trivial things, Lunars notice and, if you listen very carefully, you may even hear a tiny sigh escape their pursed lips.

Lunars have no appetite for direct confrontation, so they will send an email or memo if something is really getting under their skin. If you work with or are in a relationship with a Lunar, it is well worth paying attention to these small, quiet messages, as it is likely that the irritation is greater than it appears on the surface. Travelling further down this road, when the vital Lunar employee hands in their notice because they have finally had enough, it's of little use pleading, "Why didn't you tell me you were upset about this?", because they did tell you, quietly, and they will be able to show you when and how and exactly how many times they told you.

Still waters run very deep with Lunars and, like the Moon, they have a hidden dark side: it is possible to know a Lunar for many years and have little idea about certain areas of their lives. Once you get to know them very well, you will often find a Lunar has secret pleasures that no one knows about or would even guess at. Part of the thrill they experience is in the secrecy itself: they get a repeated frisson from the fact that they know and you don't. For example, Winona Ryder is a Lunar actress who enjoyed shoplifting. At night, we find many solitary Lunars in casinos gambling. These sorts of behaviours revolve around internal stimulation which the participant typically seeks to conceal, so we are reminded of Diana goddess of secrecy, hunting and the night.

A Lunar friend of mine, who looks as if butter would not melt in her mouth, has two specific indulgences when driving. One is to politely allow other drivers to enter the stream of traffic in front of her when she has an impatient driver tailgating her, the other one is to spray washer fluid on her windscreen so that it lands on the front of the car tailgating her. One could almost consider this behaviour to be passive aggressive.

Because they don't encroach on others, Lunars can be taken for granted in the workplace or family and simply expected to just go along with the status quo. Their only means of asserting themselves is to resist and hold their position. Often, the first time their colleagues realise how crucial a role the Lunar plays is when they go on holiday and no one can find anything. They don't make a big song and dance about their contribution, but when they turn off the tap then the system grinds to a halt.

Lunars are far more clearly aware of what they don't like than what they do like, and this holds for people too. For this reason, Lunars make wonderfully true and loyal friends; once they have decided you pass muster, they are constant and will be especially supportive in a crisis because they do not waste time and energy on emotional dramas. The process of building a friendship with a Lunar can mystify other types: there is a slow exploration and respectful sharing of interests; things begin to warm up emotionally; they become more talkative and you may to share a few in-jokes. There then comes a critical point where the friendship is established in the heart of the Lunar, and at that point they stop talking to you! To a Lunar, once they have established a friendship, all the tiresome effort is done and they can now relax and be quiet. Lunars deeply respect other people's privacy and space, and now you are friends you can leave each other alone. It is not difficult to imagine how a Jovial reacts at this point. Lunars offer and in turn appreciate low-maintenance relationships; if you are looking for ongoing drama or fireworks, then look elsewhere. However, if you value deep and lasting friendship that doesn't need constant injections of emotional energy to survive, then this is where you will find it. By understanding the different ways that types relate, we can experience deeper, richer and more fruitful relationships.

If a Lunar lets you in on their quirky sense of humour and wacky world view then you are in for a real treat, as they notice and relish the foibles of other people that most people miss. Jane Austen and Thomas Hardy were Lunar authors whose minutely-detailed observations of human nature are the core of their timeless literature.

William Benham had this to say about Lunar creators:

> *Such subjects, when describing some creation of their fancy, will not omit an iota that can make the picture complete. The subject is apt to be orderly in dress and surroundings and extremely likely to be sensitive and ready to take offence at trifles.*

Woody Allen is a classic Lunar whose oeuvre was almost completely based on his own neurotic awkwardness around human relationships and who neatly fits Benham's description:

> *He is constantly a prey to his imaginings, thinks he is ill, and has diverse ailments, is fickle, restless and changeable. It is hard for him to settle down to humdrum life for he is always yearning for things beyond his reach… He is slow in his movements, phlegmatic in disposition and extremely sensitive. He imagines slights when none are intended and shrinks into himself and away from company. He does not love nor seek society. He realises he is different from other people, so he retires to secluded places where he can enjoy himself by himself… He is never generous; to him selfishness is innate…The Lunarian is lacking in self-confidence and feels his unfitness for the active pursuits of life.*

Their steadfastness and persistence make Lunars the 'quiet heroes' in organisations and in families, ever present in the background to offer guidance and support, when appropriate. If they decide to take on a project, then they will see it through until the end. They take a long-term, ground-level view; they are planted on the Earth and know how to proceed step by step to their destination. The parable of the tortoise and the hare neatly captures this approach, the tortoise being a Lunar animal that retreats into its shell when threatened and carries its defence on its back at all times. Lunars have this ability to fall back on their own resources, knowing full well that no one is equipped or inclined to do the task at hand as thoroughly as they are and that the outside world can be a randomly threatening place.

Lunars are the most meticulous people in their dress and work habits and are able to live and work quite comfortably in a compact space. Disorganisation is quite disturbing to them and as children they were very likely to have enjoyed tidying their room and found security in routine and structure.

We find Lunar attention to detail and high standards in Priya's story.

Priya is a Lunar type who has found a specific niche for her innate skills: she is a teacher of ancient temple dances, a discipline that requires intensive training and involves sustained presence and self-awareness. She talks about the self-control that she exercises in her work:

I take extensive notes on every detail of a routine and spend hours planning a lesson; it is vital to coordinate the external movement and internal awareness and one must apply total presence or it all falls apart. In some routines there are separate movements and rhythms for the head, hands and feet and an intentional focusing on attention, all happening at once. If I drop one element I feel totally wrong and when it all comes together I feel I'm 'getting myself right'. I am constantly assessing myself and others and have very high standards; I had a trained musician in my class who could do the external form correctly but could not manage the inner focus, they looked good from the outside but I knew it was just the form and it drove me crazy.

Because Priya has spent many years on personal development, she is able to bring a forensic focus and precise awareness of her inner contradictions:

There is a real paradox to my work in that there is the possibility to find real peace internally and be free of my ego, but it's my ego that wants to do the movements perfectly. I feel trapped in that I'm either doing an exercise right for the wrong reasons or doing it imperfectly for the right reasons! I observe myself judging other people and then I immediately judge myself for doing this because 'it's wrong to judge people.' I find myself filtering my responses through many layers of 'shoulds' before I respond to a question, and I find it difficult to be spontaneous.

Priya's friends find her utterly delightful and easy to be around. I asked her how she finds relief from her rather strict inner critic:

When I am with friends who are humorous and playful, I can relax, let go, and stop taking myself so seriously. Recently, my husband left some spots of soup on the stove so I spent an hour cleaning it; internally I was complaining about him but I couldn't say anything because it is 'wrong' to complain! My friends and I laugh about this and then I relax and have a new perspective. We even joke about the fact that sometimes I try hard to be humorous and spontaneous, as if joyfulness is yet another task that I must get right. When I am away from my native Taiwan it is easier for me to relax as the rules are different from my own culture, so I am aware of fewer things that I can get wrong.

Lunar children can have difficult childhoods if their parents are of another type and do not understand them or accept them as they are. Western European and North American popular culture idealises the Mars male as something men are supposed to aspire to and Lunar boys, in particular, have traumatic experiences when they are forced or expected to act like sporting heroes or warriors. This shoving of a square peg into a round hole can do lasting harm to their self-esteem, especially if coupled with a sense that the father is ashamed of the 'weakness' of the son.

If you are reading this and have identified your child as a Lunar, please give then space; don't push them; drop your agenda, and appreciate their unique qualities. Under no circumstances try to 'toughen them up', 'jolly them along' or 'bring them out of their shell'. This is painful to them, producing stress and generally resulting in a more determined withdrawal. Instead, quietly and patiently make them aware of the value of engaging with people on their own terms and support them in building their confidence at their own pace. When they set themselves on a path, they will persist. Recognise their sensitivity and allow them to unfold naturally. It may be that they need solitude after a social interaction. It is as if they grit their teeth, meet and greet and then reward themselves with peace and quiet.

When I present this material to groups and invite delegates to explore identifying their own type, it has been my observation that approximately 60 per cent of Lunar males seek to identify themselves as Martials, due to growing up with this residual pressure to conform to external expectations. It is always a delicate and emotionally-charged moment when the group feeds back to them that they are seen as Lunar. The clearest example of this dynamic on the world stage is when Vladimir Putin appears in photos bare chested on horseback or engaged in a dangerous activity; he is a textbook case of a Lunar who wants to be a Mars.

I once presented this system to a global insurance company that had a lot of international clients and wanted to promote cultural understanding and sensitivity. I was describing the Lunar type in a fairly sensitive manner as there were several Lunar men in the room and we were aiming to also bond the team. About halfway through my description of a typical Lunar, a Mars male with flaming red hair leaned back in his chair and bellowed at the ceiling, "Oh God! Who would want to be one of them?" So much for sensitivity with our dear friend Mars in the room.

A Lunar's inner focus can extend into an obsessive preoccupation with their digestion and lead them to follow rather bland faddish diets which are 'good for you' and involve simple ingredients. Macrobiotics is therefore a prime example of Lunar dietary practice – lots of brown rice and a few vegetables.

Words that inspire Lunars include precision, procedure, process, principles, departmental, spreadsheet, clear-cut, task and defined role.

Words that disturb Lunars include surprise, party, left field, rapid response, frontline, multi-tasking and high visibility.

The other types judge Lunars as being cold, distant, nit-picky, sullen, finicky, serious, boring loners.

Lunars judge the other types as loud, intrusive, immature, sloppy, invasive, impolite, careless, impatient, pushy, compulsive and clumsy.

It is no wonder that they prefer to spend time by themselves or with their fellow Lunars!

Lunars see themselves as being clear-minded, precise, consistent, persistent, reliable, highly principled, patient, committed, mature and focused.

Core attribute

The core attribute of a Lunar is Wilfulness. Wilfulness is the awesome power of unshakeable determination and laser-like focus.

At the healthy, functional end of the spectrum this attribute means that when a Lunar decides upon a course of action they will not be swayed. Wilfulness means Lunars doggedly continue until they succeed in their endeavour; any obstacles only serve to strengthen their resolve, and delays are grist to the mill and simply serve to sharpen their focus. 'Persistence pays' is a Lunar motto which certainly applies in Simon's story. Simon is a Lunar property developer who designs and develops property to a high level before renting or selling. He told me about his working style:

I structure a property project quite methodically; this is quite a weight to bear as there are so many factors to consider in giving shape to the project. I find it taxing to mentally arrange the multiple processes, so I make lists to get the information out of my head. I need peace and quiet to do this so I can sit and look into the future and decide on the order in which elements of a project need to occur. Once this is done, I feel a sense of relief, because when the plan is in place all I need to do is just get up and bloody well do it – step by step. I hate to wake up in the morning without a clear plan because I cannot get started until I have worked out what to do. My analogy for the roles of a project is a ship: someone is steering, the rowers are rowing and the managers make sure it's all happening. I apply a large amount of persistence to a project, like an oil tanker plodding along – slow and steady wins the day in my book.

We talked about how Simon applies a Lunar attention to detail when it comes to signing off on a project:

I chip away until I get a flat looking how I want it; I have spent four entire days snagging a four-bedroom flat because I see things that most people miss. When I have gone through a flat looking for details that need to be corrected it is covered in notes stuck in every room. My aim is to create an experience for the occupier that passes what I call the blink test – when someone walks into a room, they say, "Oh lovely!" before they have time to blink. I'm designing to have that sort of impact. I own up to having nit-picky and control freak tendencies but I do weigh-up the amount of hassle that is required to create the experience I'm aiming for, and let go when it doesn't add up. I do get tradesmen that question my choices and at the same time I get feedback from clients that the level of finish is extraordinary when the job is done. I carefully gather a wide range of craftsmen with a narrow depth of focus and aim to deliver the experience I planned without driving myself crazy.

I asked Simon how his friends would describe him in a few words:

I imagine they would say I'm analytical, individualistic, curious and creative in finding better ways to do things and a bit of a misfit – especially when it comes to my offbeat sense of humour.

When imposed upon by others, Lunars will resist: the greater the external pressure, the greater their resistance. Many an active type has learned at great cost the futility of trying to budge a determined Lunar. When an irresistible force meets an immovable object, the irresistible force will eventually get tired and give up. Lunars do not lose their cool in a crisis: the pancreas serves the function of dampening the activity of the adrenal glands and so they remain unflappable. In fact, the increasingly dramatic reactions of others serve to produce an even deeper calm inside the Lunar.

They become, in the words of Shakespeare in his sonnet 116 "an ever-fixed mark that looks on tempests and is never shaken."

Lunars have a strategic approach to challenges akin to that of chess players – they aim to win the long game. A Martial, for example, may overpower them and win a brief battle, but it will be the Lunar wilfulness that ultimately wins the war. With a grasp of small print and procedure and their patient focus on the end result, Lunars make a formidable opponent in office politics and on the world stage. Wilfulness harnesses the power of quiet commitment and Lunars can be remarkably successful using this discipline: Mark Zuckerberg's career is a good example of this.

At the unhealthy, dysfunctional end of the spectrum, the attribute of wilfulness appears when a Lunar has taken a position and cannot be flexible. This is a refusal to participate in the flow of life and, when threatened, bribed, reasoned with or persuaded, they will dig in their heels and say no! Once they are in this posture, the attribute has possessed them and it is not possible for them to shift; the situation feels like a life-or-death matter to them and it is important for other people to respect their stance. A child growing up is essentially at the mercy of the parents: they decide what and when the child eats, where they live and so on. The first time a child asserts itself is usually when it learns to say no to the parents – this produces a reaction and at that moment the child is in charge of the situation. Lunars are typically impinged upon by the other types and it is by saying no that they gain some breathing space. For some Lunars, this becomes habitual behaviour and their lives get progressively narrower and smaller. Howard Hughes took this attribute to extremes.

Herman Melville's tale, 'Bartleby the Scrivener', captures this habit when taken to extremes. His central character simply responds to every request or demand with the phrase, "I'd prefer not to", until his life reduces to an absolute minimum. It can be deeply frustrating for other types to suddenly find a normally quiet, compliant Lunar opposing them and refusing to budge. It is vital to recognise that the attribute of wilfulness is now in charge and to resist your desire to push harder – it's much better simply to give them time and space.

Another element of this attribute is that a Lunar may become fixated on one arena of life to the exclusion of all others; they bring a disproportionate amount of time and energy to a hobby until it becomes an obsession. We see this loss of perspective in some train spotters, bird watchers, collectors, 'Trekkies' (the character Data from *Star Trek* is a Lunar character played by the Lunar actor Brent Spiner) or builders of absurdly-detailed scale models. This obsessive focus on details at the expense of the bigger picture truly fits the ancient term 'moonstruck'.

Relationship to rules

Lunars flourish when structure and guidelines are clear, because they value the sense of order and security that is engendered when people adhere to the rules. They usually keep rules to the letter with their typical thoroughness and they expect others to do the same. If other people flout the rules, Lunars will tut and shake their heads. Lunars fear that if they themselves break the rules they will get caught and this will lead to public exposure and embarrassment. On occasion, their attribute of wilfulness can produce a secret rebellion, where they quietly subvert an organisation while presenting a compliant facade to those in power. They cover their tracks carefully and may well get away with their campaign of quiet sabotage for many years. An unhappy Lunar in an organisation will subtly devote time and energy to engineering a situation where they can take a fixed stand on a technicality in order to passively assert themselves. This can look like a chess move to an outside observer and is often an act of resistance to unfair treatment. This sort of behaviour is a red flag to anyone managing the players involved and it will need to be addressed sensitively and privately, as there is a lot more dissatisfaction brewing than is showing on the surface. Lunars are absolute masters at patiently using the rule book to trip up those who have annoyed or bullied them.

Social situations

Lunars do not generally enjoy chaotic social events and will tend to avoid them if they can do so without making waves. If they do end up being cajoled to attend a party, they will arrive on time or slightly early so they do not have to make a highly visible entrance and they will stand either alone or with a fellow Lunar so they can both criticise the food, music or other guests. They may well engage in a supportive task in the background that enables them to avoid excessive interaction. They will probably leave early after picking at the few buffet items that are permitted as part of their current restrictive diet. They do not enjoy the limelight, crudity, small talk or the unexpected – so throwing a massive surprise party in a Lunar's honour will drop them directly into their idea of hell!

Professional environments

Lunars flourish in a working environment where the following factors are present:

- Precise tasks
- Defined roles
- Continuity
- Routine interaction
- Detail
- Peace and quiet
- Remote supervision
- Solid territorial boundaries
- Clear outcomes
- Single focus.

We find Lunars happily working as accountants, bookkeepers, secretaries, librarians, bank clerks, research scientists, engravers, data analysts, architects, draughtsmen, health and safety inspectors, archaeologists, compliance, quality control officers, horologists, lab technicians, finance directors, computer programmers, proof readers, actuaries, surgeons and miniaturists. Bonsai is a typically Lunar pursuit too.

Lunars make a unique contribution to the wellbeing of others when they bring their particular precise focus to the human body, as we see in Sarah's story. Sarah is a teacher of improvisation using movement and voice and an accomplished teacher of the Feldenkrais Method – an approach which focuses on movement and awareness in order to learn easier ways of moving, acting and being in the world. Sarah is clearly a Lunar type and it is evident that she practises what she preaches, as she has a calm, grounded presence and is precise yet flowing in her movement and posture. She talks about her practice in exploring the way a client moves:

> I use touch as well as my visual sense to investigate how a person moves. I find that using my hands clarifies the complex and often confusing information coming in visually. I have always loved movement and had a revelation when I started taking Five Rhythms classes that the freedom I found in dance could be a big part of my life. The combination of movement and being in my internal world of sensation is blissful for me. When I discovered Feldenkrais I knew I wanted to explore it more deeply. Through exploring this method and learning to choose what feels easy, I have come to recognise my tendency to push through regardless and to know when it's time to take a break.

Sarah was intrigued to discover that Luna or Diana is the goddess of secrecy and talked of her own love of solitude:

> As a child I spent a lot of time alone and it's a comfortable place for me to be. I love detail and used to do a lot of Vipassana meditation, which involves sitting in silence and observing one's inner sensations. I love travel but feel most at home in nature and internal stillness. When I have been in an intensely busy period and I have a day off, I sometimes feel that I can't even get out of the front door! It goes beyond simply not wanting social connection to the point where I feel I couldn't be around people, it feels like a strong need to come inside myself and replenish.

I wanted to explore how Sarah addresses peer pressure or obligation and she gave me a crystal-clear description of the subtle process of Lunar wilfulness:

If I feel someone wants something from me that I can't give at that time, then something rebellious happens within me, within my thinking. It is difficult for me to come straight out with my reluctance. Externally I will go along with things and internally I am rebelling and blaming the other person. Once the discomfort grows to a certain point then I will speak up for myself and it's a real relief when I do.

Famous examples: These include Kristen Stewart, Miles Davis, Wen Jiabao, Nate Silver, Pee Wee Herman, Mahatma Gandhi, Rosa Parks, Robert Mugabe, the Mona Lisa, Damien Hirst, Olive Oyl, Heinrich Himmler, Rowan Atkinson (his Mr Bean is a Lunar character), Pete Doherty, Andy Warhol, Vladimir Putin, Tim Burton, Helena Bonham-Carter, Jimmy Carter, Gary Numan, Marc Almond, Meg Tilley, Bob Dylan, the Puritans, Eeyore from Winnie the Pooh, Bud Cort (who played the ultra-Lunar Harold in the classic movie *Harold and Maude*), Alice Cooper, Stephen Hawking, Elvis Costello, Donald Pleasence, Noomi Rapace and Rooney Mara (both of whom play the Lunar central character in versions of *The Girl With the Dragon Tattoo*), Giancarlo Esposito (the icy Lunar villain Gus Fring in *Breaking Bad*), Marilyn Manson, Myra Hindley, Emperor Hirohito, Ann Boleyn, Terry Leahy, Helen Worth (Gail in *Coronation Street*), Paul Simon, Pope Paul the Sixth, Pope Benedict, the Madonna, Florence Nightingale and Captain William Bligh of HMS Bounty fame.

Lunar animals include mouse, donkey, mole, rabbit, woodlouse, snail and tortoise.

Predominantly Lunar countries and cultures include India, Tibet, Bhutan, Singapore (it's a good idea to obey the rules when visiting Singapore!), Belgium, the Pygmies, the San people of Southern Africa, Switzerland and China.

The culture of China is a study in Lunar characteristics: their medicine and artwork is intricate and precise; they built a huge wall to keep out foreigners and refused invitations to engage in international trade for centuries. The word inscrutable has become a cliché when used to describe the lack of emotional display inherent in public. China has a permanent seat on the UN Security Council and automatically votes 'no' on any UN resolution that they see as affecting the internal affairs of another nation. The 2008 Beijing Olympics broadcast a mixed message to the rest of the world: on one hand, they invited everyone over to their new place for a big party; on the other hand, guests were not allowed to wander about freely, to look in certain areas or to ask embarrassing questions about a long list of forbidden subjects. The Chinese government were on a knife edge between courting stage-managed acclaim and visibility, while avoiding public humiliation in front of a global audience.

During the negotiations between Britain and China regarding the handover of Hong Kong, the British delegation appeared at the board table one morning wearing identical ties, each with a snail embroidered on them; this was a subtle, polite (and very British) message to the Chinese delegation that perhaps things could move just a little more quickly, please.

We love Lunars for their persistence, coolness, eccentricity, practicality, commitment, decency, propriety, dependability, tenderness, fragility, orderliness, respect for our privacy, delicacy, subtlety, light touch, politeness, ingenuity, determination, finesse, diplomacy, attentiveness and their unique and quirky sense of humour.

How chaotic and loud the world would be without Lunar, embodiment of the goddess of secrecy, hunting and the night to organise and focus us.

Alma VENVS *dicor Cœli gnata atque Diej:*   *Aufpicijs dantur gratia amoriq̃ meis.*

Venus

In mythology, Venus was the Roman goddess associated with love, beauty and fertility. She is connected to nature, abundance, nurturing and child-raising and is the equivalent of the Greek goddess Aphrodite.

The classic five-pointed star drawn by children the world over is an ancient symbol for Venus and has always been connected to nature, growth and regeneration. Ancient astronomers are known to have monitored the movements of Venus very closely. The planet Venus' orbit and rotation periods are such that the average interval between successive close approaches to the Earth is almost exactly equal to five Venusian solar days. Five Venus solar days between close approaches to Earth, five pointed star – coincidence?

There are numerous classical sculptures and depictions of Venus as a voluptuous woman, usually with her children at her side. In fact, some of the earliest works of art are the Venus figures dating back as far as 35,000 years and thought to depict the Great Goddess or Mother Goddess. The most famous of these is the Venus of Willendorf, discovered in Austria in 1908. Hundreds of these figures have been found in settlements throughout the prehistoric world.

In the English language, we find ourselves in interesting territory, due to the effects of cultural attitudes changing through time. Historically, the Latin noun form 'venus' means 'love' and 'sexual desire' and connects to 'venerari,' meaning 'to honour; to try to please' and 'venia' meaning 'grace, favour'. In Sanskrit, 'vanas,' means 'lust, desire'. Venus' name may embody the function of honours and gifts given to the divine when seeking their favours, acts that can be interpreted as the attempted seduction of the gods by us mortals.

In post-Puritan modern English, the word now has mostly negative physical connotations, such as 'venereal', meaning 'of, relating to, or involving the genitals, sexual intercourse or erotic desire', or 'venial', meaning, in terms of sin or mistakes, 'excusable; trifling; minor: a venial error'.

Yet we seem to retain traces of the original sacred roots in the verb 'venerate', meaning 'to regard or treat with reverence.'

In astronomy, the planet Venus is sometimes called Earth's sister planet, as it is of a similar size and gravity.

Venus appears in the night sky as the morning star and evening star, second in brilliance to the moon. It has always been described as beautiful and sensual and many ancient sacred sites monitored the movements of Venus. It takes 243 days to rotate on its axis, which is by far the slowest rotation of any of the major planets. Although Venus is the closest planet to Earth, it is very difficult to observe as it is covered in clouds of sulphuric acid. The atmospheric pressure at the planet's surface is 92 times that of the Earth.

The astronomical symbol for Venus is a stylised version of Venus' hand mirror, symbol of beauty.

In endocrinology, the Venus type corresponds with the parathyroid glands which control the amount of calcium in the blood and within the bones and teeth. A deficiency of calcium in the bloodstream causes muscle spasms, while an excess of calcium causes extreme lethargy, confusion and weakness.

Physicality

Venus women tend to be soft and rounded, their skin is velvety and sensuous, their hair is dark and thick and they may have a lot of body hair. Their eyes are typically brown and large and inviting, their lips are plump and full, their breasts are often large and their hips wide. Kim Kardashian – I rest my case! This is the second type that Western European culture labels as overweight and, while Jovials are apple shaped, Venus is classically pear shaped. These are the archetypal nurturing Earth Mothers, with all sharp angles smoothed away. Their voices are soothing and melodious and relaxing to listen to.

Venus men are large all over, with a lot of dark body hair and soft facial features. They often carry weight in their legs and thighs and have a grounded feeling – picture Forest Whittaker or a sumo wrestler. Venus men tend to keep their hair into old age and it sometimes stays jet black, with little greying. They may be physically very large yet have a soft gentle voice and harmless manner. I have on occasion met Venus people, male and female, who are so soft that they feel as if they have been filleted.

There is something about Venusians that invites us to drop our guard and just relax in their easy-going, laid-back presence or, to be more precise, their lack of presence. A Venus friend will almost invariably be delighted when you appear unannounced and will drop whatever they are doing (which probably won't be much) to focus on you. You will not need to bring anything with you or to do or say anything to impress them. This is the Goddess of Love after all and it is as if you are doing them a favour by showing up and providing someone for them to love. Male and female Venus people have an inviting feminine quality that is refreshing and nurturing to those around them. Whereas a hug from a Jovial feels like a well-stuffed leather couch, hugging a Venus friend feels like being engulfed in a warm vertical waterbed as you sink into their languid sensuality.

Those of us fortunate enough to have steadfast Venusian friends have a readymade haven from the stresses of modern life in their cluttered, informal living room, where we can totally unwind and soak up the glorious healing vibrations that Venus emanates as naturally as breathing.

William Benham:

> The Venusian type then, stands for love, sympathy, tenderness, generosity, beauty, melody in music, gaiety, joy, health and passion, an array of forces which place it on the pinnacle of attractiveness and render it liable to many temptations and dangers.

Venus traits

Venus is the slowest moving of all types, sometimes to the persistent annoyance of the faster types. They don't see time as a linear track with fixed points dotted along it. Martials, in particular, see time as a dead straight line along which they march, ticking off targets as they hit them, then marching on directly to the next one. Lunars see time as an agreed-upon structure that keeps everything running perfectly as long as things happen when arranged. Venus, on the other hand, sees and experiences time as something more akin to a fluid that everyone drifts through; if you drift up against someone else, then you can float together for a while then drift on. For someone who is predominantly Venus, this fluid may well have a thick syrupy quality, which means that they are habitually late for appointments and can't quite see why everyone else gets so stressed about it. If you invite a Venusian to dinner at your house at 8pm, there is an expectation on your part that they will arrive in time to eat dinner at 8pm. The Venus hears the words 'dinner 8pm' they start slowly getting ready at around (probably after) 8pm in order to go out for dinner. When they arrive at 10pm they are mystified to find everyone finishing dessert. If a Venusian invites you to dine at their house at 7pm, it's best not to show up too hungry, because you can expect them to start cooking at around 9pm, once they have listened to all your news.

The lifestyle of a Venus is much more concerned with being than doing, so they just go with the flow, assuming that wherever they end up and whenever they arrive, it will be just fine. This outlook shows up in unconditional acceptance of others: they are prone to see the best in even the worst people. In the eyes of a Venus, most people are basically good inside and will act decently if treated well. They seem to believe that love cures all and are willing to take care of those that most people would have given up on long ago. In fact, the more outwardly unlovable someone appears, the more the Venus will shower love on them. They possess a unique ability to reach wounded people and support them in developing their potential. In this process of rehabilitation there is no such thing as a last chance; a miscreant in the care of a Venus will be accepted as they are, and any glimmer of hope is lavishly praised and rewarded.

David is a classic Venus type, with dark hair and big brown eyes; he is a successful professional speaker who helps his clients focus on their goals and the deeper meaning of those goals. He performs a delicate balance in his life between his corporate clientele, his work with young people and a challenging home situation – his wife is disabled and his son is autistic. Those who know David are universal in their appreciation of his humility and caring and his 'what you see is what you get' approach:

> In my work with CEOs I am known for being down to earth and real. There is very little in the way of image or achievement that I present to them. Very often they find it refreshing that I am not seeking to impress them or to be impressed, but simply to offer acceptance, challenge and support. I find that CEOs are able to drop the mask of being omnipotent

and powerful around me and discover goals that have depth beyond the material. It may seem ironic, but the more I dedicate myself to my mission of helping young people, the more successful I am with business leaders. I love my family, and we all make sacrifices to function as we do. For the first eight years of his life, my son had a habit of waking up at 3am ready for action, so a combination of the energy given in my work and a challenging home situation has had negative effects on my own wellbeing. I am very grateful for what I have.

Venus is drawn to healing the downtrodden and disaffected of society without thought of reward or acclaim. This can sometimes cost them dearly, as happens when they fall into the trap of identifying so closely with life's victims that they themselves become disempowered. For example, a successful Venusian businesswoman I knew in the US became passionate about helping homeless people and fighting for their well-being. She became so involved that she neglected her own business to the point where she went bankrupt and became, you guessed it, homeless.

Manipulative people are able to play Venusians' good nature and drain them dry, emotionally and financially, before moving on to the next one. In a distorted mirror image, a Venus will often lose interest in someone they have nurtured back to independence: once that person can stand on their own two feet, the Venus can no longer play their accustomed helping role and so moves on to find someone else to take care of. Stepping back from the victim/helper dynamic, it is sometimes difficult to see who is using whom.

There is another core factor that fuels the Venusian willingness to let others set the agenda – their identity is more rooted in their sense of 'we' than in their sense of 'I.'

When you ask a non-Venus type "How's life? What are your plans?" they will typically answer along the lines of, "I'm working hard, made my targets and I'm buying a new car and going on holiday."

Ask a Venusian, however, and the answer will be more like, "Our team made the targets; the family is all well; we're buying a new car; my son got into university and we're going on holiday."

The difference is that Venusians see the world through the prism of 'us' or 'we', while the other types see through the prism of 'me' or 'I'. Western European and North American culture and economy is built upon the latter viewpoint: I know who I am and what I want and I am going to get it for myself. Venus cultures do not approach the world in this way at all and Venusians can find it hard to adjust their natural tendencies in order to succeed in a non-Venus culture.

A few years ago, I presented in a school for Navaho children in Northern Arizona. The Navaho have a profoundly Venusian tribal culture. When asking the class a question, I soon realised that the child who knew the answer would squirm and avoid eye contact, hoping that they would not be called on. The reason behind this was that they did not want to excel and thereby make the other children look bad. The opposite dynamic was at work in my schooldays in England, where the child squirming would be the one who did not know the answer and so wanted to avoid being shamed, while those who knew would be thrusting their arms to the ceiling desperate to compete in displaying their knowledge.

In non-Venusian cultures, we seek to show our status by acquiring goods for ourselves and competing to get bigger and more stuff; we try to 'out-get' the competition. Venusian cultures, on the other hand, show status by competing to out-give their neighbours. The term 'potluck', referring to a shared communal meal, has its roots in the word 'potlatch' from Native Americans of the northern Pacific coast, meaning a festival at which gifts are bestowed on their guests in a show of generosity that the guests later attempt to surpass.

The sense of self that is tied up with 'we' more than 'I' means that Venusians are oriented to family, tribe, company or team; they do not like to stand out from the crowd and may hide their talents in order to fit in. More than any other type, Venus needs other people to enliven and invigorate them and can almost go into a state of suspended animation when not connected to and engaged with others.

The vagueness of defined boundaries between 'I' and 'we' that Venusians experience shows up in a very specific behaviour pattern: observe a Venusian in company asking people if they want a glass of water; if no one does, the Venus looks a little confused, and after a short while will ask again. They will continue asking, with mildly increasing urgency until someone says 'yes', at which point they will bring the person a glass of water and, while they are at it, get one for themselves. Watching the Venusian gulp down the water, it will be obvious that they had been thirsty for some time. Most of the other types would simply recognise their own thirst and get a drink. Venusians, however, do not easily register their own needs, for them there is a recognition that the sensation of thirst is somewhere in the room and they want to help. It is only by a process of elimination that it dawns on them that they themselves are the thirsty one; it is usually the last place that they look!

This focus on the needs of others is described with great clarity in Heather's story. Heather is a Venus type through and through and is highly aware of her internal dynamics; she is the CEO of a charity dedicated to helping families with a terminally-ill child to live life as normally as possible. She talks about her devotion to being in service to others:

> I would say I was born this way: as the eldest of three with two younger brothers, it was just expected of me to help at home and I naturally took on that role. I was always involved in groups and became a cub leader at 15 years of age; being part of something bigger than me was always important to me. This can present challenges as a leader because I think more in terms of 'we' than 'I' and in my role I have to push myself forward more. My brother has monumental self-belief (he is a Mercury type!) and it has been quite a journey for me to acquire some of that sort of confidence for myself. I am not strongly internally driven and I respond well to external pressure and deadlines. In my work I see many demanding situations and, while I empathise, I put my own feelings aside and I focus purely on what our organisation can do for the families.

At this point in the conversation we both became aware that every time the subject was Heather herself, she very skilfully steered the focus back to her family or the organisation. I asked about her personal life and she came out with a phrase which could have come from a textbook on the Venus type.

> In my personal life, my sense of responsibility overrides just about anything I want to do. Even when someone else is telling me I am doing too much for another person, I can't stop – I feel I have no choice. For

*example, I readily cancel plans, even when they involve others, if someone
close to me unexpectedly needs help or support whatever the reason –
health, childcare, financial… I do not give this a second thought and I
have cancelled trips away and meals out because it's important to me that
I do what I can for others. I sometimes have to manage my objectivity as I
generally have too much empathy for other people.*

It can be a difficult and ongoing challenge for a Venusian to discover who
they really are and what they really want. Serious self-enquiry can be
bewildering for a Venus type; it is usually a sense of discontent which
prompts other types to look within and Venusians can usually avoid
discontent by simply adjusting their expectations and requirements
downwards. This can give a sense of vegetation and lethargy to a dispirited
Venus (we are reminded that an excess of calcium in the bloodstream, a
Venusian trait in endocrinology, creates despondency). It can come as a shock
to a Venus type to wake up and realise that they have spent a decade doing
very little. Part of the ballast holding them down if they begin to move
towards self-determination is a feeling that they are somehow being disloyal
to their tribe or family by acting 'selfishly' and pursuing their goals.

It is highly unfortunate that some young Venusians develop a taste for
smoking cannabis, a drug that fits only too well with Venus sensibilities: the
haziness, blurred boundaries, increased appetite, lack of motivation and
delayed synaptic action feels great to a Venus and it just happens to be
exactly what they already have too much of! The clannish bonding of pot
smokers with their shared language, music, costumes and rituals can lead a
Venus into a lifetime spent 'vegging out' in a haze of inaction and stupor.
Venusian Grateful Dead fans were momentarily shocked into alertness by the
death of Jerry Garcia; for a while they were a tribe without a chief until they
found a new band to follow and everything settled down to normal again. As
Lenny Bruce said, "There is nothing sadder than a 40-year old hipster."

Their deep affinity with the regenerative forces of nature draws us to Venus
people: they can take a shrivelled and neglected houseplant and, with kind
words and regular watering, transform it into a gigantic healthy plant in no
time. A Venusian woman will pick up a crying baby and it will instantly
become quiet and contented. Stray animals will not be turned away from their

door and the glossy purring housecat on their sofa really is the same skeletal stray kitten that was hiding, traumatised underneath it, just weeks ago. Venusians come the closest that human beings come to embodying unconditional love; an outpouring of quiet love without expectation of repayment from the recipient.

One person I interviewed had found ideal outlets for his loving nature and I can attest to feeling calmer and more positive from simply talking to him on the phone and capturing his story. Paul is a Venus type in his early fifties who has had an extraordinary journey from childhood neglect and abandonment to a successful career as an author, broadcaster and consultant specialising in issues of diversity and inclusion. He has escaped from the Venusian trap of being stuck in feelings of worthlessness to find roles which are aligned with his life purpose of healing others. Paul is also a Christian pastor and teacher. He radiates a peaceful calm and his mission is 'to channel God's unconditional love for all humanity'. Paul talked about the two strands of his work – the consultancy and ministry:

> There is a connection between my professional and my spiritual work. When I work with an organisation, I talk about the business of inclusion and help them to see the dividend that accrues when their people feel included within their corporate environment: when people feel included they are able to give their best; when they feel excluded they will be less productive. In my pastoral work, I teach that God is in the inclusion business. Everybody is included under the canopy of God's love; nobody is excluded. Exclusion is perverse, so it is perverse for an employer to exclude an employee because of race or gender. I maintain a separation between my business discussions and pastoral conversations, yet within me they are totally congruent. My work focuses on performance and morale and in my pastoral work my message is "God loves you exactly as you are – regardless of performance or morals."

Paul has an interesting phrase to describe his work history – he calls it 'number two syndrome' and it is a succinct description of the Venusian approach to work:

> My dream scenario in a commercial relationship is to work with someone who I respect and admire because they are smarter and more experienced

than me; I can then focus exclusively on how I can best support us and the organisation. I don't necessarily want to lead, but historically I have ended up as the smartest person in the room and reluctantly found myself in charge when actually my goal is to be second in command. Many people aim for the top, but I aim for one step down and have consistently failed to achieve that until recently – so I ended up on top! In my current company it has finally come together: my business partner is twelve years older than me, more qualified and widely recognised. It is the perfect partnership because I handle the creative writing and sales presentations and he brings gravitas and has clarity about driving the intellectual proposition.

It is clear from Paul's description of his business partner (six feet tall, former decathlete, chiselled features, barrel chest) that he is a Saturn-Mars and indeed this is a powerful working partnership.

I asked Paul about his experience of being overlooked in his personal life. After decades of personal development he has a clear insight into Venus 'non-existence':

Right now you are asking me questions and I am simply answering them with what I think or feel. If this conversation had been taking place twenty years ago, my first thought would not have been 'what's the answer?' but 'what does he want the answer to be?' My own answer would have been irrelevant. It has taken me many years to change this pattern. One of my all-time favourite lines in a movie is spoken by Julia Roberts in Pretty Woman when Richard Gere asks her name and she replies, "What do you want it to be?" That is how it was inside for me for most of my life.

Deep down, Venus, the Goddess of Love incarnate on Earth, believes that love cures all, that the damaged wrongdoer can mend their ways through being loved and held. When we see Venusian love in action, in the caring touch of a nurse, the kind words of a friend or the patience of a mother with her child, we are reminded that perhaps the objects that we are working so hard to acquire for ourselves are not ultimately that important; that we can step off the hamster wheel of materialism and recall those moments when we too have truly loved and been loved unconditionally:

Love is patient, love is kind. It does not envy, it does not boast, it is not proud. It is not rude, it is not self-seeking, it is not easily angered, it keeps no record of wrongs. Love does not delight in evil but rejoices with the truth. It always protects, always trusts, always hopes, always perseveres. Love never fails… And now these three remain: faith, hope and love. But the greatest of these is love. 1 Corinthians 13

Words that inspire Venus types include team, us, family, we, caring, together, help, heal, support, community and growth.

Words that turn off a Venus include cut throat, dog eat dog, reject, agenda, argument, front runner and me.

Other types judge Venusians as being lazy, vague, lost, adrift, spineless, doormats, slovenly, soft touch, do-gooders, unmotivated and pushovers.

Venus judges other types as being hyperactive, selfish, pushy, greedy, materialistic, isolated, backstabbing and ungrateful.

Venusians see themselves as kind, peaceful, easy-going, helpful, cooperative, supportive, patient and friendly.

Core attribute

The core attribute of Venus is Selflessness or Non-Existence.

At the healthy, functional end of the spectrum, this attribute of selflessness enables Venusians to have their attention totally focused on serving other people. By not asking for much for themselves, Venusians can become highly valued in an organisation and be the cohesive force which holds teams or families together through turmoil. They are also instrumental in developing the latent talents of others. They can be there for and with the other person 100 per cent, without any thought of their own wishes or needs. No other type is able to do this in as effortless and sustained a manner as a Venus can. They listen without judgement or condemnation for as long as it takes for the other person to feel better. This selflessness has a healing quality without any external action needing to occur. They make a conscious choice to put themselves second so others can be held and nurtured physically, mentally and emotionally and feel the stress of life ebbing away. Life on earth would be far colder and harsher without this patient selflessness in our lives. 'Don't mind me!' is a Venus healing phrase, giving the other person permission to relax and do what they need to do in order to return to wholeness.

If you have a Venus child, then they are likely to be 'low-maintenance' and even play a mothering role to their siblings. It is vital to help them to clarify their individual sense of self and to foster an awareness of their own needs. This is not as easy as it sounds, as their habitual automatic focus is on 'we' and not on 'me'. Let them know it is OK to be 'selfish' and recognise that they will have difficulty knowing what they want. It is actually a skill they will have to learn. Avoid the temptation to take a short cut and just decide for them. It is as if they need to have an internal circuit activated to make them aware of what they need and affirm that they can verbalise their needs. This investment of time and persistence will pay dividends in their adult life in making them more likely to stick up for themselves and lead a more satisfying and purposeful existence.

There is more poetic version of this offer in this extract of Rumi:

> *Come, come, whoever you are. Wanderer, worshipper, lover of leaving*
> *—it doesn't matter. Ours is not a caravan of despair. Come, even if you*
> *have broken your vow a hundred times. Come, yet again, come, come.*

Josie is a Venusian woman with a calm and caring nature who has found a specific niche for her healing talents. She is an art psychotherapist working with children and young people who have experienced trauma. Some of her clients have witnessed or experienced highly traumatic events and may even be called as witnesses in criminal trials. Here, Josie explains why she chose to work with this particular demographic:

> *My clients are unpredictable and challenging; you never know what*
> *they will say. They can be hilariously funny and can also evoke a wide*
> *range of feelings in seconds. When I work with a young person I have*
> *no agenda, I follow their lead, tailor the session to their needs and pace*
> *myself to match them.*

I asked Josie how she managed her own internal reactions when a child is talking about severe violence or even murders that they have seen. Her response spoke clearly of the tightrope that Venus people sometimes need to walk in order to protect themselves from over-empathising with the feelings of others while supporting them:

> *I focus totally on the child and observe them closely. I ground myself physically and consciously stop my mind thinking thoughts such as "What if that happened to me? How would I cope with this? What if my family was like that?" I am aware of my own reactions but make sure they are not the primary focus of the session by making an effort to feel my feet on the ground. Occasionally I need to stop myself crying so as not to take attention from the child. Sometimes, when my stress level is high, I will spend my tea break thinking about coming home, wearing comfortable clothes, dancing or eating a nice meal (all typical Venus pleasures!). Part of my work involves knowing when to pause the interview process during pre-trial preparation because the child is becoming overwhelmed; this is very delicate work. I tune in to the child, their breathing and eye movements and sense when to call for a breather.*

After some prodding, Josie talked about the personal benefits of doing this stressful work:

> *My best moments are when a perpetrator is convicted and imprisoned; I know I have played a role in protecting the victim from further harm and also protecting other children. I often support children post-trial in processing their emotions and memories and it is satisfying to see them come through the worst and become lighter and more playful. I have an ability to reach children who find it difficult to trust simply by being patient and non-judgmental for as long as it takes and it is wonderful to see them blossom in their own way.*

At the unhealthy, dysfunctional end of the spectrum, the attribute of non-existence is an abandonment of self in exchange for being seen as doing good. Venusians at the mercy of non-existence have no idea what they want or who they are and need other people to define them and give them purpose. This can go way beyond low self-esteem or self-sacrifice: there appears to be no self here to esteem or sacrifice. The body is present but the personality is absent; they may not 'show up' for their whole life. They need to be needed and can actually drive people away by compulsively taking care of them, while sighing loudly. The phrase 'don't mind me' takes on a whole different tone of toxic victimhood and sullen blame as Venusians run themselves into the ground while rejecting all offers of assistance.

Marlon Brando was a Venusian actor and his iconic monologue which begins; "I could have been a contender, Charlie" is a cry from the heart of a Venus who has sold himself out for another's agenda. Under extreme prolonged duress a Venus may snap and explode into uncontrollable rage. The more sociopathic elements of society have antennae which are finely tuned to home in on Venusian neediness; by pushing the right buttons, telling the perfect sob story and showing just enough signs of progress, sociopaths are able to exploit a Venus type to the point of total depletion before moving on to the next one.

In my observation, the vast majority of women who marry prison inmates after meeting them as pen pals are Venus women. Here is an actual news item from June 2010 which captures the loss of perspective caused by extreme non-existence: "A British woman married to a prisoner on America's Death Row says she will never again have a relationship with a man awaiting execution." This revelation came shortly after Sandie Blanton's second Death Row marriage ended in the execution of her husband Reggie by lethal injection! Sandie is still writing to 30 other prisoners.

Relationship to rules

Venusians have a laissez-faire attitude to the rules, generally going along with them as long as not too much effort is required. If someone else breaks the rules, they are usually not bothered enough to take action to enforce them and would rather overlook infractions than rock the boat. This is why reporting a crime in Mexico or Spain can be a highly comedic and ultimately pointless exercise.

Social situations

It is a safe bet that a Venusian will arrive late, having baked cakes and brownies and written cards for everyone. They will avoid the spotlight and happily spend every moment serving food, listening to sob stories, giving back rubs to those who are stressed and taking care of the kids. If the event is at someone's home, they will be able to offer the full Venus treatment, which will involve watering the plants and taking care of the pets. They will also stay and do the washing up before giving lifts home to the stragglers. They may not even show up at the event at all, having forgotten it, put the wrong date in their diary or been side-tracked into helping out in a family drama. One side effect of Venus selflessness or non-existence is that in the social arena it is easy to forget their name or overlook them. Notice how frequently it is the Venus in a group whose drink or food order doesn't arrive and notice that they generally don't mind – absolutely not the case when, as rarely happens, a Jovial is overlooked!

Professional environments

Venusians flourish in a working environment where the following factors are present:

- Teams
- People to take care of
- Plenty of time
- Immobility or lack of movement
- Obvious needs to be fulfilled
- Stability
- Regularity
- Appreciation
- Gossip.

So we find Venus types happily employed as nurses, massage therapists, bouncers and doormen in areas where management seeks to defuse conflict, museum guards, kindergarten teachers, personal assistants, hair dressers, manicurists, school dinner ladies, social workers, counsellors (especially in drug and alcohol rehab), cooks, gardeners, care assistants, waiters or vets.

They make fine actors and singers when given strong direction and management. Possibly the most Venus profession in the world is working in a shelter for abandoned or abused animals.

Famous examples: Famous Venusians include Jennifer Lopez, Gabourey Sidibe (she is possibly 100 per cent Venus), Nigella Lawson(the Domestic Goddess), Camila Batmanghelidjh (founder of the charity Kids Company and extremely Venusian), Alfred Molina, Monica Lewinsky, k.d.lang, Demis Roussos, José Mujica (president of Uruguay who gave 90 per cent of his salary to charity), Venezuelan President Nicolaás Maduro, Droopy Dog, Al Capone, Alexei Sayle, Liv Tyler, John Sentamu (the Archbishop of York), Bishop Desmond Tutu, the Venus de Milo, Ernest Borgnine, Marina Sirtis (who played counsellor Deanna Troi, the empath in *Star Trek, the Next Generation*), Luciano Pavarotti, Nana Mouskouri, Will Sampson (who embodied non-existence as Chief Bromden in *One Flew Over the Cuckoo's Nest*), Barry White (the Love God), Mama Cass Elliot, Elvis Presley, Dylan from *The Magic Roundabout*, Roseanne Barr, John Belushi and Claude Debussy (whose lush music oozes with Venus sensuality).

Venus animals include sloth, koala bear, slug, seal, chocolate Labrador, manatee, Persian cat, bloodhound and cow.

Predominantly Venusian populations are historically found in areas where physical survival did not require too much effort, where there was an abundance of natural resources and clothing was optional. These are the places on Earth that we come to think of as akin to Paradise (that is before the Martials showed up and ruined them!). So we find such Venus countries and culture as Hawaii and Polynesia, the Caribbean Islands, Maoris (not every warrior is a Mars, and vice versa), Samoans, Australian aborigines, Mexico – any culture that has a siesta and a 'mañana' attitude has a strong Venusian element. In North America we find, amongst others, the Sioux, Navaho, Hopi, Cherokee and Blackfoot tribes; the Pima of Arizona have been found to carry what is known as the thrifty gene, which stores any available fat and makes this tribe highly prone to obesity.

Opposites attract

With Venus, we come to a point on the circle of types where we have already explored the type that is opposite them. Mars is directly opposite Venus and opposites attract each other like North and South poles on magnets. Mars, God of War and Venus, Goddess of Love, were lovers in mythology and these two have an intense physical attraction. The tough, lusty, sexually-charged drive of Mars is propelled directly at the soft, succulent yielding sensuality of Venus. 'Love at first sight' is primarily a function of opposite types meeting and naturally finding in the other everything that they are looking for. When there is on-screen chemistry, the audience recognises that the actors are of opposite types and the attraction doesn't just look good; it feels real. We can see how the attributes of Destruction and Non-Existence can complement and support each other in healthy ways. In gender specific terms, we see the hard-working Mars father protecting and providing for the family, coming home to be nurtured and supported by the Venus mother and the children, knowing that they are safe and loved. There is warmth and caring in a home that has strong boundaries and a solid foundation. At the unhealthy end of the scale, we see Mars destruction fuelled by alcohol taking out his violent frustration on the selfless Venus, who just puts up with it.

A deeper examination of the relationships between types will be found in the next book in this series.

We love Venusians for their patience, kindness, care, support, loyalty, tolerance, nurturing, benevolence, gentleness, grace, charm, softness, forgiveness, encouragement, amiability, comforting, acceptance, beauty, sensuality, constancy, sensitivity, cooperation, empathy, sympathy and affection.

How harsh and cold the world would feel without Venus the goddess of love to soothe and heal us.

MERCVRIVS
Ioan . Strad . inuen .
Ioan . Collaert . ſculp .
Phls Galle excud .

6

MERCVRIVS Iouis & Maiæ chariſsima proles ,   Alatus ſuperis nuncia porto Dijs .

Mercury

In mythology, Mercury is the winged messenger, god of trade, communication and travel, guide of the dead and protector of merchants, shepherds, gamblers, liars and thieves. Words such as merchandise, mercenary and mercantile have their etymological roots in his name. He is the Roman equivalent of the Greek god Hermes. In paintings and sculpture, Mercury is depicted with wings on his helmet and heels, symbolising his rapid movement, and as carrying the caduceus, an ancient symbol for commerce. The element mercury or quicksilver is named after him; this is the only metal that is liquid at room temperature and, as befits the god who protects liars and thieves, it slips through your fingers. Fittingly for the god of communication, Mercury has the most eclectic collection of correspondences between his name, his mythological characteristics, linguistics, folklore and the planet itself.

In the English language, mercurial means:

1. Changeable; volatile; fickle; flighty; erratic: a mercurial nature.

2. Animated; lively; sprightly; quick-witted.

3. Pertaining to, containing, or caused by the metal mercury.

4. Of or pertaining to the god Mercury.

5. Of or pertaining to the planet Mercury.

In etymology we find mercurial as meaning 'sprightly, volatile and quick', from supposed qualities of those connected with the planet Mercury, probably partially by association with quicksilver.

In astronomy, Mercury is the innermost and smallest planet in the Solar System. The orbit of Mercury has the highest eccentricity of all the Solar System planets. Its orbit deviates the most of all the planets from being a perfect circle. It completes three rotations about its axis for every two orbits. Mercury is bright when viewed from Earth, but is not easily seen as it orbits close to the Sun and is normally lost in its glare. Unless there is a solar eclipse, it can only be viewed from the Northern Hemisphere in morning or evening twilight. Mercury is never above the horizon of a fully dark night sky. As befits the planet named after the god who protects liars and thieves, comparatively little is known about Mercury – it is difficult to even catch a glimpse! Ground-based telescopes reveal only an illuminated crescent with limited detail, and the Hubble telescope cannot observe Mercury at all, due to safety procedures which prevent its pointing too close to the Sun.

The astronomical symbol for Mercury is believed to be a stylised version of his caduceus or of the caduceus and winged helmet.

In endocrinology, Mercury corresponds to the thyroid type. The thyroid gland controls how quickly the body uses energy and makes proteins by producing hormones which regulate the rate of metabolism and affect the growth and rate of function of many other systems in the body. The thyroid hormones also control how sensitive the body should be to the effects of other hormones. In simplistic terms the thyroid is like the carburettor in a car which adjusts the air-fuel mixture entering the cylinders. Mercurial people tend to run fast and hot!

Louis Berman wrote of the thyroid type:

> *During childhood he is quite healthy, thin, but striking robust, active, energetic, fair complexioned with nose straight and high bridged, eyes rather 'poppy', teeth excellent, regular, firm and white. These children are always on the go, never get tired, and require little sleep.*

Physicality

Mercurial men are wiry in stature, often with a V-shaped torso and the physique of a sprinter or acrobat, with narrow hips and small hands and feet. They are usually of medium height; their hair is dark, sometimes jet black and shiny and often wavy; their eyes are large, brown, bright and flashing, and set above fine cheekbones. Their teeth are often white and even and their facial features are sharp and well defined. Barack Obama is Mercurial, as was Bruce Lee. They like to dress well and appear dapper.

Mercury women are fairly short with trim figures, smallish breasts and narrow hips and waist. With their black hair, large dark eyes and perfect white teeth, they know exactly how and when to flash their dazzling smile and how to consciously use it to good effect. For someone so compact, a

Mercurial woman may well have a surprisingly strong, powerful voice, like Amy Winehouse and Diana Ross.

Both male and female Mercurials will have a youthful appearance and this gap between their real and apparent age may actually widen as they grow older, with or without cosmetic surgery.

Mercury Traits

Mercury is the fastest moving of the types: physically, emotionally and mentally, they are filled with restless, nervous energy which courses through them from the moment they open their eyes in the morning. Mercurials are almost incapable of going directly from A to B; they don't want to miss anything so they will continually and compulsively deviate from a straight path and often forget the intended destination. Their attention is constantly moving as they scan their environment and flit from one situation to another, propelled by their fizzing rapid internal reactions.

We all have a monologue inside our minds, the running commentary that accompanies and occasionally torments us most of the time. The chatter inside the mind of a Mercurial is relentless and actually speeds up when they are under pressure, as they seek to filter and rearrange their mental universe while on the go. Some of the time we may even have an inner dialogue, with one voice, for example, saying "time for the gym" and another voice saying, "better to sit and watch TV". Mercurials can easily have four or five voices going at once! Mercury is the god of communication and ideas and Mercurials are certainly full of ideas: every new one sparks several more novel connections, and it is utterly impossible for any other type to keep up with a Mercury when their creativity is activated. It is best to just sit back and watch, while occasionally writing down the gold nuggets which are flying thick and fast. They are a one-person brainstorming team, a whirling dynamo scattering concepts to the ether, juggling and plate spinning and loving the thrill of it.

Naji is a financial advisor and the absolute epitome of a Mercury type, with dark wavy hair, sharp features and a dazzling smile. He is utterly charming and speaks so quickly that it is hard to determine when he actually breathes in! When I first met him I was looking for my flight at Heathrow airport and he invited me to jump the queue and join him, explaining, "It's the Lebanese way." When I asked Naji about his work, it was clear he has a fundamental Mercurial spin on selling financial services:

> *From my perspective I do not simply sell insurance or services; what I do is I help people live with dignity and leave a legacy to their loved ones. I get to know my clients and I find out their dreams so I can help support them making their plans for the future. The most satisfaction in my work is when I see the peace of mind that comes when a client signs a contract and they know that their family is protected against disability and loss.*

As Mercury is the god of communication, speed and commerce, it came as no surprise to hear Naji express the ultimate moment when he knows he is on track:

> *For me the greatest feeling in my work is when I give a settlement cheque to someone who needs it. I make sure this happens more quickly than expected and they are always relieved and surprised.*

I asked Naji about how he deals with a client who is reluctant to sign up to his services; his reply was typically Mercurial and spoke to his larger mission in life, which perfectly fits the Mercurial ability to inspire change in people:

> *When a client says no to me I just love it because I have to find new ways to convince him; I must use all my skills and total focus. This motivates me to get him to say yes. When a client says no, it is a temporary situation; my energy level increases 100 per cent. I have to find more and more possibilities and I love the challenge. I have to master my thinking to keep my mind fresh and ready to find new solutions. I am always attending seminars, reading books, exercising and keeping my thoughts focused on the positive so my relationships are healthy and I have a positive impact on the people in my life. I have no time for negative people and on many occasions I have motivated people to change their careers and lifestyles by getting them to think differently.*

On the physical plane, Mercurials are frequently passionate about their hypochondria. They are indeed prone to stress-related conditions, but they simply will not let go and slow down; preferring instead to chew a handful of indigestion tablets with their lunch (which of course is eaten standing up in five minutes between appointments), while complaining loudly about their stomach ulcer. They may pursue a bewildering array of therapies, treatments and diets in a search for an optimum state of health which always seems to elude them.

It may be difficult for a Mercurial to sit still for more than a few seconds; they fidget and tap their feet, crane their necks to see what is behind them, while drumming their fingers on the nearest table top. It is not difficult for us to imagine the palpable tension in a classroom where a Lunar schoolteacher, lover of quiet decorum and control and their Mercurial pupils are destined to spend countless hours in close quarters.

Mercurials have an unerring instinct for the tender spots on the psyche of another person and once they know the button to push to get a reaction they can never resist the urge to keep pushing it, usually while keeping a look of affected innocence on their face.

William Benham:

> *The Mercurian is the quickest and most active of all the types and this activity is not confined to his physical agility but applies to the mental as well. He is like a flash in his intuitive faculty and enjoys everything which puts his quickness to either a mental or physical test. In all games he is proficient and he plays with his head as well as his hands, winning because he plans his plays and shrewdly estimates the ability of his opponent.*

Mercurials are habitual game players. Being able to think more quickly than other types makes it almost impossible for them to go into any situation or negotiation without being strongly compelled to get one over on the other party. A Mercury will bring the following tricks to the negotiating table: bluff and double bluff, move and counter move, gambits, emotional blackmail, threats, pleading, misdirection, innuendo, verbal smokescreens, planting seeds of self-doubt, playing divide and conquer, maximising the value of their contribution while minimising the value of the other parties contribution, misinformation, grandstanding, offering worthless concessions, pulling rank, playing favourites, delaying responses while demanding immediate replies, flattery, laying guilt, affecting disinterest, appearing to zone out, fainting, denial, ambushing, entrapping, seduction, impatience followed by glacial stalling tactics, use of inside information, bribery and histrionics. That is just a small sample of the likeliest opening moves during the early stages of discussion! Mercury is just warming up at this point, seeing how you react before bringing out the big guns.

As the stakes are raised and decisions need to be confirmed, then a portion of their dramatic capabilities are unleashed; they will be using many of the preceding techniques while simultaneously acting as if they are naive, senile, unwell, forgetful, confused, misinformed, distracted, mentally unstable, not authorised to make a decision, broke, hamstrung by red tape, outvoted by the board, morally outraged, forbidden by their religion or finally – their perennial favourite – that they are legally constrained from making a firm commitment until they have consulted their accountant, lawyer, stockbroker, tribal elders, calendar, union, chairman, spirit guide, manager, spouse, priest, homeopath or their shareholders. They may even have to consult all of the above, several times. It may well be that the amount of time and energy expended in coming out on top bears no relation to the fiscal result. To a Mercury that is not the point; the purpose here is not to lose face.

Observing two Mercurials in a negotiation is an experience that leaves one doubting the evidence of one's own senses. Having engaged with Mercurial people intimately, recreationally and professionally for over twenty-five years, I am increasingly aware of how little I know of the labyrinthine Mercurial mind. One navigates a section and feels satisfied at having grasped a portion, only to realise that what appeared to be a map is actually a fractal and that there are dimensions of mystery layered and concealed within a fraction of that portion. It is akin to walking into a hall of mirrors and not being totally sure which image is really you and which is just a reflection – or a reflection of a reflection. The Middle East is an area swarming with Mercurials and I heard an anecdotal tale of a five-day long Arab-Israeli peace talk session during which the first three days were spent negotiating where representatives of the parties would sit at the table!

Another element of not wanting to lose face shows up in how Mercurials' dress. They are deeply concerned with their appearance and often power dress in red, black and white. They are social chameleons, able to adjust their appearance, persona and views instantly to whatever situation they find themselves in. It is great fun to go from a business meeting to an informal event with a Mercurial colleague and observe them changing costume and gestures on the run.

I have a great friend, Paul, a successful business owner who is about 98 per cent Mercurial. On one occasion, we were attending three events together in one day: a business meeting, a networking event, and then a comedy workshop in a grotty pub. He met me at the business meeting, briefcase in hand, shirt and tie on and highly-polished shoes on his feet. He played the managing director role to perfection with his peers. On route to the networking event he took off his tie, rifled through his briefcase for a fistful of business cards and proceeded to work the room. No one works a networking event like Mercury, the god of communication and commerce! On leaving, Paul stepped into the gents toilets to make his next transformation. The briefcase was dual purpose: by rotating it and pulling out hidden straps it became a backpack. Out of the backpack came a pair of trainers and a casual sweater, into the backpack went the smart shoes and business cards. *Et voilà*! Before your very eyes – an instant blue collar comedian.

Mercurials do not enjoy being in situations that they do not control and will hedge their bets and gather background information before committing to show up at an event. If you invite a Mercurial friend to a party, it is unlikely that they will give a straight yes or no; they will grill you first, wanting to know who will be there, when it starts, dress code, whether the buffet is gluten free and so on. If satisfied, they will make a firm commitment – to get back to you once they have checked their diary.

Mercurials will typically line up an escape hatch so they can make a speedy exit at any point. They often pay careful attention to the person who is in charge of a situation or may hold access to opportunities for them. They can be very seductive and persuasive, having a way with words and a finely-tuned instinct for saying exactly what others want to hear. They may instantly break off a conversation with you if someone more interesting shows up, and they have mastered the art of scanning a room while appearing to listen to you.

Mercurials thrive on attention and are built for being on a stage; they can entrance almost any audience with their natural flair for showmanship and drama. They can deliver a well-worn and over-rehearsed line as if it is a totally spontaneous ad lib; they can also make a it look as if they have spent many hours practising and honing a presentation when they are actually doing it off the cuff.

Their relationship to human attention is worth examining: Mercurials naturally love attention and thrive on adoration from a crowd, but it goes beyond that: they can mould and direct the attention of a group of people as if it is an energy force or a plastic substance. Their timing and delivery is so intuitive that they can hypnotise an audience into focusing on one spot on the stage and completely missing what is happening in plain view in another spot. Thus Mercurials embody a facility for being highly-accomplished stage magicians and hypnotists, fooling and misdirecting audiences again and again and sometimes appearing to let the audience in on the secret only to fool them at a deeper level.

The almost magical ability to sculpt the very material of reality enables Mercury types to bring another unique gift to their fellows: a Mercurial can turn their clarity of perception and ability to make surprising connections to the inner world of other people. This means a Mercurial can make a rapid appraisal of who you are, how you come across, your talents and capabilities and immediately show you new possibilities about yourself that had never occurred to you. This insight serves people by helping them find new direction in their life and convincing them that they have the capabilities to achieve their dreams. Mercurials are truly inspiring when they function in this way and it comes to them as effortlessly as breathing. They won't want to be there for the details or the nitty-gritty of implementing the change and they may well have forgotten the conversation next time you see them, but they will have provided the spark and enthusiasm to get you started on a new chapter in your life.

Mercurials can work this same magic between people too: they collect contacts with a vast range of skills and services and they find utter delight in bringing together the ingredients for new enterprises. They will connect an artist with a manufacturer and an importer and a branding consultant, stir the mix and create a whole new business that none of the players would have dreamed of collaborating on. If it looks feasible, they will bring in a venture capitalist, and if it looks like being lucrative, they will want a few shares; most of all they are putting it all together for the thrill and the challenge. It is as if Mercury is saying to us, "Look over here, right in front of you is a pot of gold, dive in!"

Chris is a talent and business development consultant, facilitator and coach who hosts an internet radio show where he interviews business experts and high achievers from a range of disciplines. He is a Mercury type, with youthful features and an infectious boyish enthusiasm; his work certainly aligns with the god of commerce and communication. Here he talks about the joy he finds in sharing knowledge on his radio show:

> *I love to connect thought leaders from around the world with each other. My radio show goes out to over 50 different countries and in our best month we were just shy of 100,000 listeners. I get to spend time with people I would never normally have access to and find great satisfaction in bringing valuable ideas to a wide audience. For many of my guests, the experience of being on the show has helped them to clarify what it is that they offer so they also find benefit from sharing their expertise – for many guests this is an unexpected win/win. There is a structure to every show so that the guest and I are clear on the message we are getting across, while at the same time we are free to explore interesting points along the way. When I get excited about an idea we can go off at a tangent and then come back to our destination. I find I can quickly assess whether a guest likes to wing it or wants a tight structure and generally find a happy medium where we can stay on track and keep the listeners engaged. On a Friday afternoon, before recording the show, I may feel tired by a busy week, but once we are on the air and the communication is flowing I find my energy level rising and I just don't want it to end.*

With their bright persona and engaging talents, it may seem from the outside that Mercurials have it made, flitting through life from one light-hearted success to the next, dazzling another audience, creating another project and heading off to another party. If we scratch the surface and get to know Mercury, then we sometimes get a different picture behind the scenes: they have this rapidly calculating mind which appraises other people and looks for an edge over them; they don't want to lose face or be tricked, but in their mind everyone is doing what they are doing. They maintain a positive external image while internally feeling insecure, needing reassurance and not wanting to show this need. In Farsi there is a word *ta'arof*, which loosely translates as making promises purely to please the listener, while having no intention of doing whatever was promised. In Iranian culture, it is accepted as normal that everyone is doing this, Iran being a Mercurial nation par excellence, so no one expects any different.

A Mercurial who is doing business in Saturn-Mars Northern Europe finds it impossible to believe that most people are pretty much telling it as it is and that there is very little subterfuge. They can get lost in their own hall of mirrors, spending sleepless nights analysing every nuance of a conversation to ferret out the subplot and avoid being conned. Using their own shifting internal landscape as a reference point does not help gain stability and they can tip over into paranoia, trusting nobody, especially themselves, and frantically speeding up in order to get ahead of the impending imaginary disaster.

It is deeply unfortunate that some Mercurials develop a taste for cocaine, the supposedly clean, classy drug that is taken by sophisticated and successful people to give them a bit of a boost. It is actually the worst possible choice they can make: while under the influence they initially speed up even more, open their minds to extra possibilities and feel supremely confident and accomplished. Before too long this tips into compulsion and extreme paranoia; they are already hyper so cocaine just makes all of it worse. Not wanting to lose face and admit to being out of control, they will cover up the problem until their whole life falls apart. The Mercurial Al Pacino overacted this descent in the movie "Scarface".

When large sums of money enter the equation then things just get ugly. Money plus cocaine plus Mercury equals disaster; witness Wall Street in the 1990s, followed by the banking crisis of 2008. Ideally, banking would be in the capable hands of Lunars: reality based, boring as hell, but functional. When Mercurials got into unregulated banking and began bundling then selling bad debts as assets, we found ourselves watching a show where the surprise at the end was not pleasant. In the book *Whoops! Why Everyone Owes Everyone and No One Can Pay*, John Lancaster captures the more expedient side of the Mercurial approach to legal matters when he writes: "Bankers treated the rules as things designed by thick people to slow them down and hamper their rightful profitability."

Words that inspire Mercurials include latest, cutting edge, under the radar, close to the wind, exclusive, opportunity, connection, deal, visibility and action.

Words that turn off a Mercury include follow through, regulations, delay, details, procedure, consensus decision and eventually.

Other types judge Mercurials as being evasive, expedient, slick, manipulative, insincere, insecure, devious, scheming and pushy.

Mercury judges other types as being lazy, slow witted, too literal, boring, petty, passive victims.

Mercurials see themselves as creative thinkers, dazzling, witty, confident, highly motivated and inspiring synergists.

Core attribute

The core attribute of the Mercury type is Power. It is played out in the ability to influence the actions of other people using words and ideas.

At the healthy, functional end of the spectrum, this attribute conjures new possibilities from existing situations and inspires people to explore and express their untapped potential. Mercurials use their power to make breath-taking leaps of imagination and invite us to follow their lead; they refuse to accept our limiting beliefs and can actually sell us a different version of ourselves. They invigorate organisations with their relentless high energy and pioneer new methods of engagement and communication. In many ways, we are living in a Mercurial age, with instant global communication and where the buzz of a catchy homemade video can spread virally in seconds.

At the unhealthy, dysfunctional end of the spectrum, the attribute of power shows up as facile manipulation and subterfuge. Mercurials who are gripped by the attribute of Power see other people as dull-witted sheep who deserve to be misled and fleeced. Seducing with empty promises and moving on to the next victim when things get too hot, these are the conmen and snake oil salesmen, the hucksters and scammers of the ancient and modern world, acting without scruples, purely for their own ends. Niccolo Machiavelli was a Mercurial type whose advocacy of political manipulations gave his name to 'Machiavellian', which describes the employment of cunning and duplicity in statecraft or in general conduct.

Mercurials may aspire to positions of great power in the corporate world, where they gleefully embrace the worst excesses of modern capitalism, backstabbing and lying in pursuit of the almighty dollar, while carefully presenting a benign progressive image. In popular culture, Mercurials are the type most often cast as the villain, with furtive eyes and pointy black moustache – this goes back to the silent film era, pantomime and vaudeville. Shakespeare drew vivid Mercurial character sketches of Iago, Shylock and Cassius, with his "lean and hungry look". More current versions include Charles Ponzi, proponent of the Ponzi scheme, and his contemporary understudy Bernie Madoff.

Relationship to rules

Flexibility is a polite way of putting it! Mercurials see the rules as something put in place for the welfare of the slow-thinking people. They see themselves as being of a different breed, duty-bound to reinterpret the rules in a creative way. Mercurials are compelled to bend the rules, look for the loopholes and feign innocence if and when caught. This is not to suggest that they are innately or uniquely criminal: for a great many Mercurials, the fear of public humiliation attached to an arrest and conviction keeps them well within the law. They simply question the solidity and literality of the rules and are prone to testing the boundaries now and then. Few experiences are more thrilling to a Mercury than getting one over on a rigid system.

Social situations

If a Mercury type has completed their checklist of qualifying questions and decided to attend a social event, they will generally arrive fashionably late. One can almost imagine them outside ticking off the seconds until the perfect time to enter. They are born for the spotlight, so will make an energetic entrance and head straight for the action. If they have not established beforehand who in the room has access to the most power and opportunity, it will not take them long to sniff it out. Having charmed the hostess with compliments and air kisses, they will graze the buffet for a few nibbles and turn on the show, cracking jokes, teasing, making introductions, wheeling and dealing, spinning yarns, palming off people who bore them onto other bores, appraising the value of the furniture, flirting, networking and generally performing.

As soon as they feel they have exhausted all potential leads and entertaining possibilities, it will be time for a dramatic exit as they head off for the next exclusive party. No type can electrify a room in as dazzling a fashion as a Mercurial and no type will disappear as quickly when their attention wanders. Mercury is the spoilt grandchild in this system and, once bored with their toys, they drop them and move on. If you want to have a bit of fun with a Mercurial at a party, keep them talking for just a few minutes longer than they find interesting and watch them looking over your shoulder for something more sparkly.

Professional environments

Mercurials need

- Change
- Speed
- Communication
- Pizzazz
- Flexibility
- Movement

- Influence

- Glamour

- Image.

Louis Berman had this to say about the Mercurial type:

> *Noticeable emotivity, a rapidity of perception and volition, impulsiveness, and a tendency to explosive crises of expression are the distinctive psychic traits. A restless, inexhaustible energy makes them perpetual doers and workers, who get up early in the morning, flit about all day, retire late and frequently suffer from insomnia, planning in bed what they are to do the next day.*

Mercurials happily work as salespeople, PR agents, estate agents, lawyers (especially on high profile cases, Johnny Cochran being a prime example), politicians stalking the corridors of power, fashion designers, morning DJs, auctioneers, stock market traders, theatrical agents, music agents, spin doctors (Peter Mandelson, for example), jockeys, telemarketers, motivational speakers (see Tony Robbins book *Unleash the Power Within*), actors, magicians, dancers, mime artists, jugglers, advertising executives, marketers and yes, charity muggers.

If your child is Mercurial, they will be a bit of a handful and not averse to capturing the attention of any potential audience. They are likely to have a flexible relationship to 'the truth' and have an ability to lie convincingly. The classic mistake parents of Mercurial children make is to insist on 100 per cent honesty from them. This is not productive. Please avoid grilling them and putting them on the spot by demanding the straight story. This creates great inner turmoil within them. A nod and a wink will go a long way here; try praising their creativity and leave them some room. Let them know you realise there are shades of grey and that you are not totally buying their spin. Let them become aware of how you feel when they fool you – that it doesn't feel nice – and leave it at that. This gives them time to refer to their own inner moral compass and room to edge a little closer to 'reality' without fear of punishment or shame. Let's not pretend this is an easy tightrope to walk along!

Stephanie is a family solicitor and most definitely a Mercury type. She is slender, with dark hair and eyes and a restless upbeat energy. She uses her communication talents to resolve the legal side of family issues and disputes. I asked how she addressed the more high stakes moments that occur:

Part of my time is spent doing advocacy work in court which is predominantly connected to protecting women or children who are in difficult situations. For instance, I will prepare an application for a non-molestation order and present this in court. This is not my favourite part of my job as I feel that I can be put on the spot by the judge and called upon to clarify specific points. This feels nerve wracking as I know the client and what is at stake so I want to present the case well and get the intended result. My preparation is meticulous and I try to mentally anticipate every possible question, so when I walk into court I am mentally juggling massive amounts of information while also managing my nerves. As this is such a crucial time I also try to appear calm and collected in order to reassure my clients – who are invariably nervous. This is not easy!

It is obvious from our conversation that Stephanie is devoted to getting the best outcome for her client and is therefore willing to go through this legalistic version of stage fright:

When a case comes together, it is exhilarating. I feel great and I'm glad that I threw myself into it and got a good result. It is massively nerve wracking and also thrilling. At school I never really applied myself, but when I first found the law it got my attention and I focused on learning. The real attraction for me was that the law provides a means of helping people that is cut and dried; I like applying the technical aspects of law to real life.

I asked Stephanie about how she manages to relax and unwind – this is a loaded question to ask a Mercury type as they generally are running at twice the speed of other types:

I find it a real challenge to turn my brain off at weekends and can be quite uptight, often thinking about work and turning it over in my mind. It is really hard to switch my brain off! The best remedy I have found is

133

to be around my family and especially children, when I can be a bit silly and forget that I'm a grown up for a while – it's a relief to step out of my serious role.

Another loaded question I asked was about Stephanie's own relationship to rules. I was not surprised that her high regard for the black-and-white nature of the legal profession went through a Mercurial shift to shading to grey in her personal life:

I don't drive much anymore but when I did I sometimes found it hard to follow the little rules, for instance sticking to speed limits. It's paradoxical – I have a genuine reverence for the law while at the same time I get a little thrill from bending petty regulations, just as long as I don't get caught!

Famous examples: These include Jon Stewart, Zoe Saldana, Justin Bieber, Niccolo Machiavelli, Snoop Dogg, Eddie Murphy, Michelle Yeoh, Tony Blair, Silvio Berlusconi (he was indicted for numerous criminal offences while in office) Nicolas Sarkozy, Richard Nixon, Diana Ross, Charlie Chaplin (superbly played in the movie *Chaplin* by the Mercurial Robert Downey Jr), Marcel Marceau, Sepp Blatter, Victoria Beckham, Freddie Mercury (who was at least 99 per cent Mercurial!), Naomi Campbell, Colin Farrell, Joan Rivers, Adolph Hitler, Mother Teresa, Chuck Berry, Steve Coogan (his character Alan Partridge being an acutely observed study of Mercurial attitudes), Lena Horne, Jim Carrey (Private Walker from *Dad's Army*), Tom Cruise, Melanie C, Spike Lee, Lena Olin, Lenny Bruce, Charles Manson, Simon Cowell, Derren Brown (indeed most stage magicians and hypnotists), Sandra Bullock, Speedy Gonzales, Bugs Bunny and the Road Runner.

Mercurial animals include chihuahua, hyena, parrot, magpie, mackerel, Jack Russell, fox, squirrel, coyote (the trickster of Native American mythology), mosquito and the wasp.

Predominantly Mercurial countries and cultures include Iraq, Vietnam, Afghanistan, Grenada and Panama (anyone see a pattern here?), Hollywood, New York, Romani 'gypsies' (who are conjectured to have been familiar with this system through their affinity with palmistry), Japan and Iran – the most gloriously Mercurial country that I have ever had the good fortune to visit.

Opposites attract

Mercury is opposite Jovial on the circle of types and opposites attract. These two have a relationship of play, drama and humour: the warm expansive Jovial throws parties and the Mercury shows up to network and entertain. Their dynamic is akin to the bond between an indulgent jolly grandparent, the Jovial, and a naughty spoilt grandchild, the Mercury. Only a Jovial has a mind that is expansive enough to accommodate and keep up with the twists and turns of Mercurial trickery. This relationship is the foundation of almost all successful comedy double acts: Morecombe and Wise, Johnny Carson and Ed McMahon, Little Britain, the Two Ronnies, Laurel and Hardy, Blair and Prescott, Little and Large, French and Saunders, Fry and Laurie, Little and Large, Hale and Pace, Mel Smith and Griff Rhys Jones, Ant and Dec, Reeves and Mortimer – you get the point.

This pairing can also make for some serious excess, occasionally with the bill being paid by third parties: Ferdinand and Imelda Marcos are a case in point, where the Mercurial Ferdinand generated the income while the Jovial Imelda bought the shoes. Conrad Black and Barbara Amiel were similarly creative in maintaining their indulgent lifestyle at the expense of other people, except he is the Jovial and she is the Mercury in this duo. Dick Dastardly and Muttley played this one out nicely.

All of which brings us cheerfully to the second plug for the next book in this series, which will be entitled *The Art and Science of Reading People 2: the Relationships* (It would be remiss of me to end a chapter on Mercury without a bit of upselling!)

We love Mercurial people for their sparkle, wit, playfulness, dash, glitter, panache, cheerfulness, creativity, boldness, daring, spellbinding charisma, rapid minds, gleeful puncturing of pomposity, bending of the rules, multi-tasking, exquisite timing, penetrating insight, teasing, tightrope walking and plate-spinning flair.

How flat, dull and rigid this world would be without Mercury, the god of communication, trade and thieves to fascinate and inspire us.

SATVRNVS *Cælo genitus Vestáq; parente,*   *Ex me prognatam deuoro Opis sobolem.*

Saturn

To the Romans, Saturn was the god of agriculture and harvest, and in medieval times he was known as the god of dance, agriculture, justice and strength. He was depicted holding a sickle in his left hand and a bundle of wheat in his right, symbolizing the harvest. The Roman mid-winter feast of Saturnalia is reflected in our Christmas celebrations. Saturn was the father of Ceres, Jupiter, Veritas, Pluto, Juno and Neptune, among others. Saturn's temple on the Forum Romanum contained the Royal Treasury. He was identified in classical antiquity with the Greek deity Chronos, and the mythologies of the two gods are intertwined. Chronos has been merged with the name of Cronus, the personification of time in classical antiquity. During the Renaissance, this combination of Cronus and Chronos give rise to the image of 'Old Father Time' wielding the harvesting scythe, which in turn has been connected to the personification of death as the 'Grim Reaper'. In Hindu mythology and astrology, Saturn is called Shani. He is embodied in the planet Saturn and is the Lord of Saturday. Interestingly, Shani and his brother Yama are judges; Shani delivers the results of one's deeds through one's life via punishments and rewards, while Yama grants the results of one's deeds after death. According to the Gnostics, outside the circle of limitation described by the orbit of Saturn, there was a realm of freedom and immortality.

In the English language, Saturnine means

1. Sluggish in temperament, gloomy, taciturn; dark, dour, glowering, glum, moody, leaden.

   Literally 'born under the influence of the planet Saturn'. Medieval physiology believed these characteristics to be caused by the astrological influence of Saturn, which was the most remote known planet from the Sun at that time and thus coldest and slowest.

2. Suffering from lead poisoning, as a person

3. Due to absorption of lead, as bodily disorders

The planet Saturn was symbolically seen to have been made of lead, being heavy, grey and cold.

In astronomy, Saturn is the sixth planet from the Sun and the second largest; it is the outermost of the visible planets. The rings are the most obviously striking element of Saturn and are composed mostly of ice, with some rocky debris and dust. Sixty-two known moons orbit the planet, of which fifty-three are officially named. There are also hundreds of 'moonlets' within the rings. Titan, Saturn's largest moon, is larger than the planet Mercury and is the only moon in the solar system to possess a significant atmosphere.

The astronomical symbol is Saturn's sickle or scythe.

In endocrinology, the Saturn type corresponds to the interior pituitary type.

This gland is sometimes referred to as the master gland, as it regulates several physiological processes, including stress, growth and reproduction, and it acts upon organs including the adrenal gland, liver, thyroid gland and gonads, as well as bone. The anterior pituitary gland is regulated by the hypothalamus and by negative feedback from these target organs. A benign tumour of the pituitary gland, called an adenoma, produces excess growth hormones which cause children to become extremely tall, a condition known as gigantism. In adults, this causes a condition called acromegaly, the symptoms of which include distorted bone growth. Abraham Lincoln is believed to have had this condition, as did the actor Richard Kiel who played the character Jaws in the James Bond films.

Physicality

Saturn women tend to be tall and bony with a long face and neck and long, slender arms and legs. If they are Caucasian, they will almost invariably have blonde hair and blue eyes. Saturn women of African descent are tall, slender and graceful, with eyes that may have a greenish tinge. Some Saturn women have coolness and a masculine or androgynous feel to them. Picture the archetypal cool Nordic blonde. This is the physical build that is currently idealised in Western media as fashion models and the 'bikini ready' body. Elle 'the body' Macpherson summarizes this cultural bias; in other words, this is the body to strive for. Saturn women typically move in a poised and deliberate manner.

Saturn men are tall and long limbed with a bony chest; the face is long, narrow and craggy, with a high forehead and prominent nose, chin and brows.

Caucasian Saturn men have fair hair and piercing, deep-set blue eyes. They move slowly, hold themselves in a commanding manner and may appear dry and aloof. Abraham Lincoln is the epitome of this type, while the Maasai are an African Saturn people.

Louis Berman:

> *The masculine pituitary personality, the man with a dominant anterior pituitary gland, is the ideal virile type. They are generally tall with a well-developed strong frame large firm muscles, and proportionately sized hands and feet, the head is flattened at the sides, face is oval more or less with thick eyebrows, eyes rather prominent, nose broadish and long, lower jaw prominent and firm. They have prominent bony points like the cheekbones, the elbows and knees, the knuckle joints of the hands and feet. The teeth are large, especially the upper middle incisors, and they are usually spaced. The arms and legs are hairy.*

Saturn Traits

In this system, where Lunar is seen as the child, Venus the Earth mother, Mercury the exuberant grandchild, Mars the warrior and Jupiter the indulgent grandparent, we see Saturn as personifying the father. The associations that we find connected to Saturn in the realms of mythology, legends and linguistics are intricately linked: the concept of Father Time, time being absolute and immutable; the concept of limitation and restriction, of Saturn monitoring and recording human activities, setting boundaries and regulations, and ultimately showing up as Death himself, wielding his scythe and personifying the final inescapable barrier.

Saturn people simply feel tall, and not just physically: they have an overview of other people's affairs and effortlessly exude a natural sense of authority, so that other types instinctively look up to them. They have a strong affinity with the concept of justice and may work tirelessly for causes connected to fairness. In fact, they have a strong antipathy towards injustice of any kind and are often drawn to large organisations which actively promote fair play. The English High Court judge, grey and bony, his long countenance peering out sternly from under his wig as he dispenses justice having long considered the verdict and sentence, embodies Saturnine sternness. We are reminded of the god Saturn himself, standing erect with his scythe in one hand, a bunch of wheat stalks in the other reminding us, as he has for millennia, of the message 'You reap what you sow.'

Saturns seem to feel that the world would be a better place if only everyone else were a little bit more like them; they can't help themselves giving off an air of being slightly disappointed with the rest of us, as if we are not quite as mature or principled as they are. They have high standards of morality and behaviour and make great efforts to live up to the standards that they set for themselves. There is a lack of hypocrisy around this, as a Saturn will not expect another person to live up to standards that they themselves do not uphold in their personal lives. You can be pretty sure that if a Saturn has recommended a diet or exercise regime for your well-being, they have followed the same regime themselves diligently.

Saturns have an inbuilt tendency to be ascetic; if you study the motivations of a Saturn carefully you will find that they feel inspired when they see their journey through the world as a long march down a narrow, straight path. Long, straight and narrow being the key words here – there is something in the make-up of a Saturn that relishes the prospect and the sense of security they find in mapping out a clear path. There is usually a lofty goal at the end of this path and they expect themselves to make continual personal sacrifices along the journey. These sacrifices are undertaken for the purposes of a higher cause and Saturns like to expect the same sort of sacrifices to be made by other people.

They believe that they simply know what is best for other people and generally they do have good insights into what would benefit another person, especially in the realm of direction. Saturns display a strongly altruistic nature which finds expression when they can offer the benefit of the overview that their extra height gives them. This extra height is not simply physical – it is often psychological, mental and emotional. Saturns have a far-reaching clarity of vision which they offer to those they believe are in need of it. They radiate a paternal feeling of safety which other people feel when in their presence; they like to take lost souls under their wing and offer them astute guidance. They are always immensely proud of the achievements of their protégés, seeing positive changes as the result of their guidance as reflecting a higher purpose.

Laurence is a corporate trainer, coach and a classic Saturn type. When he first encountered the Reading People material he recognised himself immediately and told me that he was a fan of systems like this in his own work. Here he talks about his working methods:

I facilitate organisational change by helping senior managers and directors understand and change their behaviour, using simple models to bring about a shift in understanding. I use tools of mindfulness, creativity and awareness to promote problem solving and conflict resolution.

Laurence has an intriguing take on structure in his work which is essentially Saturnine in his intentional balancing of different forces:

I find myself holding an ambivalent attitude towards structure. An unstructured flow allows the self-organising intelligence of a group to emerge, yet at the same time it is having structure that creates the security for this process to occur. Personally I always used to rebel against structure, but nowadays find myself loosening up as I embrace structure – it's rather paradoxical. At my best I construct an environment where I can communicate effortlessly, pierce my own seriousness with humour and embrace times of silence in which a certain grace descends and there is a stillness which serves the deeper aims of the group, or the project, or whatever it is I'm working on.

In his personal life Laurence is, in his words, 'almost forensic' in his understanding of his own internal processes and desires:

I have a love of purity and wish to act from an integrity that assures me that I am doing things for the right reasons. This means I tend to hold myself to high standards. For example, when I feel I've over-indulged or lost my clarity I will balance myself out through abstinence, and I will sometimes fast for one or two days a week, which helps me return to connection with myself. For the same reason, I am often aware of distinguishing my actions in terms of whether I am acting from a real wish (my body wants a cup of tea), or from what I call a concept (my

THE ART OF READING PEOPLE

mind thinks another cup of tea will give me a boost). This is what I think of as not being 'pure' or true. Yes I can be rather ascetic! In the past I used to be harsh and critical of others who do not aspire to the same standard as me, sometimes to the point where I have found it painful within myself. These days I am a lot softer with myself and others.

Like Lunars, Saturns are not an emotionally demonstrative type; the emotion that other types most often experience emanating from them is a benign paternal tenderness. The flipside of this emotion, which is evoked when other people do not meet the standards that Saturns set, is a feeling of sniffy disapproval and disappointment. In fact, other types frequently sense that Saturns are looking down on them; it is amusing to observe a whole roomful of people unconsciously sit up just a little bit straighter when a Saturn silently enters.

William Benham:

The Saturnian type keeps the Jupiterian, the Apollonian, the Martian and the Venusian from going too fast and from being carried away by their excessive spirit. These brighter types, while adding gaiety to the world, need the Saturnian to restrain and hold them back. The Saturnian is a prudent, wise, sober necessity greatly needed among the types. The Saturnian is the repressor, who lays his hand on the shoulder of enthusiasm and bids it take a view of the dark side before leaping.

Saturns may have difficulty loosening up and just having a good time, preferring to spend time and energy in purposeful activity or conversation, rather than going to a party and dribbling their attention away on small talk. Saturns much prefer cerebral puns to broad earthy humour and their minds process jokes in such a way that they appreciate the structure of a joke as being mildly amusing rather than the content being rib-ticklingly funny. Their home life reflects this dry, purposeful focus and they would generally much prefer their living environment to be uncluttered to the point of austerity. They may well have an active distaste, bordering on horror, for knick-knacks and cheap souvenirs, choosing to have one or two high quality items on display instead of lots of stuff.

William Benham:

> *In all his surroundings he likes soberness and grey, black or brown will be apt to dominate in all his apparel, nor will his home have any startling colours in it.*

The physicality of a Saturn is reflected in their psychological make; the visible bone structure of the body can be seen as a picture of the structure of their thinking. Saturns have well-ordered minds and an attraction towards logical systems; they value routine and regularity in their diet, work habits and behaviour. This relationship to structure, both internal and external, lends itself to the creation and maintenance of vast and intricate systems of government and procedure; this faculty makes Saturns the masters of delegation. Their ability to view an organisation as a machine and to see people as parts of the machine makes them highly valued in leadership positions. The phrase 'A place for everyone, and everyone in their place' was very probably coined by a Saturn. There would be no doubt in the mind of the Saturn that their own place would naturally be at the top of the organisation, as no other type quite has what it takes to see things as clearly as they do.

Elizabeth is a tall, elegant Saturn type. She has had a Saturnine career as a teacher and then fifteen years as a secondary school principal. Her school has consistently been rated as outstanding despite having a catchment area that includes economically-deprived neighbourhoods. Elizabeth is greatly loved by her colleagues, students and their parents, largely due to her dedication to holding all staff and herself to the highest standards. Here, Elizabeth talks about her mission in education:

> *It's about making a difference and making sure that the children have the best opportunities possible to pursue their dreams in the future. As a head teacher, I have influence over spending and hiring, and this means everything can be aligned with my vision of doing the very best for the students. When we get the feedback from parents about how children have progressed, it is a euphoric feeling; teaching is not the highest-paid profession, but the rewards are not something that money can buy. I am still in touch with a student I taught in another school over twenty years ago. During one lesson, I set him extra work and, when the other*

students made fun of him for this, I let them know that this was ambition fuelling a drive for success and this was a light bulb moment that he never forgot. He is now a senior economist in a major company – that is what teaching is about for me.

Elizabeth talks about her reaction to teachers who do not share her level of commitment:

I get angry inside. I try not to show it, but when teachers short-change children I have to address this. Children only get one chance at education and my staff knows exactly what is expected of them. I have very high standards and a new teacher knows on day one that this is hard work and they are accountable. When someone meets the expectations, I will coach and mentor them and have helped an assistant become a teacher and then go on to become head of department. I'm retiring soon and I know my legacy will continue through the people I have coached.

Elizabeth also has high standards in her personal life and a typically Saturnine approach to delegating grocery shopping:

My house is well organised. When I had my children it was a bit of a mess, but they are family so I got over it! I plan the social calendar; I remember all the birthdays and my husband does the shopping in a very specific way – every week I give him a list which has all the items we normally buy from the supermarket laid out in the same order as they are in the store; I tick off the list and he goes and gets everything. It's a highly efficient system. It works because he doesn't like shopping but he has to pull his weight and all he has to do is follow the list – rarely does he come home with something that is not on the list!

Saturns are renowned for their ascetic nature so, as an experiment, I asked Elizabeth about her idea of self-indulgence:

My only real indulgence these days is a second glass of wine, but when I retire I'm going to exercise more. I plan to be much fitter than I am now.

Only a true Saturn would consider going to the gym to be an act of self-indulgence!

The word 'properly' resonates deeply in the heart of a Saturn; it stiffens their spine and makes their nostrils flare. When people do things properly and with good manners, it creates an atmosphere of decency, respect and decorum. The British Empire was a thoroughly Saturnine institution: the British imposed their standards of discipline, structure and order upon most of the world and they achieved this largely by showing up in other people's countries, telling them what to do and jolly well making sure they did it properly. For over 300 years, the inhabitants of one small island exported their language and religion along with their systems of law, commerce, education, class segregation and communication, blithely assuming that this was best for all parties concerned. The archetypal Victorian explorer, striding purposefully with a stiff upper lip through swamp, desert and jungle, secure in the knowledge that God himself was surely an Englishman, can only have been a Saturn, with perhaps a touch of Mars. For the natives, it must have seemed as if the concentrated essence of 'Dad' had appeared to check up on everybody! Rudyard Kipling's classic poem 'If' is an elegy to Saturnine stoicism; the original Stoics were themselves Saturns, as we can see from the following quotes:

> *Freedom is secured not by the fulfilling of one's desires, but by the removal of desire.* Epictetus

> *The happiness of your life depends upon the quality of your thoughts: therefore, guard accordingly, and take care that you entertain no notions unsuitable to virtue and reasonable nature.*

> *If you work at that which is before you, following right reason seriously, vigorously, calmly, without allowing anything else to distract you, but keeping your divine part pure, as if you were bound to give it back immediately; if you hold to this, expecting nothing, but satisfied to live now according to nature, speaking heroic truth in every word which you utter, you will live happy. And there is no man able to prevent this.*
> Marcus Aurelius, Stoic philosopher and Roman Emperor

The belief that we can best live our lives according to a system of principles rather than by following our own impulses is fundamental to the Saturnine outlook. Saturns may strive to master their desires in order to follow logic and reason rather than their emotions. This can leave them feeling stiff, pious and controlled in comparison to the other types; spontaneity does not come easily to them. The Desert Fathers were hermits who withdrew from society and lived in the Egyptian desert around the third century. They lived a life of extreme asceticism, renouncing all the pleasures of the senses, rich food, baths, rest and anything that made them comfortable, believing that they were practicing a pure form of Christianity. Their founder Saint Anthony the Great was certainly a Saturn.

We often see Saturns engaging in physical pursuits which require steadfast endurance rather than speed or brawn, so they can be found running marathons, rowing, fell running, long-distance cycling and trekking solo through desolate terrains. In the realm of personal development they are drawn to demanding austere regimes such as fasting, challenging yoga routines and week-long silent meditation retreats.

Words that inspire a Saturn include order, procedure, system, principle, reason, sacrifice, clarity, far-reaching, long term, equality, just rewards and patience.

Words and concepts that turn a Saturn off include get rich quick scheme, close enough, whatever, snap decision, touchy-feely, mega and free for all.

Other types judge Saturns as being grey, dithering, stingy, judgmental, puritanical, stuck up, boring, gloomy, rigid, frigid and hide-bound.

Saturns judge other types as being undisciplined, compulsive, self-indulgent, short-sighted, shallow, immature and frivolous.

Saturns see themselves as reliable, fair, highly principled, self-disciplined, aesthetic, sober, refined, cultivated, astute and well balanced. The writings of the Roman emperor and philosopher Marcus Aurelius provide clear access to Saturnine thinking.

Core attribute

The core attribute of the Saturn type is Dominance. This is a willingness to take responsibility for oneself and offer leadership to others.

At the healthy, functional end of the spectrum, this attribute brings a strong, constant yet benign paternalism which lends the ability to take charge and delegate in a logical, organised manner. Dominance brings an aura of calm authority, which can help lead organisations and individuals to a better way of life. With patience and wisdom, Saturns offer considered guidance and never ask more of others than they do of themselves. With the able hand of a Saturn at the helm, the other types are inspired to raise their standards.

Louis Berman said of this type:

> *High-grade brains, the ability to learn, and the ability to control; self-mastery in the sense of the domination of the lower instincts and the automatic reactions of the vegetative nervous system, the rule by the individual of himself and his environment are at their maximum in him. The ante-pituitary personality is educable for intelligence and even intellect, provided the proper educational stimulus is supplied. Men of brains, practical and theoretical, philosophers, thinkers, creators of new thoughts and new goods, belong to this group. Men like Abraham Lincoln and George Bernard Shaw belong to this ante-pituitary type.*

In an era when the word 'expert' is applied a little too readily, Michael is a genuine expert and a widely-acknowledged pioneer in his field of analysing and understanding culture for commercial purposes and applying global insights to brands. He is a Saturn type, well over six feet tall, and brings this natural overview to his work, which includes published works and worldwide lectures on his insights. Here he talks about his professional life:

> *I consider myself fortunate that I am pragmatic and independent minded and go with what I find interesting as long as it provides the means to get by materially. I am not hugely ambitious and it is by grace that my interests coincided with a way to make a living. I feel that those who are pioneers are people who are not under the control of pre-defined concepts about the way to do things and are not anxious to please their parents. I am labelled a visionary in my field because, on top of a thorough cultural and intellectual grounding, I have good reason to trust my own intuition in seeing the big picture accurately and with a personal twist that can inspire others to think creatively and join in to build a shared vision.*

During the interview, I drew Michael's attention to the fact that he had quoted five authors and artists, with meticulous attribution, in a short stretch of time:

> *Prior to my current career I was a professor of literature, so in my work I see myself as perpetually crossed by quotes and concepts which flash across my screen. Many ideas that I hold true have been expressed very elegantly elsewhere and I feel drawn to pass on the sparks of magic which have impact.*

He then quoted another author, Bruno Latour, to back up his contention that we almost never come up with our own truly novel insights.

> *In the words of Bruno Latour: "We are surrounded by floating bits of truth and beauty." For me, quoting other people is my attempt to capture these moments. Part of my mind is constantly processing imagery and ideas to find the bliss beyond the structure. TS Eliot talked about "a raid on the inarticulate, with shabby equipment always deteriorating". [Another quote!] I enjoy the craft of maintaining or creating the best equipment.*

In summary, Michael articulated his underlying values, which could almost be a blueprint for the higher principles that Saturn types hold dear:

> *I'm creating a vision into the future; I really want to simplify, to remove complexity. I'm about communication, peace and reconciliation, activism, helping us move beyond selfishness and greed and reconciling my/our inner contradictions with as much good grace as possible.*

At the unhealthy, dysfunctional end of the spectrum, the attribute of dominance makes a Saturn become repressive, isolated and cynical. Convinced of their own moral and intellectual superiority, they look down on the rest of us with a supercilious and despairing air. They see all of humanity, except for themselves, as lost and pathetic children and the planet Earth as a cold and desolate place. They become dogmatic, grey, bitter and constipated, seeking to dominate other people purely in order to exercise power and demonstrate their own superiority.

The classic mediaeval depiction of a miser is a Saturn, ruled by Dominance and controlling the people around him. Saturns can sink into a very bleak and judgemental place. They may become obsessed with dominating and controlling their own bodily desires, viewing the physical body as something animalistic that needs to be repressed. We see this behaviour in the Penitent Brothers of New Mexico, who practise self-flagellation rituals to atone for their sins. Self-denial becomes a warped form of self-indulgence and their publicly-displayed humility a form of arrogance.

Relationship to rules

Saturns make the rules, because in their minds only they know what is right, fair and best for everyone! Because they are taller than the other types, only they can fully see the big picture and make the all-important and far-reaching decisions. Saturns deliberate in a methodical and thorough manner before pronouncing their decisions. Most other types are willing to defer to a Saturn in matters of justice, instinctively recognising their genuine ability to adjudicate fairly. Saturns are primarily guided by principles above all other concerns, which makes them almost immune to lobbying, pressure or threats from external parties. They can be relied upon to take an unbiased viewpoint when resolving disputes. With their sober and realistic assessment of the dynamics of power, they astutely put in place intricate checks and balances. The masterful Saturnine George Washington ably demonstrated this skill when presiding over the writing of the US Constitution in 1787.

Social situations

Saturns are generally slightly awkward in social situations. They find parties just a little too frivolous for their liking: purposeless small talk does not engage their formidable mental powers; gossip is distasteful to their refined sensibilities, and most jokes just don't hit the spot. Over indulging in food and alcohol does not fit their ascetic habits. Chaotic and noisy environments just give them a headache. They much prefer calm, measured discussions with like-minded people, in other words, other Saturns. At a social gathering, you are likely to find a clump of Saturns sipping fine wine together and philosophising quietly. A solitary Saturn at a social event may seek out a lost soul in need of their wise guidance and spend the evening rearranging their life for them, whether the other person has requested this service or not.

William Benham:

> *The Saturnian is physically built so that he cannot be carried away with enthusiastic, joyous or frivolous amusements. No matter how much he may want to be, he cannot be other than the Saturnian that he is. He sometimes writes excellent ghost stories or tales in which morose heroes go into a monastery. For amusement, the Saturnian seeks his books and the studies which take him away from the haunts of man. He is opinionated, does not like to be contradicted, is independent and dislikes restraint.*

Professional environments

Saturns flourish in a working environment where the following factors are present:

- Order
- Discipline
- Agreed principles
- Common purpose
- Higher calling
- Sacrifice
- Respect
- Decorum
- Structure
- Opportunities to demonstrate leadership
- Planning
- Good manners.

So we find Saturns happily working as strategists, teachers, judges (for example, Lord Denning), executive coaches, management consultants, company directors, scientists, philosophers, theorists, evangelists, museum curators, captains of industry, airline pilots, mediators, basketball players,

CEOs, head masters (Mr Chips being a Saturn played by the Saturnine Peter O'Toole in the 1969 movie), undertakers, pathologists, charity organisers and scout masters.

I have a good friend who is a Saturn and he may have found himself the perfect occupation. He buys a neglected house, moves in, renovates the house and then sells it. This process involves him living in a series of houses which lack basic amenities. As soon as the house is finished and habitable, he moves into the next shell. As part of this process he also gets to manage various craftsmen, while living in uncomfortable circumstances. So he gets to live in an atmosphere of self-deprivation with a long-term goal, while juggling the art of delegation. When he is not working, he travels the length of Britain in a milk float to raise money for charity, so his hobby involves making long journeys under difficult circumstances – but all for a good cause!

If your child is a Saturn then the task in hand is to encourage them to be a child; they are prone to becoming prematurely sober and responsible. There is nothing innately wrong with this manifestation of their type of course, but balance is important and it is useful to remember the aphorism 'all work and no play makes Jack a dull boy'. A Saturn child can fall into parenting their siblings and even their parents and miss out on the play and wonder of childhood. Taking them out in nature is helpful as they can simply be in the glorious chaos of the natural world, unable to tidy it all up. They will delight in finding the patterns in the natural world and let go of seriousness. Do try to let them know that academic qualifications and test results are a tiny fragment of the make-up of an individual. As a last resort, present them with evidence that laughter and humour are good for them, so they can justify enjoying themselves. Let them know that you are doing your best to be fair, but total justice is simply not possible so they may as well enjoy the ride.

Famous examples: Among these are Ebenezer Scrooge, Charlton Heston, Peter Fonda, Katherine Hepburn, Prince Phillip, Lurch from *The Addams Family*, Uncle Sam, Ralph Waldo Emerson, Agyness Deyn, Dr Harold Shipman, Carly Simon, Keira Knightley, Vanessa Redgrave, Sven Goran Ericsson, Maggie Smith, Generals Kitchener, Montgomery, Jackson, Booth and Gordon, Elle Macpherson, Greta Garbo, Farah Fawcett, Claudia Shiffer,

Iman, John Kerry, Walter Thesiger, Trinny and Susannah (Susannah is a little more towards Mars than Trinny), Michael Jordan, Randy Johnson, James Joyce, Willem Dafoe, Lawrence of Arabia (another portrayal by Saturn actor Peter O'Toole), Mr. Spock, Roger Moore, Meryl Streep, Sherlock Holmes (played by Basil Rathbone), Vanessa Redgrave, Saints Paul, Peter, Patrick, Christopher (in fact almost all depictions of male saints and Jesus are pictures of Saturns, and Saint Augustine captured the inner life of a Saturn in his writings; female saints are almost invariably depicted as Lunars), Peter Tosh, Seal and Heidi Klum.

Saturn animals include giraffe, stick insect, garfish, longhorn cattle, heron, stork, ostrich, Great Dane and bald eagle.

Predominantly Saturn countries and cultures include Holland, Switzerland, parts of Scandinavia, the Turkana, Watusi and Samburu tribes of North East Africa, New England and Stoic philosophers.

Opposites attract

Directly opposite Saturn on the circle of types is the Lunar type. The paternal Saturn is drawn to the quiet Lunar in a relationship which may have shades of a parent/child element. Saturn makes the rules and Lunar keeps them. This relationship tends to be stable and long lasting, without an excess of drama, and is set against a neat tidy backdrop. Neither of them likes surprises or noise and they are likely to be highly considerate of each other's space and whims.

Their humour is often quirky and highly intelligent; we occasionally see them form double acts, such as Peter Cook and Dudley Moore and Mitchell and Webb. The conflict comes when their core attributes encounter each other in a battle of willpower. Saturn dominance will attempt to overpower Lunar wilfulness in the certainty that they are correct in the action that they are insisting upon. Lunar wilfulness will resist being pushed at all costs and they become locked in a slow grinding struggle. An irresistible Saturn force meets the immovable Lunar object. An exquisite portrayal of this dynamic is at play between Harold and his mother in the film *Harold and Maude*. The main characters in *A Room with a View* spend most of the film in this exchange.

On a far larger scale we see the Lunar Mahatma Gandhi defy the Saturn British Empire with Satyagraha – non-violent direct action. This movement tapped into the core attribute of wilfulness embedded in the psyche of the predominantly Lunar country, India, and changed the course of history by appealing to the Saturn sense of justice and fair play. More recently the Saturn actress Joanna Lumley has gone to great lengths to obtain justice for Lunar Gurkha war veterans (as I've said before, not every warrior is a Mars). The impromptu press conference where she skewered Phil Woolas, the Lunar Member of Parliament, on this issue is a masterpiece of skilfully timed and applied dominance.

We love Saturns for their decorum, sense of justice, deliberation, high standards, patience, reliability, commitment, stability, self-discipline, wisdom, guidance, stamina, order, principled approach to life's conundrums, integrity, honour, vision, clarity, calmness, common sense, responsibility, leadership, trustworthiness, resilience, doggedness and caring nature.

How chaotic and narcissistic the world would be without Saturn, the god of good governance, to guide us.

CHAPTER 7: Combined Types

Thus far we have examined one type at a time in clear isolation in order to get a sharply-focused picture of each type. A useful analogy would be to see these types like primary colours in the colour wheel, with each type being distinct and unadulterated. It is extremely rare to encounter someone who can be considered to be a pure type, having 100 per cent of the characteristics of one type with no elements of another type evident. To take the colour analogy further, the combined types can be visualised as a blend of two adjacent primary colours.

In each of the examples of famous people that have been given so far it is possible, with careful observation, to determine shades of another type along with their predominant type. It appears that each human being embodies a combination of two adjacent types in varying degrees on the continuum Mars-Jovial-Lunar-Venus-Mercury-Saturn-Mars. It is possible to be a Mars-Jovial or a Jovial-Lunar, but not a Mars-Lunar, for example. The combinations are only possible with the types next to each other on the circle. We can calibrate these proportions fairly precisely on the circle of types. So we may determine, for example, that someone is between Lunar and Venus and observe that they are closer to Lunar. This means they will embody mostly Lunar traits with some Venus. With practice and application, it is feasible to place someone quite accurately on the circle of types and get a sense of the proportions that are blended in their makeup.

We will now examine each of the combinations of types in turn.

Mars-Jovial

The direct bluntness of Mars is softened by the tact of Jovial to produce an almost irresistible combination of drive and charm with a distinct tendency to develop a strong taste for excess. What both Mars and Jovial have in common is that neither do things by halves, so restraint and subtlety are not words that spring to mind when these two types are blended within one person.

Mars-Jovial men are often of ruddy complexion with a tendency to be physically robust and stout; they tend to lose their hair at an early age and in fact could be the poster child for male-pattern baldness. They also sweat a lot, particularly from the head. A Mars-Jovial man may be athletic in youth and fill out as they grow older. Sean Connery and Ted Kennedy are examples of this combination.

Mars-Jovial women are large, direct and energetic and likely to be noticed in a crowd. Their combination of clear Martial boundaries and Jovial grandeur means that they effortlessly radiate an aura that announces that they are not to be trifled with. A Mars-Jovial woman may be very happy to drink like 'one of the boys'. Janis Joplin was a Mars-Jovial who took this a little too far. They make outstanding charity fundraisers: with Martial determination, they target wealthy potential donors, draw them into their uplifting Jovial orbit and then charm them into donating freely. As girls, young Mars-Jovials may have received tremendous social pressure to be more feminine.

Mars-Jovials embody a tremendous inner conflict: the forceful combativeness of Mars must somehow coexist with the diplomatic, harmonising force of Jovial. Martials may not actively seek conflict, but are certainly invigorated when conflict arises. Convinced that they are in the right, Martials wade into the thick of things and take no prisoners. Martials like to call a spade a spade and they respect a strong challenge from the other party. Raw Mars energy is impulsive, fierce and impatient, so they just get bored when things are peaceful. Given an either/or choice, many Martials would prefer to be feared rather than liked.

Jovials, on the other hand, relish a harmonious environment where people respect and encourage each other. Jovials gloss over the differences between people in order to create an atmosphere of inter-personal warmth. Conflict between people they like causes them great internal discomfort. Jovials view arguments as something that small-minded people indulge in to waste their time and emotional energy.

In short, a Mars-Jovial must reconcile the conflicting urges of the Mars desire to move against people and the Jovial desire to engage with people. When a Mars-Jovial can make best use of these desires, they can become successful through being highly interactive with those people that serve their best interests. To watch a Mars-Jovial networking when they are on form is a master class in personal effectiveness: with Mars focus and determination, they pick their target carefully, approach them directly and then give them both barrels of Jovial charm at point-blank range.

At their best, their Jovial side makes grand promises to other people and their Mars integrity fulfils the promises. The combination of Martial drive and the Jovial love for opulence and money can be a potent recipe for material success and a cheerful shameless enjoyment of the trappings thereof. High-functioning Mars-Jovials demonstrate a particular flavour of emotional intelligence, combining the crystal-clear clinical perceptiveness of Mars with the expansive heart and forgiving nature of Jovial. Their humour is often provocative and highly intelligent, Jovial sensitivity having softened Mars crudeness into a celebration of human nature. Eddie Izzard is a prime example of this combination. Mars finds the deep absurdity in human behaviour with forensic skill and Jovial helps us celebrate with laughter rather than to judge and attack these contradictions. Loyal, hearty, generous and spontaneous, a Mars-Jovial makes a great friend and is the aunt or uncle whose visits the children look forward to.

The inner world of a Mars-Jovial holds a delicate balancing act; it's vital to have clear boundaries so the Jovial generosity does not get taken advantage of, while making sure that the Mars side does not drive people away and leave the Jovial side feeling lonely. We sometimes encounter Mars-Jovials who appear to have two distinct personalities: at work they are driven, perhaps even hostile Martials and at home they are just Jovial teddy bears. We may know someone very well and yet only see one element of their type due to the circumstances in which we spend most time with them, so it may be surprising to us to see the other type emerge. If someone is predominantly a Jovial, they may be extremely easy going for many years and suddenly explode with Mars rage when their tolerance finally runs out. By the same token, someone who is predominantly Mars may well have a hidden caring charitable side, which is where their Jovial plays out.

Emotionally unhealthy Mars-Jovials are the combined type that most benefits from learning to count to 10 before expressing their anger. They may cause themselves tremendous emotional grief by lashing out at people close to them in Mars defensiveness and later finding their Jovial side mortified by the pain their harsh words have caused. The Mars-Jovial alcoholic is an archetypal cliché. Mars typically likes to drink and Jovial likes a lot of everything, which can combine into a deeply-tormented person stuck in a harmful vortex. Jovials love the warmth and camaraderie they feel after a few drinks, but after a few more drinks Mars belligerence may well be unleashed, turbocharged by the Jovial capacity to remember every emotional slight they have suffered. This volcanic mix leads at a minimum to inflicting deeply-wounding insults on those closest to them and, at its worst, to physical violence. Jovial charm will then attempt to heal the wounds once the storm has passed by begging for forgiveness and another chance, but unfortunately this very act of contrition simply becomes stored as another blow to the vanity of the Jovial and will be extra fuel for the next explosion. Once this pattern is established in the life of a Mars-Jovial, the only feasible remedy is to remove the alcohol. This may prove difficult, as the Mars attribute of destruction has turned to self-destruction; the Jovial tendency to excess has raised the stakes, and the attribute of Jovial vanity always knows what's best.

An out-of-control Mars-Jovial can wreak absolute havoc in a family or organisation as they refuse to relinquish control and would rather take everyone down with them than admit that they are in the wrong. Workaholism, uncontrolled spending, drug addiction, obesity, compulsive infidelity and stress-related illnesses are all potential risks, and I have met Mars-Jovial men who exhibit all of the preceding tendencies simultaneously. A Mars-Jovial who has sunk into self-pity is like an emotional black hole; they are simultaneously wounded and hostile. The safest way to deal with an enraged one is to quickly give them a very wide berth as their temper can be volcanic.

Well-balanced Mars-Jovials make superb generals and politicians. Winston Churchill is a splendid exemplar of this type, the Martial defiance and Jovial eloquence of his speeches rallying the British people against all odds in World War II. They love to run successful companies, especially those which have a family feeling, and they often have a refreshingly frank and open love of money. Due to their reckless and hearty bonhomie and wide network of friends and contacts, they bounce back from downturns and many people consider them lucky. It is thrilling to be around a Mars-Jovial who is successful and doing what they love, for they radiate an aura of confidence and of endless positive possibilities. Life to them is a fabulous journey and they've made room on the bus if you want to join them – just remember to show them plenty of gratitude and do so frequently, loudly and publicly!

As managers and team leaders, they are extremely loyal to their team, hugely proud of their team's achievements and can be quite spiteful to those who defect. They see someone leaving their team as an act of betrayal. Mars-Jovials enjoy active team sports that have plenty of possibilities for violence and alcohol-fuelled celebration, soccer, rugby, ice hockey or American football being ideal.

Famous examples of this combination include Robbie Coltrane (Hagrid from *Harry Potter*), Hells Angels, Sarah Ferguson, Renee Zellweger, Dean Norris (Hank from *Breaking Bad* is a great example of this combination – a driven police officer who brewed his own beer!), Boris Yeltsin, George Gurdjieff, Henry VIII, Bette Midler, Ice T, Oliver Reed, 'John Bull', Jaime Winstone, Ray Winstone, Hilary Clinton, Ted Kennedy, Brian Blessed, Herman Goering, John Prescott, Mo Mowlam, Michael Moore, Generals Norman Schwarzkopf, Burnside and Colin Powell, Brian Dennehy, Barbara Bush, Les Dawson, Bernard Manning, Sam Kinison, Richard Burton, 50 Cent, Victor Hugo, Ma Rainey, Leadbelly, Boris Johnson, Prunella Scales, Catherine the Great of Russia and Oliver North.

A fair number of dictators have been Mars-Jovials, as they are adept at gathering gangs of subservient followers and leading them to engage in destruction. Benito Mussolini, Herman Goering, Idi Amin, 'Emperor' Jean-Bedel Bokassa, Marshall Tito and Slobodan Milosevic are all examples of this combination.

Mars-Jovial animals include rhinoceros, bison, pit bull, grouper, giant triggerfish, wild boar and grizzly bear

Mars-Jovial people are often found in Bavaria, Poland and the Czech Republic.

Professional environments that suit this combination have targets, activity and lots of personal interaction, so sales is a frequent outlet for their talents, especially on high-ticket items or big orders. Mars-Jovials make great operations managers, as they approach their projects like a military campaign with their team on board. As managers, they are able to give the message that people are lucky to be on their team and likely to be in trouble if they let the team down. Most rock band roadies are of this type. Both genders make superb teachers, with a mix of warmth and discipline, so their classes are lively and interactive, yet with clear boundaries of acceptable behaviour.

Mars-Jovial women, in particular, as mentioned earlier, make outstanding fund raisers for charities. Mars-Jovial women are also active in events management and as HR directors; they are often the pioneering women who make inroads into historically male domains, such as professional speaking and delivery of training programmes

Blacksmiths are almost invariably Mars-Jovials and if 'Country Squire' was a job description, then most middle-aged Mars-Jovials would apply for the position!

Jovial-Lunar

The expansive interests and warm sociability of the Jovial is tempered by the cool detached Lunar ability to maintain focus on a task. Every Jovial-Lunar that I have met has a high IQ: the closer they are on the circle to Lunar, the less likely they are to tell you this without prompting, whereas if they are more Jovial they will be only too happy to refer to their membership of Mensa!

Jovial-Lunar men are not as robust as Mars-Jovials, though they will sometimes try to emulate them, as Martials are seen in North West European culture as more 'manly'. Their face will be roundish, with the jowls of a Jovial, and the weak chin of a Lunar, giving them a distinctly 'moonish' or 'owlish' appearance. They may well have a paunch on a medium frame and have small hands and feet. Their voice will usually be softer than a pure Jovial. Mikhail Gorbachev and Benjamin Franklin, for example.

Both male and female Jovial-Lunars tend to have weak eyesight and wear glasses – often those round gold-wire-framed ones, with cords attached!

Female Jovial-Lunars have a roundish face and their physique is often best described as pleasingly plump; they seem to embody a neat balance of Jovial expansion and Lunar containment. Chelsea Clinton is pretty much a 50/50 blend of Jovial and Lunar. They may give off a slightly 'proper', prissy air, which can quickly turn to hearty delight at a risqué joke and then return swiftly to calm detachment: it's as if the Lunar has suddenly put the lid back on the Jovial. One female Jovial-Lunar cultural icon is the teenage Goth, dressed in black leather and frilly lace with a pale face and thick black eye liner.

Jovial-Lunars embody an inner conflict in connection with other people: their Jovial side loves company, spontaneously connecting with lots of people and holding forth as the centre of the Royal court; their Lunar side, on the other hand, prefers quiet solitude and resents intrusion. Their challenge is to find the ideal orbiting distance from their friends and family and colleagues: too close to other people and the Lunar feels encroached upon; too far away from other people and the Jovial feels lonely. Most Jovial-Lunars solve this by having an erratic or elliptical orbit, being out and about for days on end, then isolated at home, not even answering their phone as they swing from Jovial to Lunar. This can be bewildering to other types: having connected with the Jovial side of a Jovial-Lunar, they are puzzled and may feel rejected when they encounter Lunar coolness; conversely, having formed a sedate relationship with the Lunar side, they may feel overwhelmed when they are suddenly engulfed in Jovial warmth. It may be no easier for the Jovial-Lunar to understand these apparent contradictions within themselves.

To other types, Jovial-Lunars can appear highly intelligent and a little eccentric. Internally, the Jovial love of arts and culture and the depth and sensitivity of their feelings can be well served by the Lunar strengths of persistence and commitment. This can combine to produce creative breakthroughs as the heat and passion of the Jovial emotional enthusiasm is focused through the Lunar laser beam of attention to detail and clarity of purpose. Jovials love to get excited and start projects, but their Achilles heel is periodicity – once the initial excitement wears off, it is far more thrilling to start a new project then to finish the current one. Lunars derive deep satisfaction from completing a project, so when a Jovial-Lunar can draw upon both of these talents, we find sublime genius, such as the works of Johann Sebastian Bach and William Shakespeare. Jovial-Lunars best embody this unique ability to be simultaneously deeply engaged while utterly detached.

Jovial-Lunars are therefore often called upon for their expertise and can be found quietly playing the role of innovators and inventors, finding great satisfaction in being recognised for their talents in the process of doing things differently. If they work as business consultants, Jovial-Lunars are able to synthesise diverse sources of information and produce surprising solutions to challenges. They can have an almost obsessive flair for linguistics, logic problems, brain teasers and cryptic crosswords, and they may well spend much time studying obscure chess openings. This combination may lose perspective and devote large amounts of time and energy to relatively unimportant subjects. Jovial-Lunars are drawn to humanitarian and philanthropic endeavours, where their Lunar sense of what is right and wrong is fuelled by their Jovial love for humanity, and they may become deeply committed to organisations such as Amnesty International.

The Jovial-Lunar author Charles Dickens encapsulated minute observations of human behaviour and misdeeds within his sweeping novels. The greatest concentration of Jovial-Lunars I have encountered was at a climate change conference, where at least 95 per cent of the attendees and expert presenters were of this combination, seeking to care for humanity by discussing the science behind the threats to our planet. The second greatest concentration of Jovial-Lunars that I have experienced was at a conference for vicars.

On the downside, when the core attributes of Jovial and Lunar combine in unhealthy ways, we find individuals who are socially isolated and left publicly awkward by their Lunar wilfulness and, at the same time, feel lonely and frustrated by their lack of connection to other people. Their Jovial vanity and sensitivity can lead them to feel that they are being deprived and rejected by society and that they must seek to meet their emotional and tactile needs in more furtive ways.

Internet addiction is common amongst this combination of types, as the expansive Jovial mind explores cyberspace in monkish Lunar solitude. Hacking of security systems is another outlet for their frustration as they wreak havoc and take revenge on those they see as having something that they themselves lack. There is also a payoff for Jovial vanity in having beaten a system by applying their Lunar focus. The Lunar discomfort at being the centre of other people's attention, when combined with Jovial depth and sensitivity, can leave this type lacking in social skills, while feeling simultaneously inferior and superior to other people. We have the recipe for a serious misfit here, with an unhealthy blend of secrecy, charm, manipulation and sexual frustration. It is this author's totally subjective observation that a disproportionately high percentage of male paedophiles are Jovial-Lunars; a contentious comment, I know, but one that is easily put to the test by an online image search 'convicted paedophiles'.

In Western Europe, Jovial-Lunars constitute a fairly small proportion of the population and are easily misunderstood by the other types, who tend to see and engage with the Jovial bulk and jollity, while rejecting or judging the cooler Lunar qualities. This is especially true for Jovial-Lunar boys, who are socially pressured to speak up more and 'toughen up and be a real man', which essentially means act like a Mars.

Jovial-Lunar humour is quite cutting and judgmental, yet wrapped with warmth and good nature, so it really sits on a razor's edge. Ian Hislop and Paul Merton have delivered this gourmet comedic treat superbly for many years on *Have I Got News for You*. American comedian Steven Wright is a master of Jovial-Lunar one liners and British DJ Steve Wright is an icon of on-air quirky humour.

Famous Jovial-Lunars include Bill Hicks, James Spader – the fabulously wealthy and intensely secretive Raymond Reddington in the TV series *The Blacklist*, Cheri Blair, Evanna Lynch (appropriately cast as Luna Lovegood in the *Harry Potter* movies), Gordon Brown, Jenny Murray, Kim Il Jong, Mr Magoo, Stephen Fry (his Jovial Broadway debut was scuppered by Lunar stage fright), Mrs Tiggywinkle, Agatha Christie, Queen Victoria – hence, "We [Jovial] are not amused!" [Lunar], Tim Brooke Taylor, Bernadette Peters, Mervyn King, Alistair Darling, the Dalai Lama, Oliver Hardy, Prince Edward, Bob Newhart, Margaret Rutherford, Robert Morley, Joanne Woodward, Boy George, Dan Brown, Garrison Keillor, Stephen King, Timothy Spall, Ivor Cutler, Chastity Bono, Gary Larson and Matt Groening.

A great number of highly successful film and theatre directors are Jovial-Lunars, as they are able to gather a large and diverse crew and apply meticulous detail to the creative output. Examples include Steven Spielberg, Peter Brooks, Peter Hall, Mike Leigh, Francis Ford Coppola, Sofia Coppola, George Lucas, Pedro Almodovar, Orson Welles, Terence Malick, Tobe Hooper, Stanley Kubrick (he refused to allow *Clockwork Orange* to be shown in Britain for 30 years after it attracted public criticism – now that's wilfulness!), Ron Howard, Peter Jackson, Alfred Hitchcock, Peter Ustinov, Mick Napier, Jane Campion, James Cameron, Del Close, Robert Altman, Cecil B. DeMille and Ken Burns.

Gorillas, hippopotami, pufferfish, hedgehogs and owls are Jovial-Lunar creatures.

Russia, Korea and Finland are all Jovial-Lunar countries. Part of the challenge that the USA finds in engaging with Russia is that the Jovial warmth and openness is approachable and feels European to literal-thinking Martial Americans, while the Lunar privacy and watchfulness feels more Asian and inscrutable.

Professional environments that suit the Jovial-Lunar combination have elements of secrecy, clarity and precision with reasonable amounts of human interaction and warmth. The old school 'Captain Mainwaring' type of bank manager is a classic example: dependable, fussy, jolly and polite. Jovial-Lunars are especially talented at maintaining long-term relationships with clients in financial services, even to the extent of handling the portfolios of multiple generations within wealthy families. Jovials enjoy and relish abundance, while Lunars tend to be risk averse, so this combination provides a safe pair of hands to steadily grow the wealth of a small group of select clients. A successful Jovial-Lunar will wear high-quality accessories that do not attract attention; they prefer a subtle display of wealth that will only be appreciated by those perceptive enough to recognise the value of the item.

They may be highly adept social workers, able to reassure unsettled people while maintaining an emotional distance to protect their own well-being. We find them working at senior levels in housing associations, where they provide stability and support to their staff and exercise astute political savvy in their own careers.

A lot of twitchers are Jovial-Lunars, finding a certain cool companionship in their largely solitary and highly-specific pursuit, which involves patient persistence in observation and building a network of fellow enthusiasts willing to tip them off about the latest rare bird to appear.

The Jovial-Lunar combination often has a particular fascination with sound and a love of technology. Their Jovial side responds to the emotional element of music, in particular, while their Lunar side relishes the science involved, one example being record producer and inventor of the 'wall of sound', Phil Spector. Working as a professional speaker, I almost invariably find that the sound technician at a conference is a Jovial-Lunar, and their role is a perfect balance of being involved in proceedings while sitting at the back of the room fiddling with technology. They love it when I go to say hello and let them know I'll be presenting and then it is time to leave them alone to do their thing until the event is over. They are especially happy to be thanked for their support after the event – this is usually forgotten in the rush at the close of play. Indeed any audiophile environment is filled with Jovial-Lunars, who can be passionate and vain about their level of expertise; I have a Jovial-

Lunar colleague who can tell you which microphone a singer used in recording a song. Any record shop that specialises in obscure music will be populated with Jovial-Lunars enthusing about bands that no one else will ever hear. The Jovial-Lunar Brian Eno has pioneered ambient music. Their auditory focus makes them tremendous voice coaches, both in singing and presenting.

Lunar-Venus

The cool, withdrawn nature of the Lunar type is softened by the warmth and nurturing of Venus. Combining the calm stillness and economy of movement of a Lunar with the slow speed of operation of a Venus means this type can quite happily lead a sedentary lifestyle, and it is easy for more active types to overlook their supportive contributions and take them for granted.

Lunar-Venus men have pale roundish faces with the archetypal weak or receding Lunar chin. Their hair is often mousey brown. If they are predominantly Lunar, they will tend to be slender and quite delicate; if they are closer to Venus, they will be plumper or even a little 'doughy'. Humphrey Bogart and Kevin Spacey are found here. Lunar-Venus men are never sharply masculine in their physique or demeanour and may well spend time at the gym trying to look like their opposite, the culturally idealised Saturn-Mars male. This combination has a particularly strong inclination to avoid physical confrontation by shrinking into the background. Childhood may be a gruelling ordeal for a Lunar-Venus boy, if raised in an environment where it there is an expectation to be sporty or manly. They may well be teased and called 'sissies', especially if they are raised by Martials!

Lunar-Venus women are often a living embodiment of femininity, with the fine bones and delicacy of a Lunar overlaid with the softness and sensuality of Venus. They may well have a pear-shaped figure, with a slender Lunar upper body and the rounded hips and thighs of a Venus. If they are predominantly Lunar, they will appear quite fragile; if they are predominantly Venus, then this combination is exceptionally soft and rounded. The actress Meg Tilly is closer to Lunar, while her sister Jennifer is closer to Venus; it is interesting to look at images of them and see their respective places on the circle. Maggie Gyllenhaal is about 50/50. In religious iconography, the Virgin Mary is invariably depicted as a predominantly Lunar, though Lunar-Venus, woman who epitomises virtue, purity and nurturing. The Western cultural archetype of a Lunar-Venus woman is the 1950s suburban American housewife with a spotless home, who is totally focused on serving her upstanding citizen of a husband and their neatly-dressed and polite children. The modern imaginary version of this icon is the sweetly-subservient Asian mail-order bride.

As with all combined types, we find an inner conflict, and in the case of a Lunar-Venus, this shows up especially in relationship to other people. Lunar types have a strong sense of a separate identity; they are not comfortable in front of people and much prefer to keep to themselves, even when in company. Venus types, on the other hand, tend to live through other people and can feel totally demotivated when they are not connected to their friends, family or tribe. Lunars can feel drained by the needs of other people, while Venus types feel invigorated by taking care of others. So there is a push-pull conflict within Lunar-Venus people, with finicky isolation at one extreme and sensual engulfment at the other extreme. Lunars have very clear personal boundaries within which they operate, while Venus types have permeable or fuzzy personal boundaries, to the point where they are sometimes unable to distinguish between their own needs and the needs of those around them.

A Lunar-Venus who is predominantly Venus will be agreeable and accommodating most of the time, with an occasional and unexpected retreat into wilfulness. A Lunar-Venus who is predominantly Lunar will be cool and self-contained, with an occasional foray into caretaking and nurturing. This combination has a tremendous stability and consistency, with finely-developed notions of selfless service to other people and organisations. Both Lunar and Venus types shun the spotlight, preferring to play supportive roles and allow others to take credit rather than attracting attention to themselves. Lunars value self-reliance and frugality and have a remarkable ability to minimise their personal needs: I knew a Lunar who would eat plain oat biscuits for lunch every day of the working week!

Venus types are often unaware of their own needs, so it is common for Lunar-Venus people to be overlooked, neglected or marginalised in companies, organisations and even in their own families. It is often the case that the true value of the contribution that a Lunar-Venus type makes in these circumstances goes unrecognised until they are not around. People just get used to Lunar-Venus people always being there in the background and keeping things running.

Lunar-Venus people make wonderful friends, constant in their understated affection, willing to listen and steadfast and supportive in a crisis. They do not ask for much in return and if you upset them they will withdraw until you figure out the error of your ways and make amends. It is well worth spending the time to discover where they find pleasure in life and to share their quiet joys with them. There is a soft innocence to Lunar-Venus people, coupled with a keen observation of nature and human behaviour. It is a delight to sit with them and see the world through their eyes, as their observational powers are employed with a refinement and delicacy of feeling. This quality is evident in the diary of Ann Frank.

The quirkiness of a Lunar and the loving nature of a Venus combine to give us a fresh appreciation of our fellow humans and this remarkable planet. At their best, Lunar-Venus people exude a calm and constant sense of service to humanity that is modest, humble and quietly uplifting. Lunar refinement and persistence coupled with Venus compassion can produce an exquisite flowering of the human spirit.

Julia Butterfly Hill is an environmental activist who lived for 738 days on a small platform high up in a 1500-year-old redwood tree in California in order to prevent it being cut down by a logging company. She was successful in this endeavour, which clearly combines the Venusian love of nature with Lunar wilfulness and persistence. It may simply be a coincidence that she named the tree 'Luna.'

On the downside, this combination can produce a specific type of victim: their inertia and lack of self-determination leaves them stuck in menial employment; they resent those who assert themselves, and seek to subtly sabotage and block the efforts of others. It is possible for a Lunar-Venus to surreptitiously undermine an organisation for decades without the source of negativity being discovered, because the secretiveness of a Lunar combined with the invisibility of Venus means they can simply fade into the background. This combination is adept at masking their true feelings of resentment in order to quietly wreak havoc. An aggrieved Lunar-Venus can work their revenge beneath the surface of a company like a fungus beneath the floorboards. If their sabotage is discovered, it will not be easy to remove them as they will know every step of the procedure required for dismissal and every detail of the compensation to which they are entitled.

We sometimes encounter this negative element playing the role of petty tyrants while embedded in admin positions in stagnant government departments. At its most extreme edge of dysfunction, it became a cliché that employees of the US Postal Service (a Lunar-Venus organisation) would show up for work with an assault rifle and kill their supervisor and co-workers after building up resentment for years. There is even a term – 'going postal' – to describe this phenomenon.

Famous examples of Lunar-Venus types include Jake Gyllenhaal, Beth Ditto, Norah Jones, Marcel Proust, David Spade, Tiger Woods (his Lunar persistence was the key to his success and his Venus sensuality got him into trouble!), Lewis Carroll, Prince Charles, Ringo Starr, Keith Moon, David Byrne, Nick Drake, George Bush Senior, Henry Winkler, Dudley Moore, Primrose Shipman, Isadora Duncan, Alec Guinness, Lakshmi Mittal, Terry Jones, Chevy Chase, Paramahansa Yogananda, Billie Jean King, Queen Elizabeth II and John Major.

Lunar-Venus animals include sheep, slow loris, panda, shrew, water-vole and Galapagos tortoise.

India is a largely Lunar-Venus country, as are Taiwan, Bali and Sri Lanka.

Professional environments that suit the Lunar-Venus combination have elements of clear procedure and structure without too much movement or change. This type is strongly drawn to serve people and organisations through being steady, reliable and organized, which makes them ideally suited for admin work in offices, especially in the realm of healthcare delivery. In the UK, we find a great number of Lunar-Venus people working in the National Health Service, both as nurses and in admin support positions.

This combination is not typically highly ambitious and may be very content to work in the same role for decades and to acquire a strong dislike for change. In office environments, their calm stability is of great value to their fellow employees. If they are taken for granted by other types, their steely determination and formidable grasp of procedure can create well-crafted traps upon which many a high flyer has foundered.

Lunar-Venus women, in particular, often find tremendous fulfilment through working in a supportive background position for powerful and successful people. Ambitious Lunar-Venus people become successful by harnessing their Lunar persistence to the Venus ability to pass unseen through the corridors of power. They take a long-term view and may well invest wisely in companies that are geared for steady and sustained growth. They do not usually use their wealth for self-aggrandisement or flamboyant displays, but focus instead on ensuring security for their family, ideally for many generations to come. They are highly adept at tying family members into intricate trusts which ensure their loyalty to the family business. Rupert Murdoch is a sterling example of this combination. Lunar distrust of outsiders, along with the Venus merging with family, is at work in the background. Once they are certain that their family is safely taken care of and their Lunar desire for security has been satisfied, they may well turn their attention to philanthropic enterprises as their Venus love of humanity comes to the fore. Bill Gates is currently playing this role with his charitable foundation. Queen Elizabeth II is a Lunar-Venus who is fiercely protective of her family's privacy and at the same time is devoted to public service. She attends many hundreds of functions every year, partly in her role as monarch and also from a genuine need to serve people.

We find Lunar-Venus people happily employed as bank tellers, post office clerks, reflexologists, massage therapists, legal or medical secretaries, school caterers, scientific researchers, archaeologists, software code writers, veterinarians, dental hygienists, manicurists, laboratory technicians, proof readers, book editors, telecommunications analysts, accountants and surgeons.

Venus-Mercury

The soft, languid, easy-going nature of Venus is toned and sped up by the drive and hyperactivity of Mercury. The Venusian ability to put aside their personality, combined with Mercurial performing skills, produces a sensual chameleon-like actor, with a flair for drama and an innate seductiveness.

Venus-Mercury women are often highly attractive, with dark or jet black hair, which is thick, shiny and abundant. Typically their eyes are dark brown, large and flashing, and if they are physically in good health then the whites of their eyes are brilliant white, almost looking like china. They have good cheekbones, perfect teeth and an electric smile. They tend to have the hourglass figure of Venus but on a more slender frame. Angelina Jolie epitomises this combination. If they are more Venus than Mercury then they will be softer, slower and more feminine; if they are more Mercury than Venus, they will be physically wirier and sharply defined, often having a strongly resonant voice.

Venus-Mercury men are the archetypal suave Latin lover, with thick dark hair, big brown eyes, good cheekbones and a winning smile. Michelangelo's David is a classic physical expression of this combination, while Johnny Depp is a more up-to-date version. If they are closer to Venus than Mercury, then they will be larger and softer, with a lot of dark hair on their head and body. If they are closer to Mercury than Venus, they will be smaller, sharper and faster. Hollywood has idealised Venus-Mercury men since the silent movie era, as they look great on camera and they effortlessly embody the sensuality of Venus and the acting abilities of Mercury. Venus-Mercury men may well draw upon their Mercury side while they are in public or at work and be fast moving and active and then relax into their slower Venus side when they are at home.

The inner conflict of Venus-Mercury people is connected strongly to their sense of self definition: Mercury people are driven to perform and to project an image; they want to show the world who they are and get attention and approval; Venus people are content to go with the flow and remain in the background. Within a Venus-Mercury person we find a struggle between the Mercurial sense of identity, grounded in 'I' as a sharply-drawn character, and the Venusian sense of identity, having a strong flavour of 'we.' Mercury people take centre stage as solo or leading performers in order to feed on the energy of the audience; Venus people are either in the audience or taking care of the performers. For a Venus-Mercury person, it can be a challenge to reconcile these two elements, so we often find Venus-Mercury actors who are dynamic and thrilling onstage or on-screen, yet seem quite dull and ordinary when they are interviewed.

Venus-Mercury types move along a continuum, with standing apart at one end and merging with people at the other end. This combination can be tremendously charming, as with Venus sensitivity to the needs of others and the Mercurial ability to adapt to fit expectations, they have an effortless and intuitive ability to tell other people exactly what they want to hear and so can easily bewitch and entrance their audience. Venus-Mercury people are also able to choose which side to present according to the circumstances in which they find themselves: it may serve their purposes to appear as an easy-going Venus or it may be more expedient for them to be an engaging and lively Mercury.

Something both Venus and Mercury types have in common is an inbuilt dislike of physical violence. Venus people are innately peaceful and Mercurials avoid direct confrontation; a Venus-Mercury may bluster and threaten, but when things start to get physical they will tend to back down or make tracks in a hurry. Venus-Mercury people much prefer to conduct hostilities with a sneak attack, where the victim does not even know the identity of the aggressor or has no means to retaliate.

A Venus-Mercury who is predominantly Venus will be slower and more relaxed in their presentation of themselves to other people; they may even come across as a little slovenly as a way of hiding their Mercury abilities. Many people have been lulled into a false sense of security by overlooking the presence of a Venus-Mercury and saying more than is prudent. Venus-Mercury people know how to use Venus non-existence as a smokescreen to cover the rapid workings of a Mercury mind. Lieutenant Columbo, as played by Peter Falk, is a superb picture of this dynamic: he bumbles about absentmindedly, appearing to be totally disengaged and then his Mercury mind strikes like a cobra with the immortal line, "Oh… Just one more thing." Here is a description of him from Wikipedia:

Lt. Columbo is a shambling, dishevelled-looking, seemingly naive Italian American police detective who is consistently underestimated by his fellow officers and by the murderer du jour. The subjects of his investigations are initially both reassured and distracted by his circumstantial speech and increasingly irritating asides. Despite his unprepossessing appearance and apparent absentmindedness, he shrewdly solves all of his cases and secures all evidence needed for indictment. His formidable eye for detail and meticulous and dedicated approach only become apparent late in the storyline.

A Venus-Mercury man who is predominantly Mercury will tend to cover up his Venus side in public so as not to be exploited for his caring nature and may be very careful only to show his softer side to close friends or family members. The actor Bob Odenkirk is a primarily Mercurial Venus-Mercury type. His character Saul Goodman in *Better Call Saul* and *Breaking Bad* has an ongoing internal wrestling match between his caring Venus side, which wants to help people, and his rapacious and expedient Mercurial side, which is purely selfish. A predominantly Mercurial Venus-Mercury woman may well employ the same strategy, especially in a male-dominated workplace, where she will adopt a 'tough broad' persona in order to compete with men. Ironically, it may be difficult for her to drop her guard and relax into her Venus side once she is safely away from the workplace, which can cause enormous internal stress.

The combined type opposite of the Venus-Mercury is the Mars-Jovial and, while these two are tremendously attracted to each other, there is also the potential for intense conflict. Mars and Venus come together as passionate lovers and Jovial and Mercury create an atmosphere of play and drama, so this relationship is never dull and may well be raucous and larger-than-life. Things can get extremely sticky, however, when the Mars element of a Mars-Jovial meets the Mercury element of a Venus-Mercury. Mars and Mercury just don't get on: Mars enforces the rules and is blunt and direct, while Mercury bends and breaks the rules and is habitually evasive, especially when pressed by a Mars! It follows that the Venus-Mercury/Mars-Jovial couple will do nothing by halves, including their arguments, break-ups and reconciliations, all of which may be very frequent and never subtle.

At their best, Venus-Mercury people are an absolute delight to be around. Warm, engaging and communicative, they nurture and support their friends and families while actively and relentlessly networking on their behalves. They listen attentively, with little judgment, and help their friends make fruitful connections both with other people and their own innate talents. Venus-Mercury people can develop, inspire, draw out and actualise hidden possibilities while taking very little credit for the positive outcomes that they help to create. Love and communication come together to develop people and communities.

At their worst, Venus-Mercury people prefer to manipulate others rather than make an effort themselves. They use their sensitivity to create doubt and uncertainty in people and take advantage of the inner conflict that they stir up. No other type has such a refined ability to blow hot and cold and to conquer the well-being of another person or an organisation, while remaining hidden or even maintaining the facade of being a positive and supportive influence. In their inner world, their non-existence and mutability may leave them with almost no sense of who they really are, which leaves them prone to self-indulgence or seductive behaviour in a futile attempt to fill their inner void. A pathological blend of the worst elements of both types is Bernie Madoff, who ruthlessly exploited his family and community connections with a suave caring Venus exterior, while his Mercurial side bilked investors of billions of dollars.

Famous examples of Venus-Mercury types include Gemma Arterton, Selena Gomez, Catherine Zeta-Jones, Al Pacino, Demi Lovato, John Travolta, Katy Perry, Robert de Niro, Jennifer Lopez, Morgan Freeman, Carmen Miranda, Tony Curtis, Rudolph Valentino, Diana Rigg, Monica Bellucci, Warren Beatty, Demi Moore, Jack Nicholson, Liv Tyler, Lenny Henry, Cheryl Cole, Carol Vorderman, Anna Nicole Smith, Antonio Banderas, Javier Bardem, Thandi Newton, Burt Reynolds, Sylvester Stallone, Tina Turner, Beyoncé, Marian Anderson, Billie Holiday, Dustin Hoffman and Jessica Rabbit.

Venus-Mercury animals include python, chimpanzee, leopard, tabby cat, chameleon, Welsh Border collie and seal.

Venus-Mercury countries and cultures include South America, Italy, Greece, the Middle East and Caribbean Islands. The Rio de Janeiro and Notting Hill

Carnivals are perfect expressions of Venus sensuality and Mercury glitter, as are most performers on the Tamla Motown label and MTV. Flamenco, rap, samba and reggae are Venus-Mercury musical forms.

Professional environments that suit the Venus-Mercury combination have elements of ongoing human contact and communication to satisfy the Mercurial need for attention and the Venus need to be needed. This combination is not suited to work in isolation: a Venus-Mercury who is closer to Mercury will want to circulate and meet a lot of people in their daily business. They will not want to sit still and will be ideally suited to sales positions, especially if this involves visiting lots of clients. A Venus-Mercury who is closer to Venus will be more comfortable with physical inactivity, but will need people coming and going around them, which makes them ideally suited for roles that require multitasking, especially in healthcare environments (they make superb medical secretaries, who can deal with half a dozen different physicians and their patients).

Every Venus-Mercury has the blood of a performer coursing through their veins and knows how to get noticed when they want to and also how to use their Venusian non-existence when they wish to be invisible. This means they can be remarkably effective private investigators, such as Jim Rockford, the character played by the Venus-Mercury actor James Garner in the TV series *The Rockford Files*.

This combination is frequently employed as cocktail waitresses, hairdressers, fashion stylists, PR agents, salespeople of medical devices or procedures, home makeover consultants, customer care specialists, networking gurus, actors, talk show hosts, make up experts, family lawyers, emergency care nurses and GPs. When a Venus-Mercury has a focus on serving other people, they can be drawn to healing professions, where their Venus caring and sensitivity combines with Mercurial keen observation and penetrating insight to create gifted doctors, counsellors, healers, hypnotherapists and therapists – in short, any profession that combines healing and communication. This particular blend of types may be especially skilled at dealing with buried trauma and victims of childhood physical or sexual abuse. Their Venus patience and kindness creates a non-judgmental atmosphere of safety while their Mercury side skilfully ferrets out the full story.

Mercury-Saturn

With this combination, the rapid mind of Mercury allied with Saturn's overview produces a type that does things their way and is a natural leader. Saturns tend to make the rules and Mercurials like to bend or break the rules. Depending on life's influences they can be deeply altruistic or, at the other end of the spectrum, white-collar criminals – literally seeing themselves as being 'above the law'.

Mercury-Saturn men have a slender physique, with long bones; their hair is dark or even jet black and their facial features are sharp, with a particularly alert look to their eyes. Their eyes are either dark brown or a piercing blue; the cheekbones and jawline are prominent, and their head is long and narrow. Their hands and feet are long and their fingers may be particularly slender and fine. Their movements are typically elegant and deliberate, and they may exude an aura of slight superiority coupled with astute inner self awareness. Think Daniel Day Lewis or Rob Lowe.

Mercury-Saturn women are slender and elegant, with a slightly masculine feel to them. Their physique lends itself to wearing high-fashion outfits in a striking manner. This makes them highly attractive to look at, but without the inviting sensuality of Venus-Mercury women. Their hair is typically dark and their facial structure is fine without being overly delicate. Their eyes are dark, and Mercury-Saturn women are particularly adept at giving a withering look of cool disdain when displeased. Cruella Deville pretty much captured this in cartoon form, while Paris Hilton does it in real life. Their movements display a tremendous elegance and self-possession, which gives them an effortlessly aristocratic air.

The inner conflict of a Mercury-Saturn arises when the Saturn desire to serve others through giving wise paternal guidance (which facilitates their protégées finding and developing their highest potential) is set against the Mercury desire to protect oneself by playing upon the weaknesses of other people. Thus the innate Saturnine sense of justice and purpose can collide with the ongoing Mercurial impatience and expediency. Saturn wants to be seen as a figurehead who provides constant support and consistent direction to a family, organisation or business; they receive tremendous validation through playing a recognisable and defined role. Saturn dearly loves to walk a long, straight, narrow path to a lofty and distant goal and, while on this journey, it is vital for them to ignore all frivolities and distractions, thereby keeping their mind focused and clearly set on their single destination. Mercury, on the other hand, has a much more fluid approach and prefers to be able to play a series of roles depending on circumstance or situation, for they are habitual chameleons and do not like to be fixed or tied down to one position. Mercury much prefers the excitement and stimulation of a spontaneous journey, where every twist and turn can be explored.

Mercury-Saturn types have a most intriguing relationship with the legal system: Saturn tends to value and venerate the rule of law as a dependable structure which potentially guarantees fairness within society; Mercury tends to view the process of law as a flexible structure designed to benefit the more creative thinkers, such as themselves, while at the same time stopping slower people (everyone else) from doing too much damage. It follows that some Mercury-Saturns have the potential to be highly-successful financial criminals, in whom the core attributes of Saturn Dominance and Mercurial Power have combined to create someone extraordinary, who is exempt from the restrictions placed upon ordinary people. They tend to express astonishment when caught and are outraged that the 'little people' have the nerve to bring them to justice. It is extremely rare for them to acknowledge or admit any wrongdoing and they will blame a flawed system or vindictive regulators for their demise. In the United States, the real estate developer and financier Charles Keating Jr was a classic example of this number – a staunch Catholic and anti-pornography campaigner, he was convicted on many counts of fraud, racketeering and conspiracy for his part in the Savings and Loan Scandal in the 1990s.

It is also the case that this combination can use their Mercurial creative abilities in the service of Saturnine higher ideals to create a life that is totally devoted to serving their fellows and making a unique contribution to society. A clear historical example of this was Raul Wallenberg, the Swedish diplomat stationed in Berlin who issued forged passports and bribed German officials to save an estimated 15,000 Jews from the Holocaust. He was a Mercury-Saturn who broke international law and ultimately sacrificed his life for a noble cause.

Mercury-Saturns often exude a dry charm coupled with extremely good manners. Other types sometimes view them as being aloof and sniffy, and indeed it can be hard for this combination to be patient with people who lack their far-reaching overview and creative mental abilities. In fact, an immaculately-dressed Mercury-Saturn waiter working in an exclusive restaurant can easily leave the average diner wondering exactly who is serving whom in their interaction! This combination seems to be born to lead others, their physical height and intellectual sharpness giving them a natural air of authority so people literally look up to them. Mercury-Saturns relish ideas, concepts and philosophies and can spend many happy hours engaged in ivory tower discussions with others of their type. Their grasp of the intricacies of language is often formidable.

The Mercury-Saturn's favourite intellectual foil is their opposite combined type in this system – the supremely erudite Jovial-Lunar; here, the expansive Jovial mind can keep pace with the quicksilver manoeuvers of Mercury, while Lunar precision is uniquely appreciative of the delicate mental structures that Saturn loves to create. The current cultural archetype for a Mercury-Saturn/Jovial-Lunar pair is the Goth couple which can be spotted in almost any shopping centre: a tall dark haired slender pale man accompanied by a short young version of Queen Victoria; they stand out as misfits and happily celebrate their 'otherness' together. This relationship does not typically have the fire and drama of a Venus-Mercury/Mars-Jovial couple; it tends to be cooler and more cerebral with the stability that comes when Saturn and Lunar align with each other. There is often a surreal edge to their conversations, brought about by the quirkiness of Lunar engaging with the playfulness of Mercury.

At their best, Mercury-Saturns bring a refined aristocratic sensibility to those around them, the high moral standards of Saturn being brought to an exquisite sharpness by the fine perceptions of Mercury. Physically, they are elegant, precise and deliberate in their movements and dress themselves crisply in muted colours. Their speech is polished and eloquent, having both the structural element of Saturn and the Mercurial facility with words. It can be an intellectual treat to keep up with the philosophical flights of fancy of a Mercury-Saturn friend, who is able to be both penetrating and challenging in their insights, while being benign and paternal in their supportiveness.

Emotionally, Mercury-Saturns hold a steadfast quiet caring in their hearts for their friends and families, which they offer with gentle humility. They are able to devote themselves nobly to a worthy cause from which they will never waver and use all their powers to espouse and support. It is difficult to resist a Mercury-Saturn who wishes to enlist your assistance with something they believe in passionately; their Mercurial mind has already sealed off all possible exits or excuses that you may offer and their Saturnine nature simply insists that you do what you know is right. Of course, it is assumed that what you know is right is in total alignment with what they have decided!

At their worst, Mercury-Saturn people hold a lofty disdain for the rest of us. Their Saturn side sees us as immature and compulsive, while their Mercury side sees other people as dull, slow witted and therefore deserving to be fleeced or exploited. They believe themselves to be better than the rest of us, they become bitter and resentful and are therefore able to justify taking advantage of others. When Mercurial rule breaking meets Saturnine dominance, we find a type capable of constructing immoral organisations which function to hoodwink and disempower acolytes. Cult leaders Jim Jones and David Koresh are pathological examples of this specific form of megalomania, fuelled by the suspicion of Mercury and the Saturn desire to control others. Believing that they alone have access to the truth, they can slip into zealotry and extremism, thereby justifying extreme cruelty to non-believers. Grand Inquisitor Tomas de Torquemada was a Mercury-Saturn. Currently we find unhealthy Mercury-Saturns drawn to control of large companies, where they can exert power and dominance at will.

Famous Mercury-Saturns include Edward Norton, Justin Bieber, Natalie Portman, Osama Bin Laden, Joey Ramone, Lord Pentland, J.G. Bennett, Angus Deayton, Grace Jones, Jimi Hendrix, Leonard Cohen, Marlene Dietrich, John Cleese, Donald Sutherland, Randy Travis, Iman, Lyle Lovett, Barak Obama, Cher, Tony Blair, Edwina Currie, David Copperfield, Stan Laurel, Tara Palmer-Tompkinson, Lauren Bacall, Bob Geldof, Racquel Welch, Vincent Price, Christopher Lee, Peter Cushing, Dracula, Celine Dion, Uri Geller, Rupert Everett, Elizabeth Hurley, Sacha Baron-Cohen, Benazir Bhutto, Oscar Wilde, Brooke Shields, Joseph Goebbels, Jamie Lee Curtis, Peter Mandelson and Spike Milligan.

Mercury-Saturn animals include greyhound, wolf, Siamese cat, Irish wolfhound, poodle, meerkat, sandeel and raven.

Mercury-Saturn countries and cultures include dry and often mountainous areas of Afghanistan, Pakistan, Ethiopia, Somalia, Sudan and Chad. Mercury-Saturn cultures tend to be found in areas where physical survival is a challenge and there is often a strict legal or moral code in place, such as extreme Sharia law. It seems that these systems reflect austere paternal Saturn dominance working to control Mercurial rule breaking.

A familiar Western cultural icon is the slender elegant city gent in a pin-striped suit.

From one perspective, we are now living in a Mercury-Saturn period in history, with the Middle Ages being Lunar and the Renaissance being Jovial. Currently we have highly-regimented and controlling government systems of surveillance and regimentation engaging with instant global communication. It is as if Saturn control mechanisms and Mercurial evasiveness are keeping pace with each other in an intricate dance. As soon as Saturn finds ways and means to keep track of people's movements, Mercury finds new loopholes to exploit. This is especially apparent in countries where the population is seeking greater freedom and governments shut down access to the Internet and mobile phone communications at the first sign of unrest.

Professional environments that suit the Mercury-Saturn temperament are those where elements of Saturnine order and structure work with Mercurial speed of communication. Mercury-Saturns are drawn to large-scale commerce, especially in realms such as futures, derivatives or commodities trading. This type does not like to get their hands dirty; they much prefer turning the wheels of power from a distance and may be highly adept at avoiding accountability for their actions. Mercury-Saturns can combine the Saturn ability to detach from emotion with Mercurial expediency in order to be quite ruthless in mergers and acquisitions and in downsizing companies. They are able to make highly-unpopular decisions and distance themselves from the emotional reactions of those affected by the decisions. This ability is a two-edged sword, enabling them to grasp the nettle in corporate wheeling and dealing, while at the same time leaving them open to being perceived as heartless and self-centred. When the passion and enthusiasm of a Mercury blends with the organisational abilities of the Saturn, it is a formula for a remarkably successful CEO, one able to steer an organisation in new directions while maintaining a sense of stability and security.

Mercury-Saturns are almost hardwired for leadership and will tend to change jobs if they are not quickly given the promotions to which they feel entitled. They are drawn to running their own businesses or finding strategies to climb the corporate ladder and create their own power structure within large organisations. Their unique blend of Saturnine paternal altruism and Mercurial flexibility finds expression in a particular niche within large charities which specialise in delivering emergency aid to chaotic areas after a large-scale disaster, such as a volcano eruption or an earthquake. This author has met several Mercury-Saturn males who play a very specific role here; they will be flown in ahead of a convoy of aid and their role is to bribe or threaten any bandit organisations that stand between those in need and the aid convoy. This is another example of Mercurial willingness to go outside the law and use all means at their disposal in order to serve a higher cause and save lives.

We find Mercury-Saturns working as consultants in leadership and organisational development, business coaches, CEOs (especially in financial institutions), waiters in fine restaurants, high-ranking police or military officers, political advisers, branding consultants, fashion models, financial advisers, trust fund managers, taxation lawyers, university deans, arms dealers, media trainers, youth ministers, civil rights advocates, charity fundraisers, architects, estate agents and old-school butlers.

Saturn-Mars

In this combination, the ascetic, ponderous nature of Saturn is turbo-charged by the direct, blunt activity of Mars to produce a driven, self-reliant pioneer who is drawn to travelling a long road to redemption while struggling against obstacles. Saturn makes the rules for the benefit of all and Mars enforces the rules, so this type has high standards which they expect themselves and others to live up to.

Saturn-Mars men have fair hair if they are Caucasian, deep-set eyes, a squarish face, a robust, lean physique, strong bones, pronounced musculature and often large hands and feet. They may well be almost absurdly physically resilient and able to endure extremes of heat, cold, hunger, sickness and exertion. Arnold Schwarzenegger built his career on this image, both on and off screen. Saturn-Mars men are built for physical work and may be almost robotic in their persistence and activity.

Saturn-Mars women are almost always blue-eyed and blonde if they are Caucasian; they have long arms and legs and are slender without being delicate. They are physically robust and active and often judged as being tomboyish when they are young. They often display a refreshing directness and self-possession and are naturally geared to physical activity, being drawn to athletic pursuits, especially tennis and golf, which often gives them an aura of vitality and good health. Angela Bassett and Cate Blanchett are here and Claire Danes captured the energy of a Saturn-Mars woman in the series *Homeland*. Western culture has relentlessly idealised the Saturn-Mars female as being the target body shape for young women to aspire to; hence, the dramatic growth of plastic surgery and even leg lengthening operations in countries like China. .

The inner conflict of a Saturn-Mars is an ongoing push-pull mechanism whereby the thoughtful and considerate Saturn seeks to rein in the impulsive and relentless Mars. Saturn wants to figure out the ideal plan of action by considering all the options carefully before making a decision; Mars just wants to get on with it – now! We can almost hear the inner dialogue whereby Mars urges immediate action and Saturn plays for time. Close enough is not good enough for Saturn, who needs to be certain before proceeding, whereas Mars finds certainty by proceeding and then encountering whatever comes along with joyful abandon. Saturn wants to move with people and with people's best interests carefully weighed up, while Mars is a very content to move against people and deal with the consequences later. Saturns do not like to hurt the feelings of other people if they can possibly avoid it and Mars likes to break eggs in order to make omelettes – in fact, they may well enjoy the egg breaking a lot more than the actual omelette making!

Louis Berman has an interesting take on this inner dynamic:

> *The distinction between men of theoretical genius, whose minds which could embrace a universe and yet failed to manage successfully their own personal everyday lives [too much Saturnine pondering without action] and the men of practical genius, who can achieve and execute, the great engineers and industrial men lies in the balance between the ante-pituitary and the adrenal cortex primarily [enough Mars adrenaline to put the plan into action].*

Too much dithering is actually unhealthy for a Saturn-Mars, as they become physically and emotionally run down by having one foot on the accelerator and the other foot on the brake. The paternal side of Saturn can be very harsh and judgmental towards the less-refined elements of Mars. Mars rebels at being judged and fights back with more misbehaviour, which evokes more Saturn judgment and condemnation. This cycle can be very self-destructive and waste the tremendous potential for positive social impact that this combination embodies. Saturn-Mars people in general do not find it entirely easy to relax and enjoy themselves; if you enjoy telling jokes, this is not your ideal audience!

Where Saturn and Mars come together is in the realm of justice. Saturns believe in the role of law and have a deep distaste for injustice; Mars has a tendency to black-and-white thinking and reacts strongly if they see something as unfair. Saturn-Mars types are capable of enormous self-sacrifice and are often seen fighting to promote the cause of justice and fairness. This combination simply will not tolerate situations which they see as unjust and will be compelled to act resolutely and forcefully to right the wrongs that they observe. A great number of environmental campaigners and activists are Saturn-Mars types and these are the ones on the front lines, scaling the chimneys of power stations and abseiling from bridges to block shipping.

This is where the clarity of Saturn decision-making creates a straight line along which Mars energy can find expression.

There is very little subterfuge with a Saturn-Mars: they meet obstacles and injustice head-on and they do not back down. Saturn-Mars types are probably the ultimate doer in this system. When Saturn planning is fuelled by Mars fire and drive this combination can be unstoppable and they are often capable of a truly extraordinary workload. Saturn sets long-range targets upon which they fixate, knowing that the goal is worthy of their commitment, and Mars adds to the mix by making sure that, upon hitting the target, this combination does not pause to reflect, they simply keep going and going. To other types, this restless and continual outpouring of energy may seem pathologically unbalanced; to a Saturn-Mars the rest of us just seem lazy and undisciplined. Saturns are willing and able to overlook their own needs when their mind is set upon a task, while Mars values self-reliance as one of their greatest qualities. This combination of self-denial and determination is actually invigorated by obstacles and sees resistance as something that calls forth even deeper reserves of energy.

Victorian Christianity was a Saturn-Mars religious manifestation; no other combination could produce songs like 'Onward Christian Soldiers' and organisations such as the Salvation Army. General William Booth, the founder of the Salvation Army, was always encouraged when his street preachers were attacked by mobs because he knew this would simply increase their commitment to the cause. Once a Saturn-Mars has convinced themselves that they are right and that they have the one-and-only handle on the truth, then any opposition serves to make them stronger. The Victorian image of God as a stern bony fellow with a beard, who wants us to follow a narrow and straight path and will punish us severely if we do not, is definitely a Saturn-Mars. It can be pointless and frustrating to expect flexibility from a Saturn-Mars who has become rigid and dogmatic with the strength of their convictions.

Julius Caesar is a fine example of a Saturn-Mars who found full expression of his talents through his role as dictator of the Roman Empire – a Saturn-Mars institution which followed Mars' conquest with assimilation into a Saturnine structure, the Pax Romana. Any tribe or nation opposing Caesar's armies was faced with a choice of either being destroyed or becoming a client state within the system. In Caesar's '*Veni vidi vici*' (I came, I saw, I conquered), we find a clear distillation of dominance and destruction working together. A core belief of a Saturn-Mars is that no one can do anything as quickly and efficiently as they can and Caesar used the might of the Roman Empire to prove this point. He was very widely regarded as being ruthless but fair, and famed for having an unbending iron will and continually seeking the next challenge against which to test his strength and determination.

As mentioned previously, the British Empire was modelled largely on the Roman Empire and sought to impose its own order and values upon the world. Explorers such as David Livingstone and Henry Morton Stanley epitomise this type, while the stiff upper lip, so widely caricatured yet admired, is an exclusively Saturn-Mars trait. The American Empire is modelled in turn on the British Empire and seeks to export justice and democracy and the American way of life around the globe. They are convinced that theirs is the only and best way for nations to be structured and they are therefore justified in using Martial force on the world stage. The archetypal cowboy is a Saturn-Mars, tall rugged and taciturn, and Clint Eastwood plays this combination in almost every one of his movies.

At their best, Saturn-Mars people seek to uphold high standards and to lead boldly by their own example. They are capable of devoting themselves totally to a cause and playing the game fairly, whether they win or lose. They have a love of competitive sports, especially those involving endurance and resilience, which test the fibre of the participant and require focus and determination. Saturn-Mars people are drawn to coaching and encouraging young people, particularly those who have lost their way and are in need of a strong parental figure. They are steadfast and sincere in their support of those who wish to turn their lives around and live more productively and honestly. They are able to guide, support and challenge their protégées to aspire to and stick with positive patterns of behaviour.

My neighbour is a retired policeman and, at the time of writing, has two broken ribs which he received playing football against a team of young offenders; it hurts, but he doesn't mind because it's a good cause and he is a Saturn-Mars!

The unique fortitude of a Saturn-Mars comes to the fore in desperate, last-stand situations: with their backs to the wall, outnumbered and outgunned, they will go down fighting and not surrender, convinced that they are in the right.

Their opposite combined type is the Lunar-Venus and, as a couple, they create a cooler, more sedate version of a Mars-Venus pairing, as both Saturn and Lunar tends to be self-contained and a little proper. This relationship tends to be stable and provides a nurturing and guiding environment in which to raise children. Conflict can arise in two places: firstly, when the restlessness of a Saturn-Mars is frustrated by the slower pace and seeming aimlessness of Venus, and secondly, when the boisterousness and impulsiveness of Mars offends the frosty propriety of Lunar. As a couple, they will tend to create a slightly quirky cosy nest in which they can both relax and unwind and from which the Saturn-Mars can sally forth.

At their worst, Saturn-Mars people are cold, judgmental, stubborn and utterly ruthless. They are able to completely dehumanise those they see as different or inferior and thereby justify acting inhumanely towards others. The blonde haired, blue-eyed Nazi *Ubermensch* is an exaggerated image of this type: strong, honest, hard-working and almost superhuman, they saw themselves as destined to eradicate the lesser races and purify the Earth. When Mars destruction is intellectually justified by Saturn dominance and the basest impulses are glorified and unleashed, the results are ugly in the extreme. Saturn-Mars people can become completely emotionally disconnected from the natural world and methodically wreak environmental havoc purely for financial gain. They can be drawn to extreme paternalistic religions which promise fire and brimstone to the unbelievers and backsliders. The dour Scottish church elder who would padlock the swings in children's playgrounds every Sunday neatly fits this bill.

Famous Saturn-Mars types include Gillian Anderson, Margaret Thatcher ("the lady is not for turning"), the Marlboro man, Jodie Foster, Ernest Shackleton, Lewis and Clark, Glenn Close, Anne Robinson, Jeremy Paxman (*"come on answer the question!"*), Queen Elizabeth I, Prince William, Linda Hamilton, Nicole Kidman, Sting, Bob Marley, Helen Mirren, Michael Caine, Generals Pershing, MacArthur, Custer and Patton, Chris Tarrant, Kirk

Douglas, Amelia Earhart, Maria Sharapova, Chris Evert, Frankenstein's monster, Sharon Stone, John Wayne, Robert Redford, Nick Nolte, Harrison Ford, Henry Fonda, Jane Fonda, Bridget Fonda, Paul Hogan, Ted Turner, Donald and Kiefer Sutherland, Julie Christie, Candace Bergen, Kurt Cobain, Kurt Russell, Burt Lancaster, Kim Basinger and Emma Thompson.

Saturn-Mars animals include golden eagle, pike, Chinook salmon, praying mantis, great white shark, Alsatian dog, Tyrannosaurus rex, barracuda, woodpecker, camel, red deer and crocodile.

Saturn-Mars countries and cultures include the Scottish highlands and islands, Vikings, King Arthur and his knights, Sweden, New Zealand, the Australian outback (see Crocodile Dundee), Alaska, Wyoming, Montana and Idaho. White supremacist groups have an abundance of Saturn-Mars members. The Canadian Mounties are a Saturn-Mars organisation that always gets their man. The phrase, 'the long arm of the law' could refer to the long bones of Saturn combined with the relentless determination of Mars to punish the wrongdoer.

Professional environments that suit the Saturn-Mars temperament blend elements of Saturnine order and structure with Martial commitment and determination. This combination flourishes in organisations where there are clearly-defined goals, a recognisable hierarchy and an overall sense of purpose. The closer to Saturn they are, the more likely they are to spend the majority of their working lives in one career or organisation; those closer to Mars will be more restless and frequently seek new frontiers. Saturn-Mars types see themselves as reformers, whose role is to sweep away the old and redundant and build new and efficient structures in their place. The more Martial they are, the more they will relish the sweeping away of the old, ideally down to bedrock; the more Saturnine they are, the more attention they will put into building viable systems.

In Western European police forces, the higher the rank of police officer, the more Saturnine they are, with the more Martial types preferring the rough-and-tumble of the front line and the sense of clarity they derive from sorting out the good guys from the bad guys. This same picture is reflected in all branches of the military, the Coast Guard, fire service and indeed all emergency services. No matter what role they play in the working world, every Saturn-Mars has a strong sense of self and would much sooner give advice then ask for it. It can be hard for them to slow themselves down for long enough to listen to input from colleagues, but once they take it on board they will act upon it with great commitment.

We find Saturn-Mars people working as ranchers, lumberjacks, test pilots, stuntmen or women, forest rangers, TV newsreaders and sports commentators, fitness instructors, high-rise construction workers, wildlife photographers, flying doctors, bodyguards, project managers, PE teachers, geologists, oceanographers, tour guides, head teachers, osteopaths, soccer and rugby team managers, snipers, expedition leaders, mountain guides, basketball players, consumer rights campaigners, company chairmen, investigative reporters, wilderness survival experts and steeplejacks.

SOL.
Ioan. Stradan. invent.
Ioann. Collaert sculpsit.
Phls Galle excudit.

Astrorum princeps, lyræ amans, SOL, siam Ioue natus. 4 Auratis mundum lustro nitens radijs.

CHAPTER 8: Solar

Up until this point we first examined each of the planetary types in turn, then took a tour round the combined types. The vast majority of people we encounter are a mixture of two types, pure types being extremely rare.

There is one more element to consider, because some people have a third influence added into the mix. This is represented by the Sun, radiating from the centre of the circle of types. The Sun is able to add a certain vibrational charge which brings a twist to the underlying combination and is referred to as Solar. Any type may have the addition of this Solar influence, which shows up in varying amounts: some people have none; others have a sprinkle, and from time to time we find people who embody a significant imprint of this influence. If an individual has readily-discernible Solar traits, then we refer to them as having three types – Solar-Saturn-Mars or Solar-Mars-Jovial, for example. The Solar influence may either soften or mitigate the underlying attribute of the planetary type or exaggerate and even turbo-charge it. When initially applying this material, it is best to pay attention primarily to planetary types and become familiar with their various physical characteristics and core attributes before looking for Solars.

Physicality

Women who have a strong Solar influence upon their type have been characterised as the archetypal fairy-tale princess: their skin is fine, pale and translucent; their eyes are bright, large and shiny and set wide apart, which may give them a look of being perpetually surprised; the neck is long and slender; their hair may have an unusual hue, being almost white or silvery; their features are fine and delicate, and they may well feel fragile and timid, with a lot of nervous energy. There is often something slightly boyish or androgynous about Solar women, which makes them highly visually attractive, but not earthily sensual. The model Gemma Ward is a striking highly-Solar Saturn.

Solar men have a similar delicacy to their features, which is often quite striking. Their eyes are open and large; their movements are typically restless and uncoordinated, with sweeping and dramatic gestures; there is often an effeminate edge to their manner, and Solar men can be almost asexual or, alternatively, have a strong sexual drive. Michael Jackson was extremely Solar and this was a huge factor in his extraordinary talent and also his inability to function in the real world. Both male and female Solar people seem to have an resistance to dirt and seem to just naturally look and feel cleaner and shinier than those around them.

Louis Berman referred to Solar as the thymus type and here he is describing a child of this type:

> There are certain individuals with excessive thymus action, foreshadowing a continued thymus predominance throughout life. The 'angel child' is the type: regularly proportioned and perfectly made, like a fine piece of sculpture, with delicately chiselled features, transparent skin changing colour easily, long silky hair, with an exceptional grace of movement and an alertness of mind. They seem the embodiment of beauty, but somehow unfit for the coarse conflicts of life. In English literature several characters are recognisable as portraits of the type, notably Paul Dombey, whose nurse recognised that he was 'not for this world'.

In this chapter I will often quote William Benham, his prose is florid and Victorian but distills his extensive observations of Solars, whom he refers to as the Apollonian type:

> The Apollonian is a handsome and manly type... the lines of the body run in graceful curves, and he is light and supple. His complexion is clear, his skin white, fine and firm in texture, and cheeks rosy. This pinkness of colour gives a clue to a healthy condition and consequent attractiveness... The eyes are large, almond shaped, brown or blue in colour, with long lashes curling up at the ends. The eyes have a frank and honest expression, which changes to sweetness and sympathy when the emotions are in play, and they sparkle with the brilliancy and life of the brain behind them, his cheeks are firm and rounded showing no hollows. The nose is straight and finely shaped, the nostrils beautifully proportioned, and dilating sensitively under the play of emotions; as is the case with all highly strung organisms. The feet are medium-size, the instep arching and high, which gives spring and elasticity to the walk.

This is a particularly distinguishing feature of the Apollonian. In this type is a picture of healthy conditions, beautiful proportions, grace and symmetry of body and to these must be linked a mind full of similar charms and attributes. From every point of view the Apollonian is brilliant, full of the love of beauty, art, colour and form.

It is worth a general thumbnail examination of each of the planetary types in combination with Solar to see how this influence colours the underlying features. Their core attribute of Naivety gives them a tendency to be blithely unaware of the negative side of life.

A Solar-Lunar will often be more talkative and sociable than a pure Lunar, as the Solar energy speeds them up and makes them more outgoing. They may well experience an internal push-pull struggle where the Lunar desire to withdraw from company conflicts with the Solar love of engagement. The combination of a weak or receding Lunar chin with large, open widely-spaced eyes is quite striking. Physically, this combination will be extremely delicate and likely to be finicky about their food. They will also have a strong affinity for children and nature. Nancy Reagan managed to combine Lunar wilfulness and Solar naivety in her simplistic "just say no" slogan as a remedy for drug abuse.

A Solar-Venus will move faster than a typical Venus and be highly attuned and open to the wishes of other people. This particular combination will have a real challenge in terms of taking care of their own needs as a Venus looks to take care of others and Solars tend to be somewhat ungrounded and unaware of their own physical desires. This type is often physically quite beautiful with large dark eyes and a grounded, sensual openness. Rihanna combined Venus non-existence and Solar naivety in her abusive relationship with the Martial Chris Brown.

A Solar-Mercury is a human dynamo, overflowing with nervous energy. Their features will be very sharply drawn and their speed of operation remarkably high. The Solar element will somewhat soften the more manipulative traits of Mercury and make this a lighter, more-trusting combination, able to effortlessly attract and entrance an audience. The artist formally known as Prince lives this number. They may well be capable of bizarre and eccentric flights of fancy and think in novel ways.

A Solar-Saturn will be very bony and slender, sometimes almost skeletal, and the eyes will be large, clear and noticeable. The dry deliberation of Saturn will be softened by the innate positivity and cheerfulness of Solar to give a combination that both believes in and works to create happy endings. With practice, their movements become graceful and flowing and they will naturally draw admiring attention when they enter a room. This is the combination most frequently found striding down the catwalk at fashion shows with a blank expression upon their superbly-chiselled facial features, like Kate Moss.

A Solar-Mars will often have large clear blue eyes and flaming hair, with pale skin and highly visible freckles. If a Mars is like a bulldog then a Solar-Mars is more like an excitable puppy, in which the drive of Mars is converted to an indomitable enthusiasm. This combination will have particular challenges around accepting that some things in life are just not fair. Mars believes in justice and Solars believe the good guy always wins; when this doesn't happen in real life, this particular combination will sulk and pout. They are also more willing to be the centre of attention than your typical Mars, Madonna being a case in point.

A Solar-Jovial will be barely able to contain their good cheer, their cheeks will be pink and flushed, their eyes wide and expressive, and life to them is one jolly adventure. This combination is actually radiant in their warmth and generosity. They have enormous challenges around budgeting, as Jovials love excess and Solars do not readily recognise earthly limitations, so they simply buy whatever they feel like buying in the moment without thought for the consequences. Solar-Jovials also switch rapidly from emotional exuberance to fits of pique, which tends to make their social life something of a dramatic rollercoaster. The Solar Jovial-Lunar, Elton John, was the subject of a documentary entitled 'Tantrums and tiaras'.

Solar Traits

Solars are a high-energy type, who may appear so sensitive that it is as if the nervous system is over-stimulated by outside influences and their pale, thin skin is not substantial enough to protect them. They are skittish and nervous in their movements and may well be extremely clumsy and collide with furniture in their excitement, giving them quite spectacular bruises. Their attention is drawn to bright possibilities and they flutter towards these like moths to a flame until they burn out with exhaustion. As soon as they wake up, they are off again on the same merry-go-round. Solars are ungrounded, even unearthly and feel like hummingbirds or hyperactive children that have found themselves inhabiting adult bodies without quite being sure how to operate them. They do not instinctively know how to take care of their bodies and lack discrimination, as they literally do not know what is or isn't good for them.

The concept of cause and effect seems to be a mystery to most Solars, so they may go for days without eating very much and have no idea why they feel dizzy or faint. A Solar friend of mine was wondering out loud why she had such a hangover and we had to remind her that it was because she had drunk a lot of alcohol the night before! Most other types see a fairly straightforward connection between drinking to excess and a hangover and between not eating enough food and feeling the effects of low blood sugar; Solars need to be reminded of these connections repeatedly and there is absolutely no guarantee that they will remember the next time.

Solars do not pay as much attention to the past as other types do; they seem to live more in the present, with hope for a bright future, much the same way that excited children do. This sunny disposition makes them very attractive to other types, who enjoy their company and their unique outlook on life, while at the same time shaking their heads with bewilderment at the fanciful notions in which Solars love to indulge. They may act impulsively and recklessly, believing in new-age mantras, such as 'the Universe will take care of me.' When they come down to earth with a bump, it is never long before they unfold their transparent wings and soar off on their next fantastic voyage. It is as if they retain the charmed aura of childhood, where anything seems possible and, if some half-baked idea doesn't work, another will soon come along for them to latch onto with their typical breathless enthusiasm.

William Benham on this type:

> *He is a spontaneous type, and versatility, brilliancy, love of the beautiful and artistic in everything, are his attributes. The dark side of life is in the background with him and, as the Saturnian was needed as a check to over enthusiasm, so the Apollonian is needed in order that darkness and gloom may not dominate. Play and diversion must follow work if we are to keep ourselves healthy and vigourous, and someone must provide these recreative things, these rests from seriousness. We must have comedians, for laughter is a tonic to the tired brain.*

Solars really do believe in happy endings, that their prince will come, the good guys will win in the end, they will find the pot of gold at the end of the rainbow, the dreams that you dare to dream really do come true – especially when you wish upon a star. They believe that sound financial investments can be made in response to unsolicited e-mails from Third World countries, the song they wrote in their bedroom will reach the top of the charts, their first novel will be a bestseller, their poetry will be discovered, their unique genius will be recognised and celebrated, sugar counts as a major food group, tattooed ex-convicts are really nice deep down inside, their guru is leading them to enlightenment and is far better qualified to handle their trust fund than they are, true love prevails, the best salesman to buy a used car from is the one with the nice smile, positive thinking is far more effective than sustained effort and that there really is a pattern to the numbers that come up on a roulette wheel – you just need the formula.

This naïve outlook makes it very difficult for Solars to learn from their mistakes, as they rush to minimise or ignore the sort of negative experiences that leave the rest of us wary. The adage 'Once bitten twice shy' does not apply to Solars; in fact they can have been bitten several dozen times by the same dog, in the same location, at the same time and still be very surprised the next time it happens. This makes the average Solar ideal prey for con artists and shysters.

Yet there is something indefinable and quite magical to be found in the company of a Solar friend, as if something within them has been untouched by difficult experiences and cynicism. Solars retain a precious innocence that can resonate with any of us who are willing to step for a moment outside the tide of negative media propaganda and revisit the openness and wonder that we experienced as children. To spend time with a Solar is an opportunity to look again at the world through fresh and hopeful eyes and to delight in the richness of our miraculous existence on this unique planet.

If we are open-minded and receptive enough, a Solar friend can remind us of the awe and excitement that we felt when we first became aware of the limitless possibilities of our young lives. There is a touching harmlessness about Solars, an affinity for the small and vulnerable and a delightful playfulness which charms the heart. Observe the exquisite joy on the face of a young child playing with a new toy; that same feeling is something that Solars experience on a far more frequent basis than the rest of us and can be triggered in them by a spider's web, a pop song or a new scarf.

Ayd is a modern Renaissance man – he is a singer, songwriter, musician, graphic designer, book publisher, philosopher, science teacher, writer and a conference speaker with a particular focus on creativity and innovation. He is clearly a Solar type, with widely-spaced large bright eyes, golden curly hair and an aura of innocent enthusiasm. I asked Ayd about his ways of accessing inspiration:

> I'll pace about, in nature, look at the sky, notice things, walk in circles, talk to myself out loud and keep moving to keep the energy flowing. I am compulsively creative; I'll create a book but probably won't bother marketing it as I'd rather just create another. It's the same with my songs; I record a bunch of songs, mix them and then have to write and record some more rather than try to sell them. I also found conference speaking could become a bit of a trap as clients would want to hear the same talk others had already heard but I'd prefer to do something new and take it further, otherwise I'd get bored.

I was intrigued as to how an ethereal Solar type would go about teaching such a nuts-and-bolts subject as science to teenagers:

> Many teachers fall into a trap – they either act like a sergeant-major, a Stanford experiment type prison guard, or they try to be friends with their students. My style is different because while I don't want to boss students around, I am not their friend – my cachet is that I am a bigger

kid than they are and I'm weirder than they are. I show up for lessons wearing my velvet frock coat and cravat [Ayd is Solar Mars Jovial]. This throws them off-centre and we can communicate differently. In my very first science lesson I showed up wearing a gas mask and World War One uniform. The subject was chlorine – I wanted it to be tangible and memorable, to mean something, to have context. I was asked to describe my teaching style and my reply was, "benevolent alien".

My students describe me as a cross between Willie Wonka [played in the original movie by the Solar Gene Wilder] and Tom Baker as Doctor Who [another Solar]. My muse is Carl Sagan: the ultimate science storyteller, he designed the gold disc that went into space on the Voyager space craft as a means to communicate with alien civilisations, long after humans may become extinct. I set this as an assignment to a class – they had to design their own golden discs that could communicate with an alien intelligence. You have to really think to be able to do that. My method is like buttering toast. Most people start in the middle and leave the edges untouched, bare and dry. I like to butter all around the edges, get the context complete first. Then you notice that the middle, the content, has taken care of itself.

Ayd has a particular talent for reaching out to disengaged students; this is a clear reflection of relentless Solar positivity and an affinity for the unsullied world-view of a child:

When a student is disruptive or bored, my assumption is that they are an unrecognised genius and I proceed on the basis that we simply need to validate the genius within. Remember, everyone thinks they're both an unrecognised genius and an unmitigated failure, at the same time. Everyone thinks that and flips between the two their whole lives. I had one challenging student who handed in her work and it was blank, she had written nothing, so I wrote in her book, "Lisa, you are an enigma wrapped in a mystery hidden in a puzzle. I have a strange feeling that you are brilliant; your talent may not even be in science; it is hidden like an iceberg is mostly hidden. I suspect you are a genius, I have no proof but the thing is, Lisa, I'm invariably right." I wrote half a page of this sort of stuff and when Lisa read it she went very quiet. In the next lesson she was totally different: engaged, making notes and asking questions, because for what was possibly the first time in a long time she was validated. I treat my students as what I hope they would be rather than as a problem (it's called the Pygmalion effect). I assume I have the next John Lennon or Einstein hidden somewhere in my class. It's my job to make sure they know I've clocked them.

Solars have an aversion to being trapped, much like a hummingbird or butterfly, and Ayd has devoted a lot of energy to maintaining his creative freedom and innovative thinking:

I was trapped in a dull job so I started my own design business; then I was trapped in my own business so I became a conference speaker; then I was trapped giving the same presentation, so I became a teacher, because it is an opportunity to constantly create new means of communicating with a demanding and vocal audience; it is a process of continual creativity with instant feedback. I believe I am able to bring dry material to life using metaphor, stories, lateral thinking and surprising connections. I can bring everything I have learned and experienced into the classroom. At an interview the first question I was asked was, "What do you think of the school?" and my reply was, "As above, so below – the signage and outward order is clear and flowing so the school must be run well according to the Hermetic principle." I doubt they had ever had that reply before! I got the job.

One identifier of Solars is their faraway look and the tendency to be 'away with the fairies'.

As a Solar, Ayd loves to embrace paradox and live in a non-literal world. Ask him if he believes in fairies and you'll get a resounding 'yes'. Probe further and you'll get a dissertation on the anthropomorphisation of nature's processes, subatomic forces and mathematical proof of multiple dimensions. His latest book project is called *A Childs Transmogrification of Magic…*

In summary, Ayd is definitely the type of teacher I dearly wish I'd had when I was at school.

Their openness, creativity and fizzing enthusiasm can lead Solars to merrily undertake projects no other type would touch. Most of us have a ready list of reasons not to do something; Solars do not have this list, so they simply forge ahead with boundless energy. They are not moderate in their passions and, while these ingredients often lead them to failures that could have been easily foreseen, every now and then it all comes together. When they are in the right place at the right time with the right energy, they can be remarkably successful, because no other type will take the risks that they blithely take. In many ways, Solars are like the Fool in the pack of tarot cards, stepping off the edge of the cliff into thin air and just assuming that they will be caught, or fly, or somehow or other it will just be fine.

A Solar friend of mine was talking to a theatre director, and hoping for a role in a play. No sooner had she explained to the director that she was a highly trained dancer than she fell down a flight of stairs. She did not get the part.

William Benham:

> *If he relied more on effort and less on brilliancy, he would reach fame more frequently and in greater degree. If he could chain his talents, his brilliancy of mind, body and endowment, down to a definite line of work, he would dominate the world. As it is, he moves among us as a brilliant possibility, a magnificent specimen physically and mentally, a joy, a pleasure, a benefit, but too often through his versatility, a 'Jack-of-all-trades'.*

Patrick is ten years old. He is highly Solar in combination with Mercury-Saturn; this makes him hyperactive, with a strong determination to do things his own way without paying much attention to the potential consequences of his actions. He has the large, bright eyes typical of a Solar, the cheeky, mischievous look of Mercury and the long bones of a Saturn. Here, his parents Joe and Claire, who are both teachers, explain how his way of approaching the world goes way beyond the typical exuberance of a child of his age:

> *Patrick is completely dreamy, with his head in the clouds all the time. He is acutely aware that there is a 'cool' crowd at school but he just doesn't care and is more than happy to be labelled as being outside the cool crowd – he actually loves it! He will go to school wearing odd socks and a bee hat and not care about being ridiculed. His dreamy*

nature can be highly endearing and entertaining and also very frustrating: he recently lost two PE kits in one week. In the actual words of his teacher, "Patrick's ability to lose things and inability to tidy up has become almost legendary."

School day mornings are an ongoing challenge:

He can't find things, even when they are in plain view. Getting ready for school is a daily ordeal, as he can't find his clothes, books, shoes or lunch. Sometimes he just gives up and wears two odd shoes all day. He becomes totally engrossed in comics or screens. When he is in his own world we have to get up close and shout his name to get his attention, at which point he snaps into the present with a startled expression.

I asked about Patrick's imagination:

Whenever we go out he is extremely sociable and talks to everyone he meets without self-consciousness or shyness. He loves comedy and plays the role of class jester. He is quick thinking and verbally inventive, but uses his thinking mostly for fun. If he is not allowed to use his computer he will simply play computer games in his mind. His attention span is short to say the least, and he won't bother to stick two pieces of Lego together or follow instructions if something isn't fun. He spends most of his swimming lessons blowing bubbles. He applies himself best to learning if he sees it as fun.

Joe and Claire were quite relieved to find there was an actual term for Patrick's way of being in the world; they realised he was not wired quite the same as his peers, but they could not put this into words. Now they can: he is Solar.

Words and concepts that inspire Solars include magical, possibilities, exciting, exclusive, entrancing, entitled, gorgeous, rare, sparkling, astral, aura, chakra, intuition, positive, golden, elf, fairy, castle, damsel, knight in shining armour, white horse, treasure chest and spell.

Words that turn off a Solar include paperwork, consequences, effort, results, sweat equity, contract, limitation, ground work, routine, realistic, weighty, nitty-gritty and boundary.

Other types judge Solars as being ditsy, petulant, airy fairy, childish, immature, unrealistic, compulsive, attention seeking and as seeing the world through rose-tinted glasses.

Solars judge other types as being negative, dull, plodding, earthbound, decrepit, limited, crass, narrow minded, blinkered, obtuse spoilsports.

Solars see themselves as light, creative, enthusiastic, positive, gifted, open, playful, other worldly, special, different, imaginative, sensitive, artistic free spirits.

Core attribute

The core attribute of the Solar type is Naivety. This gives Solars a freshness and openness, as if they are experiencing everything for the first time without comparison or negative memories. It is worth hearing how dictionary.com defines the word naive:

1. Having or showing unaffected simplicity of nature or absence of artificiality; unsophisticated; ingenuous.

2 Having or showing a lack of experience, judgment, or information; credulous: She's so naive she believes everything she reads.

3. Having or marked by a simple, unaffectedly direct style reflecting little or no formal training or technique.

Solars' Naivety means that they attempt to navigate through their lives without having solid reference points in place. Their lack of discrimination means they lack a firm sense of what to avoid in the interests of self-preservation. Their journey through life is never dull, but may take them to some unforeseen dark places and genuinely dangerous situations. Naivety is quite charming and endearing to other types, who may even envy this attribute in Solars, but the consequences can be costly. 'Live fast and die young' is a mantra that many Solars have found themselves enacting due to their inability to take care of themselves. Like children, Solars often have a strong sweet tooth and, coupled with their indifference to the nutritional needs of their bodies, this means that if they could they would live on sweets and fizzy drinks.

At the healthy, functional end of the spectrum of naivety, Solars beguile us with their charm and charisma and invite us to lighten up and be more playful. They are able to see possibilities that the rest of us jaded beings overlook or dismiss; with hearts unencumbered by cynicism, they open up delightful and inspiring vistas. When the idealism of a Solar is aligned with their intense and buzzing energy, the creative flow that they bring to the world is always surprising and often exquisite. Their innocent connection to children and animals reminds us that we can be kinder and gentler and their lack of guile is a relief to experience in our frantic world.

William Benham again on Solars:

> *All Apollonians love beauty in dress, home, business surroundings, and every walk in life in which they are found. They enjoy life by the force of their spontaneous natures, and cause those around them to enjoy it. All things beautiful and artistic appeal to them… He fairly sparkles with intuition, and seems to learn without study.*

Solar naivety at its best brings not just a breath of fresh air, but a stream from a more rarefied atmosphere which vivifies the finer instincts and nourishes and purifies the soul.

At the unhealthy, dysfunctional end of the spectrum, the attribute of naivety leaves Solars adrift in a material world for which they are ill-prepared. Finding it difficult to function at the same basic level as other types, Solars flee into their fantasy world where everything is just lovely, they don't have to work or pay rent and they are totally exempt from any limitations. Reality is just too much for them to bear, so they withdraw into their dreams and can easily be exploited by charlatans.

Naivety can create great difficulties in relationships when a Solar refuses to see the negative side of their partner and they can end up being emotionally or even physically abused. Their petulant unwillingness to learn from their prior experiences leaves them wide open to exploitation by unscrupulous people and thereby to financial and physical ruin. Their friends may well tire of seeing them repeat the same mistakes and decide to avoid them, which leaves them further adrift, not knowing who they can trust. The clichéd lonely misunderstood artist starving in a garret while producing beautiful works of art that no one will buy is a Solar lost in naivety. The Flower Power era of the 1960s attracted a lot of Solars to a carefree hedonistic lifestyle with lots of free love and drugs and a great many of them did not survive the experience.

Relationship to rules

Solars have a dualistic relationship to rules. They may well follow rules timidly in a childlike manner, hoping to stay out of trouble and be rewarded for being good, so we often find that they exhibit a quiet unquestioning compliance. Alternatively, Solars may just blithely ignore the rules and assume that they themselves are exempt because of their specialness and they will have little understanding of the potential consequences of breaking the rules. When they do get caught breaking rules and are punished, they have a tantrum, immediately forget the potential learning experience and then do it again, expecting somehow that this time the results will be different. It is not unusual for a Solar to be caught with their hand in the cookie jar, as it were, and to be let off without punishment, because their naivety is seen as so non-threatening and their expression of innocence is so natural and heartfelt.

Social situations

At social events, Solars recognise fellow Solars and will flock together like exotic birds, gasping and twittering and nibbling at canapés and sweets. A group of Solars can create such an atmosphere around them that, to an onlooker, it is as if they are hovering several inches off the ground and radiating stardust. A group of Solars entering a party that is already in full swing will always create a palpable frisson. If a Solar is alone at a social event, they will inevitably attract attention, often from some of the less desirable elements in the room, who will latch onto them and monopolise their attention. Solars find it difficult to gracefully disengage from a persistent hanger-on. It is possible to find events where the majority of those attending are Solars. Here, the energy level will be incredibly high, with plenty of drama, and there will be a tangible brittleness and other-worldly intensity in the atmosphere.

Professional environments

Solars flourish in a working environment where the following factors are present:

- Art
- Creativity
- Style
- Novelty
- Exclusivity
- Constant change
- Drama
- Intrigue
- Glamour.

Solars are drawn to jobs which allow an abundance of creative variety without too much responsibility or mundane routine. They thrive in the rarefied and exotic atmosphere of fine arts and haute couture fashion; it seems that their large eyes give them a strongly visual appreciation of life. We find them flocking to festivals, crystal shops, art 'happenings' and raves.

Solar occupations include greeters, florists, fashion designers, cheerleaders, models, children's book authors and illustrators, ballet dancers, photographers, set designers, or owners of quirky boutiques. Many Solars work as airline hosts or hostesses, which does not promote the groundedness they so often need! They are open to New Age spiritual ideas so we find Solars both working as and also engaging the services of clairvoyants, aura readers, crystal healers, chakra balancers, tarot readers, psychics, channels, mediums, gurus, dowsers, pranic healers, swamis, tantric masters and so on.

I once met a Solar who was a professional aura reader – she would effortlessly and continually see swirls of colour emanating from people as their moods changed and made her living by drawing what she saw and interpreting it. Unfortunately, she kept bumping into furniture and had problems driving, as inanimate objects like furniture or cars did not radiate colours for her and she couldn't see them so clearly!

Nikki is a Solar-Venus-Mercury, with the accent on Solar. Her eyes are widely set and sparkly and she fizzes with energy and positivity. Nikki has carved out her professional niche as an award winning charisma expert – she teaches business leaders to develop more of their innate charisma in order to raise their levels of motivation and engagement. I was intrigued to explore how she manages to persuade business owners to pick up copper dowsing rods and measure peoples 'energy fields' – not typical CEO behaviour:

> We are all energy, at the quantum level we are all packets of pulsating energy which are changing moment by moment. We all perceive other people's energy fields or auras, whether we acknowledge it or not and when our personal energy field is big then we are in alignment with who we really are. I invite people to let go of their conscious mind and tune in to the whispers of their unconscious mind. It involves them having a bit of trust in something that's a bit 'woo'. I personally find it extremely easy to let go of my conscious mind and trust my intuition 100 per cent. In a business environment I have to build a logical frame for people to start thinking about my 'weird stuff'. I'm quite logical myself, but am lead by my emotions and instinct. When I give feedback to people on what I pick up in their aura they are often quite shocked at what I can detect within a few moments of meeting them.

I asked Nikki if her intuition had led her astray in her earlier life (from meeting her I know she has had an extraordinary journey). Her initial response was a gale of raucous laughter:

> I could tell you some great stories! I have taken risks based on something feeling good and being quite spontaneous and in the moment. When I was younger and less able to manage my emotions and take care of myself I did get into a fair bit of trouble. As a teenager I was considered a model child in a model middle-class home and I rebelled and ended up in prison. For most of my life I have felt like a maverick and swum against the tide. In my early life this led me to be quite self-destructive and make poor decisions. I don't follow convention. It has not been an easy ride. When I ignored my inner guidance I had a nervous breakdown. I need to be in a state of flow.

Nikki's combination of Solar-Venus-Mercury is particularly prone to burn out when they are unaligned with their true needs. Through experience, Nikki has skilfully woven together all three elements of her combined type: the caring of Venus which wants to help people; the communication skills of Mercury to get the message across, and the positivity and trust in the invisible realms which is characteristic of emotionally healthy Solar types. She is truly an exemplar of the maxim 'To thine own self be true'.

> *It is as if I have no choice other than to follow what I feel and believe. These days I am much clearer on what I sense and I know what to trust within myself. I had a successful sales business which had gone global, but I sold it to fund my charisma project which is far less lucrative. People thought I was nuts! I see us as a mind, body and spirit and spirit is eternal. My decisions are based on nourishing my spirit and making my soul sing; money is only stuff, and my legacy is much more important than financial success. I measure my life on how many people I can positively impact on my journey – that is real success.*

I could not resist asking Nikki how 'far out' her work gets:

> *I run a regular psychic circle. I conduct paranormal investigations and I totally believe in non-physical entities. To those who think I'm crazy I point out that our unconscious mind is processing millions of pieces of information every second while our conscious mind can only deal with seven at a time. So we cannot perceive reality; everything is filtered through the limited senses and once people are in their heads they shut down access to their sixth sense. We all have a sixth sense and I have learned to tune in to subtle changes in the atmosphere which other people label as paranormal or other-worldly. I believe that if we listened to our hearts then the world would be a better place and when we are in our heads we block off the most important source of information we have. My mission is to help people listen to their hearts as I listen to mine.*

Famous examples: Below are some well-known Solar combined types.

Solar-Mars: Shirley Maclaine, Judy Garland, Brad Pitt, Bjork, Pamela Anderson, Anne Heche, Annie Lennox, Maxine Peake

Solar-Mars-Jovial: Shirley Temple, Britney Spears, Bette Midler, William Blake, Eddie Izzard, Chris Eubank, Ginger Rogers, Van Morrison, Goldie Hawn, Pink

Solar-Jovial: Chris Farley, Divine

Solar-Jovial-Lunar: Benny Hill, Gene Wilder

Solar-Lunar: Twiggy, Pee Wee Herman, Meg Ryan, Buddy Holly, Calista Flockhart, Shelley Duvall (very Solar indeed), Pete Doherty, Benedict Cumberbatch

Solar-Lunar-Venus: Miranda July, Jackie Onassis, Cicely Mary Barker, Chloe Sevigny, Emo Philips, Buster Keaton, Drew Barrymore, Bud Cort, Kate Bush, Antony Hegarty, Felicity Kendal, Lorde, Beatrix Potter

Solar-Venus-Mercury: Russell Brand, Lady Gaga, Marilyn Monroe, Liza Minelli (her character Sally Bowles in Cabaret being an exact portrayal of this combination), Janet Jackson, Elvis Presley, Lisa Marie Presley, Sophie Dahl, Clark Gable, Elizabeth Taylor, Katie Price, Kylie Minogue, Dolly Parton, Harpo Marx, Betty Boop

Solar-Mercury: Julian Clary, Little Richard, Joel Grey, Audrey Hepburn, Latoya Jackson (extremely Solar), Graham Norton, Kenneth Williams, Edith Piaf, Whitney Houston, Dame Margot Fonteyn, Sly Stone

Solar-Mercury-Saturn: Colin Morgan, Uri Geller, Macaulay Caulkin, Enya, David Bowie, Crispin Glover, Rudolph Nureyev, Fred Astaire, Grace Jones

Solar-Saturn: Christopher Walken, Paul Newman, Mathew Modine, Bo Derek, Sidney Poitier, Laurence Olivier, Kate Moss, Lyndsey de Paul, Bambi, Amanda Seyfried, Dreama Walker (extremely Solar and ideally cast as the naive victim in the movie Compliance)

Solar-Saturn-Mars: Nicole Kidman, Tilda Swinton, Princess Diana, Elijah Wood (very Solar, so plays a great Hobbit), Cameron Diaz, Robert Redford, Percy Bysshe Shelley (extremely Solar), Mozart, Bette Davis, Sinead O'Connor, Michelle Pfeiffer, Sharon Tate, Marty Feldman

Solar places and cultures: Iceland has a high number of Solars in residence; the Icelandic government postponed the building of a road so they could move an 'elf castle' rock formation to safety! The Wodaabe of Niger are a Solar-Mercury-Saturn tribe. Places include Glastonbury, Santa Fe and Covent Garden in London.

Solar animals include pink gurnard, hummingbird, butterflies, sea horses, fallow deer and alpaca.

How dreary life would be without Solars to brighten and lighten our view and show us new possibilities. I shall leave the last words to William Benham:

> *There are many people who have much Apollonian quality in them, but pure specimens of this type are rare. The Apollonian leaven that is mixed with humanity does much to brighten life and is a constant benefit, not only to the subjects to themselves, but to all around them who share in and enjoy their cheerful moods and charming manners.*

CHAPTER 9: The Chemistry between types

At a personal level, once we recognise our own type, or combination of types, there is the potential for deep insight and new life choices. We find an increased range of options in our interactions with other people and ways to realign our relationships with ourselves, our self-image, our personal history and expectations. We can stop judging ourselves for having tendencies that we can only change at great cost to our well-being. There are limits to the changes we can make using personal development techniques. We may soften our rough edges, motivate ourselves to pursue material goals and learn to have more compassion for others, but our fundamental hardware will continue to run the show overall.

As an example, I continually meet Lunar people who point to the fact that they deliver public presentations as a way of 'proving' that they are not actually a Lunar type. With a little probing it becomes apparent that they have learned to manage their discomfort in the public eye and feel an internal tightening sensation before stepping on stage. They have trained their software to function in the glare of publicity, while their hardware squirms and sends out alarm signal that they are able to override using a variety of techniques. A prime example of this is Steve Jobs, whose presentations were a much-anticipated and lauded event in the world of technology and who was seen as an accomplished presenter. Behind the scenes he would agonise for weeks about every detail of his speech. Once the presentation was over, he would head directly from the stage to a house rented for his exclusive use and lock the doors.

We can manage our hardware and may even wish we were another type – which is fairly common – but our hardware is unchangeable. Once we accept this, we can make best use of our innate qualities and align ourselves with our natural strengths while addressing the attendant weaknesses. Ultimately, the most value is found in applying this system as a template that can support us in having greater self-acceptance.

I myself am mostly a Mars type, but with enough Jovial to make me well behaved in public. Every now and then my attribute of Destruction will possess me and I will demolish an item of technology that is resisting my attempts to make it do what I want. This is irrational and occasionally costly.

On a good day, I can read the signs of an impending episode and go and chop kindling with an axe instead of stamping on a laser printer. This energy runs through my system like fire and suppression is unhealthy, so I have come to accept it as something fundamental and unchangeable – not unmanageable but unchangeable – and I no longer judge myself for this attribute. This makes it much easier for me to accept, in the words of George Gurdjieff "the unbearable manifestations of others" and drop my agenda of expecting other people to change to suit me. If I can't change an element of myself then neither can they. This awareness has brought a great deal of peace to some potentially-turbulent relationships. When we go beyond the tendency of our differing hardware systems to bump into each other and, instead, see the deeper humanity within, then life is that much richer – as in the Sufi tale of the boat at the beginning of this book.

Here are some useful strategies to avoid unnecessary friction between types, laid out in such a way that, if you know your own type and the type of the person you are communicating with, you can avoid the pitfalls and celebrate the differences. Each type has something to offer every other type, even if the gift is not wrapped in the form we would wish.

Each section here is laid out in the following order:

1. The qualities that you are likely to appreciate about a type

2. The tendencies of that type that's likely to bother you

3. How to get the best from the relationship between your type and the other type.

I'm a Mars: how do I get on with…?

Another Mars

You will know where you are with another Mars. There is no bullshit or prevarication, small print or window dressing. What you see is what you get here. You can crack bawdy jokes together, share war stories and compare scars.

Mars types tend to weigh each other up and engage in a mental test of strength when they first meet and settle down once each has appraised the other. There is, of course, the potential for explosive conflict when two Mars people each think that they are right and wish to apply forceful argument to establish the 'truth' of a situation. At its very worst, the stage is set for escalating physical violence. Once the dust has settled, assuming there are no broken bones or lawsuits pending, then two Mars types can become firm friends after a fair fight.

To get the best from this relationship it is important to be aware of the concept of positioning, so it is useful to find alignment in a common cause or purpose. Failing that, the mention of a common enemy will bring two Mars people together quite rapidly and effectively!

A Jovial

You are going to take things less seriously around a Jovial and also be intrigued by their easy-going attitude around money and success. You will both know how to celebrate together and you can even learn about enjoying life a bit more from a Jovial. You may observe how much a Jovial can achieve through personal warmth and influence as opposed to your own more pushy style.

You are probably peeved at how they can be a pushover and tend to avoid confronting people; you will see them as not robust enough and may even decide to push back at them 'for their own good'. This will usually bruise their feelings and evoke a more passive-aggressive response.

To get the best from this relationship, simply find something that you genuinely appreciate about the Jovial and let them know. They will value your honest approach and you can both quickly develop trust and rapport. You are also more likely to get invited to their fabulous parties.

A Lunar

You can appreciate the calm, straightforward nature of a Lunar and the clarity they embody. You will admire their ability to stay cool and quietly hold their ground in the face of adversity and can come to see the moral courage that a Lunar demonstrates in their quiet resistance to injustice. A superb historical example of this was the partnership of the Lunar Rosa Parks and the Martial Martin Luther King during the civil rights struggle in the US. Rosa Parks quietly and firmly said no to discrimination and Martin Luther King mobilised the more active boycotts and marches.

You are likely to be frustrated by their attention to detail and procedure and fume with impatience at their pace. In your moments of tunnel vision, you will feel that this is a personal insult and deliberate blocking of your wishes. This dynamic has the potential for ongoing torment, where both the Lunar and Mars are convinced they are right and get locked into linear thinking and prolonged sniping. The fact that a Lunar can stay calm under fire may evoke blind rage in a Mars, who wants a loud, clean fight.

Best bet is for you to breathe deeply and calm yourself. Try to adjust to their methodical ways; this can save you tripping up further down the road.

A Venus

You are naturally drawn to Venus people as your opposite on the circle of types and feel soothed and accepted in their presence. This is a person in whose presence you can truly feel safe to relax and be yourself. The Venus type has a lot to teach a Mars about acceptance and softening. In the field of social services you make a powerful partnership in action, with Mars on the front line confronting abusers and Venus healing the victims of abuse.

Their languid passivity may annoy you, as well as their apparent lack of goals or motivation. In a romantic relationship, there is going to be an underlying intensity due to the degree of attraction here. It is important for you to be responsible for managing your own frustration and expectations as it is tempting to rely on the Venus for nurturing. This can lead to deep resentment on both sides, as you feel trapped in needing their attention in order to feel better and the Venus becomes exhausted at being your sole emotional support.

This relationship is likely to feel easy and natural in the professional world, though you will feel the urge to hurry them along now and then. Avoid excess alcohol when around Venus types as this may well trigger your darker urges.

A Mercury

You relish their speed and feistiness and their love of adrenaline. You may even be in awe of the rapidity and flexibility of their thinking. If you step back and watch a Mercury in action, you will soon realise that not only do you not think like them, you actually can't think like them if you try.

This is the relationship which has the potential to cause you the greatest friction. Mercury types bend and break the rules; there can be a wide gap between their words and action, and they usually shrug their shoulders and move on when confronted with this. Your urge to enforce the rules and your version of fairness can cause huge conflict here. In fact, this is the hottest flash point on the circle of types, portrayed in Norse mythology in the ongoing struggles between the Mercurial Loki and the Martial Thor.

The wisest strategy is to recall the flaws in your own character that you have given up trying to rectify and recognise that a Mercury type has a different set of unchangeable traits that happen to severely rub you up the wrong way. By avoiding the urge to put pressure on them, you can make the most of your mutual strengths. No easy task in this dynamic!

A Saturn

You will find support from their sense of overview and direction and value the strong sense of integrity and justice that a Saturn type holds so dear. Their quiet integrity and dedication to improving the lot of humanity is something you admire.

You will be frustrated by what you see as their dithering and hesitancy when you just want to get on with things. For you, the time for deliberation is a short precursor to action; for a Saturn, the deliberation can take much longer than the action, which you will see as them avoiding making a move. There is a potential for a highly fruitful partnership, where the Saturn provides strategic direction and the Mars puts it into action –think managing director and operations director, working in harmony.

To get the best out of this relationship, take a step back and realise that a Saturn can save you from colliding with foreseeable obstacles or from one of your favourite indulgences – the habit of doing something fairly pointless with great enthusiasm. Take a breath or two and calm yourself with the awareness that you can both accomplish more in the long run by taking the sage advice of a Saturn.

I'm a Jovial: how do I get on with...?

Another Jovial

There will be loads of laughs and banter and the potential for a crackling salon atmosphere of wit and learning. You can appreciate someone who shares your love of the finer things and values quality, harmony and discernment. Watching two Jovials together is like observing splendid ripples of intellectual grandeur spread out, blend and magnify each other. Good-natured jousting and warm banter enliven the room at the best double-Jovial gathering.

Conflict arises when you see your own insecurities reflected back to you, leading to a passive-aggressive competition at centre stage. Expect sarcasm, innuendo and much damning with faint praise. You both know each other's weaknesses and are happy to press on the sore spots with a sardonic grin firmly in place.

This relationship flourishes with mutual politeness, respect and a shared focus on the qualities of the other person, coupled with an unspoken agreement to skim over the prickly bits – or at least save them for the next tiff.

A Lunar

You enjoy the quiet decorum that a Lunar brings and the fact that they are not easily impressed. You see their coolness and apparent absence of need for external approval as a strength of character that you secretly wish you could borrow for a while.

This same coolness will of course bother you when a Lunar doesn't laugh loudly at your jokes or hang on every word of your compelling stories. You push them away as a pre-emptive rejection strategy and find them an easy target for your sniffy comments and cutting observations of their lack of sartorial elegance.

To make this one work, you will need take yourself out of centre stage and access your ability to charm and listen. Still waters run deep, and you can enjoy the contrast of your drama with the quiet emotional depth of a Lunar.

Allow them to find their own spot in your professional or social circle instead of trying cast them in a role and you will both be a lot happier.

A Venus

There is no need to impress a Venus – they feel energised by your stories and schemes and are willing to play along in a supporting role. You value their unconditional acceptance and positive regard for you and love the fact that they will happily serve drinks and food at your soirees. A Venus friend is also the likeliest candidate to listen to your tales of woe when you are feeling vulnerable.

When you want a bit of input or vivacity, then the Venus will let you down. You might be disappointed by their deference to the more lively types and get tired of trying to rev them up.

The ideal approach to this relationship is to accept that the Venus is content in their role and just come to terms with the fact that not everyone needs stimulation and attention in the same way that you do. You may even find pleasure in being curious about what makes them tick and be surprised at their observations from the side-lines.

A Mercury

Here is your opposite in the circle of types. You relish their wit and humour and find great satisfaction in having a mind that is expansive enough to keep up with their cerebral twists and turns. You enjoy the arts and culture together and you will definitely want to invite a Mercury or two to your next soiree. You both enjoy the finer things in life, especially if someone else happens to be picking up the tab! The Mercurial Ferdinand Marcos and his Jovial wife Imelda played this one to perfection: he kept the US dollars rolling in and she bought the shoes!

Things get prickly and potentially unpleasant when a Mercury can't resist the urge to tease you and deflate your ego; you may even feel that they can turn your feelings on and off like a tap whenever they want to. They may well exploit your good will and generosity and you may be unsure where you stand with them.

Harmony flows in this relationship when you cast the Mercury as a co-conspirator and playmate, but maintain a little emotional distance. Finding the ideal orbiting distance between the two of you will create sparks and excitement without causing too many emotional bruises.

A Saturn

You share their love of decorum, good manners and consideration for others. You both enjoy a harmonious and respectful environment and, with some patience, you will acquire a taste for the dry and incisive humour of a Saturn. This relationship has the potential to be highly effective in business, where the Saturn provides strategy and the Jovial exercises influence to bring people on board with the programme.

Conflict may arise when you both want to help or coach a third party and each think you know best. You will see the Saturn as, well, too Saturnine and serious, while they will see you as too jovial and frivolous. You may come to resent their ethos of limitation and procedure, seeing this as boring and restrictive.

There is one infallible strategy that will get the best from this relationship and that is for you to ask the Saturn for advice in their area of expertise. It may not be easy for you to swallow your pride and do this, but it will be worth it. It will help you to visualise that the Saturn's territory is vertical and cerebral and let them own that arena, while you occupy the more emotional territory. Mutual respect flourishes when both types feel secure on their own ground.

A Mars

You will appreciate the drive and down-to-earth humour of a Mars and also share their large appetite and exuberance for life's earthy pleasures. You can understand their taste for excess and freely share the Mars love of alcohol.

There could be friction if they are impolite and speak bluntly when you would prefer a little discretion: a Mars is unlikely to flatter you insincerely and you may well find that they bruise your feelings. A Mars may just be too crude for your liking and you will have to resist the urge to scold or correct them as one would an out-of-control child. It is useful to recognise that, on the rare occasions that a Mars compliments you, it will be 100 per cent sincere and not a manipulative strategy. You can come to value the consistency of their honesty – if a Mars is willing to tell you the unpleasant truth, then any pleasantries they offer will also be accurate.

You can easily align with a Mars by sharing tales of your personal struggles to overcome obstacles, as well as having a good moan about a situation or third party. You will find both of these things easy to do and it will get a Mars to feel a sense of kinship in adversity.

I'm a Lunar: how do I get on with…?

Another Lunar

The Lunar is the type most often misunderstood by all the other types; with another Lunar you can relax a bit and not try too hard as you will naturally understand each other. You appreciate the lack of hurry or pressure to interact, while sharing that particular quirky Lunar humour. From your perspective on the circle of types, all the other types are just a bit too loud and pushy. You can enjoy sharing a sense of finding significance and pleasure in detail and even obscure interests.

The possibility of discord arises if your territories overlap in the workplace and the boundaries are unclear. Unexpressed feelings can build distrust and distance and you may find yourself simultaneously drawn to, yet repelled by, a fellow Lunar. Lunars tend to notice what annoys them about other people, so the stage may well be set for low-level simmering antipathy without any overt conflict or arguments.

To find harmony with another Lunar is going to take time. As a client, they are more likely to be talking technical rather than relationship sales. In friendship, you will find the greatest joy in looking at the world from your unique and highly-observant perspective and commenting on the absurdities of others – while carefully avoiding the temptation to turn the same critical spotlight on each other.

A Venus

You are going to feel great relief at the level of acceptance you will feel around a Venus. There will be no need for you to impress, express or even speak when you are with them; they are happy that you have simply shown up! You can be yourself and go at your own pace around a Venus, which will be soothing to you compared to your interactions with the more driven types. It will be easy for you to open up emotionally too, as there is a consistent lack of judgment here.

What will annoy you is the Venus sloppiness – clothes strewn around, dishes in the sink and appliances left unmended. The lack of definition can feel unsettling: it's as if the atmosphere is wavering and there are no clear boundaries, so you may feel emotionally engulfed as if you are in treacle and become sniffy and judgmental towards the Venus type as a defence against this sensation.

Something that can greatly serve this relationship is if you give yourself a secret mission to find out something about the inner world of the Venus – to be intrigued by them. They will be delighted that someone has taken the time to notice them and you will both find a clearer sense of who is who. You are both going to find common ground in two different flavours of common altruism – you want to quietly support people and organisations and to help them find clarity, while the Venus supports more openly and unconditionally. By spending time in the territory of service you can grow to value each other at deeper levels.

A Mercury

There are many qualities to appreciate in a Mercury, just so long as you maintain a little distance. You will enjoy dissecting their labyrinthine humour and their creative thinking in much the same way as a scientist admires the structure of a crystal or chemical compound. You will be able to sit back and let them have the limelight without feeling any pressure to perform yourself. If they strike the right note and can tease you gently, they may even bring you out to share the stage with them and demonstrate your dry and surprising wit.

The potential for irritation here is huge, however. You are going to find that many, if not most, Mercury types get under your skin. The way they sail close to the wind, bend the rules and generally act like spoiled brats will set your teeth on edge – with the added annoyance that, once they sense your reaction, they will just turn up the volume. Your irritation and disapproval will seem to bring them a certain warped pleasure and you just can't think fast enough to trip them up in public. So you fume and seethe and hope to find revenge in an environment where you hold the trump card – which is the realm of procedure. By applying the rules, you can bring the tricks and schemes of a Mercury to a screeching halt whilst pretending that it's not personal.

Finding accord with a Mercury involves surrendering to the fact that they are

THE ART OF READING PEOPLE

just faster than you in word, thought and action. It is no good competing with them and a clear sense of boundaries is essential, so recognise that they are untouchable in their realm and leave them to it. It helps to laugh at their jokes and to see that it is just as difficult for a Mercury to be quiet and follow procedure as it would be for you to belt out operatic arias on a crowded bus!

A Saturn

This is your opposite on the circle of types and opposites really do attract. You respond well to the Saturn sense of order, justice and structure and you have the patience to digest their wisdom and sweeping vision of possibilities. Both of you want things done properly and see the other types as immature and compulsive. In a word, Switzerland – a country which is primarily inhabited by Lunars and Saturns! In personal and professional relationships, you will both find stability and validation in this dynamic, in which there are no big dramas, just a commitment to doing the right thing.

When things get prickly it is usually because, in your view, the Saturn has got too big for their boots and has made decisions without consulting you. Not only that, but they expect you to meekly implement these decisions. You will see the Saturn as domineering, cold and repressive and rebel by digging your heels in. The harder the Saturn pushes and the more eloquently they try to convince you that they know what is best, the more stubbornly you will resist. The Saturn will naturally assume you have failed to see to the obvious benefits of their vision and push harder, and so on.

To find accord in this relationship, it is useful to do some internal accounting: weigh up the overall contributions that a Saturn makes to your personal or professional life against the intense irritation that is evoked by their dominance; take a deep breath and, if they are in credit, give them a little space and yourself a little time and let things settle down. A rapid method of getting a Saturn on your side is to ask for their advice on a problem; this will align you both, as well as making their day!

A Mars

The straightforward determination of a Mars is refreshing and you will find inspiration in their ability to stay focused on a target. When working with a Mars, you are invigorated by their drive.

When this relationship gets out of synch then you are going to find Mars people rude, crude and obnoxious. They will mock your attention to detail as a pointless distraction to the campaign at hand and ruffle your feathers with their offensive jokes. If they realise that this annoys you, they will then tease you for being too politically correct. This relationship has potential for great conflict when both types get stuck in their core attribute and the dynamic is like that of a Mars bulldozer crunching against an enormous rock. The clash between the finance and operations departments in large organisations can last for decades. In personal relationships, the Mars can get infuriated when their attempts to get a Lunar to 'lighten up' are met with stony indifference.

This is another relationship where the best strategy is to find an ideal orbiting distance – close enough that you can both communicate and distant enough to avoid friction. Sometimes it will be worth humouring a Mars by laughing at their jokes and antics in order to have more peace in the long term – the classic 'short-term pain, long-term gain' approach.

A Jovial

The warmth of a Jovial is a handy counterpoint to your coolness. In corporate life, this partnership can prove very fruitful when a Lunar provides technical know-how and a Jovial deals with the interpersonal side of business. A great example is when a Jovial says, 'I will bring my resident genius along' as if it is a unique treat that is reserved for exclusive clients. Both you and the Jovial can then do what you do best. You will enjoy the intelligence of a Jovial and they will like having a quiet audience for their tales. The Jovial will rise to the challenge of bringing you out of your shell when they want a companion.

This relationship does not hold much tension, though you will find the volume of the Jovial voice and the need for attention tiring on occasions and they, in turn, are liable to find you a little dull and uptight. When conflict starts to arise you will tend to separate rather than argue – the Jovial will look for a more suitable audience and you will head for a bit of breathing space or a quiet chat. Generally, you are both content to leave the other alone as you each occupy different social spaces.

You will continue to be intrigued by each other and harmony is fairly easy to achieve here: simply resist the urge to criticise a Jovial, nodding throughout their stories and laughing at the punchlines, and you will get along fine. When a Jovial is having a quiet and reflective time, then there is the chance to deepen the friendship and develop more trust.

I'm a Venus: how do I get on with...?

Another Venus

Laid-back times are afoot here, as you will really know how to relax and simply unwind together. When you are with another Venus there is not the pressure to keep up that you feel with the more active types; you can go at your natural pace without being judged as too slow. With another Venus you will be able to focus the conversation on your partners, family, team or organisation for hours on end, stirring occasionally to make a cup of tea and have another slice of cake. If one or both of you bring a child along, then the picture of Venus heaven is complete as you can fuss over the child and discuss their needs and quirks at length.

The only fly in the ointment is boredom and stagnation, as nothing much is going to happen here. You may get frustrated that the other Venus is not initiating anything and the feeling will be mutual. Two Venus people together can feel like two jellyfish trying to lean on each other and both ending up in a puddle on the floor. At a deeper level, you may see your own self-deprecation reflected back at you and find this disturbing. You may also find yourself in competition with another Venus to take care of a third party.

You are both quite accepting of others, so harmony will be the default position in this relationship. Deeper value for both parties can be found in exploring what the other really finds meaningful and encouraging each other to move towards their desires and goals. It may take a bit of prodding and poking, but you can be a supportive helper to another Venus and, as a side benefit, be reminded of your own goals and dreams.

A Mercury

Well this is fun! With a Mercury around, you can relax and be entertained for hours. You will love their wit and sparkle and the fact that you don't have to do much. The flash and glitter of a Mercury brings a dynamic movement of thought and action. You enjoy their charm and ability to connect people in a light and lively atmosphere. A Mercury is driven to get you activated too, and it is nice to be noticed and included for once. You may even secretly wish that you had a little bit of their razzle dazzle now and then.

What riles you about a Mercury is what you perceive as their self-centredness – even when they are drawing you into the party, it is all about them. You will judge the way they don't appear to care deeply about others and may just use people in a superficial way. A Mercury is prone to seeing a Venus as too vague and passive and will wonder why you can't be more assertive. You will not have the cutting wit of a Mercury at your disposal and you may feel that they are just toying with you, as you are not equipped to defend yourself against their barbed comments. The power you have in this arena is to ignore the Mercury, which drives them crazy; unfortunately, their next move is to make a cutting remark and then flounce off.

This is another relationship where the most effective approach is acceptance of the fact that here we have two types with very different ways of engaging with other people: Venus serves others and Mercury likes others to serve them as an audience. By relaxing judgment, you can allow the Mercury to do their thing, value the excitement and verve that they bring, and let them get on with it. Also, even a Mercury needs a breather now and then and they enjoy unwinding in the Venus atmosphere of acceptance, where they can turn off the performer façade and just be. So just wait for them to come to you.

A Saturn

As a Venus, you will be drawn to the Saturn realm of quiet and self-possession; they don't need that much from you and if you spend enough time in each other's company, they may even become interested in your life. You will sense their respect for personal boundaries and appreciate their patient questioning. Both Saturns and Venus types have strong parental streaks, though these are quite different. Saturn people, whether male or female, effortlessly embody a paternal nature which is upright and cool. Venus people, male or female, embody a maternal nature which is soft, warm and nurturing. In professions which focus on child welfare or development, we see a fruitful collaboration, where Saturn provides safety through structure and guidance while Venus brings caring and support.

Conflict between these types is not dramatic, but it can be slow and corrosive: the Saturn views Venus as being too soft and mushy for their own good or for the welfare of others and Venus people see Saturns as cold and heartless. This can lead to competition over the care and wellbeing of a third party and mutual antipathy, with both Saturn and Venus believing that the other 'just doesn't get it'. This tension can become fixed and habitual, as both types are slow to change.

As a Venus, you can find harmony in this relationship by looking behind the behaviour and seeing the intention: Saturns have an inbuilt sense of serving other people by offering clear and consistent guidance and standards. By seeing that you both want the best for other people, you can make room for differing styles that share the same aim. Your innate compassion can be evoked when you realise that a Saturn is even harder on themselves than they are on other people, and when they need a rest from saving the world, you are the ideal person to connect with.

A Mars

This is your opposite on the circle of types and there is some serious attraction going on here! Mars is a robust, driven and lusty type, highly masculine and full of energy. Venus is soft, succulent and sensual, so you will be drawn to each other at a visceral level. Regardless of gender or sexual orientation, Mars and Venus are magnetically attracted to each other and in mythology Mars and Venus were lovers. Mars finds a foil for their blunt exuberance in the company of a Venus and Venus finds their earthy languid nature invigorated and validated in the company of Mars. 'On screen chemistry' in a movie almost always involves this pair – Jake Gyllenhaal and Heath Ledger in *Brokeback Mountain* is a good example. You will relish the strength, honesty and determination of a Mars and you will both share an earthy sensuality.

The potential for conflict here is huge and can be extreme. You may find being around a Mars exhausting and their possessive demands for your affection can become obsessive in a romantic relationship. Mars can get extremely frustrated because their typical self-reliance is undermined by their dependency on the stress relief they can only find in the company of Venus. At its worst, this dynamic shows up as crimes of passion and physical violence, especially when alcohol adds fuel to an already volatile situation. This is the archetypal 'can't live with them, can't live without them' dysfunctional relationship.

To get the best out of this personal relationship as a Venus, your best tools are a sense of perspective and some clear boundaries – double check your actions and reactions with trusted friends so you do not get swept up in the slipstream of a Mars agenda. Make sure you are not just along for a ride that is steered by the Mars! At the emotional level, Mars is well served by having a variety of outlets for their ongoing frustration. If they repeatedly come to the Venus for help in unwinding, resentment builds on both sides. Make sure the Mars has firewood to chop and other physical activity to let off steam. Plus, avoid excess alcohol at all costs!

A Jovial

You relate to the personal warmth and love of harmony that is natural to a Jovial; they will invite you to their gatherings as a counterpoint to the more rambunctious guests. You enjoy their charm and humour and share their interest in other people and the fact that you both feel more alive around others than when alone. You are content to let them 'hold a room' while you relax into the background and just soak up the positive atmosphere.

Something that will grate on you is what you see as the Jovial neediness for attention and putting themselves centre stage. You may tire of their desire for you to support and validate them, while they quickly lose interest in your situation unless it is an exciting and well-narrated drama. You may secretly envy their confidence in effortlessly engaging people, while maintaining their own high self-regard. There is a low potential for conflict here unless you both compete to play slightly different caretaking roles with a third party – you will want to offer unconditional support, while the Jovial will have an eye on taking credit for having helped someone.

Simply compliment the Jovial and do your own thing. At the very worst, you are going to gently step on each other's toes emotionally from time to time, but this is typically a warm, low-maintenance dynamic in both the personal and professional realms.

A Lunar

You will respect the way that a Lunar leaves people to their own devices without being pushy or intrusive. You may well admire their ability to focus on a task until it is finished and wish you had the same level of perseverance in your own affairs. You share a sense of stillness and patience, and are able to work alongside each other in a calm environment.

What may bother you is that a Lunar gives the impression that they really don't need anything from you and at some level you need to be needed and have an accurate antenna for other people's wants. You may be baffled by what you perceive as their coldness and distance from other people and feel rebuffed in your attempts to reach out and create friendship. The potential for conflict is quite low in this dynamic: a Lunar does not go looking for trouble and generally withdraws from turbulent scenes and you just get along fine with most people and like it that way.

To find satisfaction in this relationship, your best strategy is be aware of your own need to be liked and realise that a Lunar is highly unlikely to spend their time gushing with praise over anyone – it's not personal. Patience and space is the ideal approach and you may well be surprised to find out later (sometimes in a crisis) how deeply your Lunar friend or colleague cares about you – they just don't make big song and dance about it.

I'm a Mercury: how do I get on with…?

Another Mercury

This is a turbo-charged duo! Whether in friendship, business or in love, you will cherish the rapier wit of a fellow Mercury and there is the experience of having found a playmate, someone who can keep up with your rapid twists and turns of thought, word and action. You witness your own abilities mirrored back to you and, like Narcissus, you can fall in love with your own positive reflection of poise, confidence, panache, glitter and dazzling repartee. With another Mercury, you feel like a co-conspirator, ever ready to pull the wool over the eyes of the slumbering public at large and then disappear in a puff of smoke.

Of course, the very same attributes you admire in a fellow Mercury have a tendency to greatly irritate you. You may wince at their superficiality and expediency and find yourself distrusting their motives. How easily the speed of their thinking becomes a potential threat to your well-being! You may find yourself analysing their every move and remark and stepping into a psychological hall of mirrors, with paranoia lurking around the corner. Two Mercury types can find themselves caught up in a psychological Mexican stand-off in which neither party is willing to walk away until they get in the last word or land the final jab.

This relationship flourishes when you, as a Mercury, can ease up on yourself and embrace the dark and light within with less judgement. This is more easily said than done, but stops the process of being triggered by another Mercury, allowing you to have a more light-hearted bond. By acknowledging your shared insecurities, you can drop your facades and simply relax with each other.

A Saturn

You will rise to the challenge of piercing the seriousness of a Saturn with your cheekiness and value the paternal indulgence that they give off when you succeed. Their sense of order and long-term planning intrigue you and get your strategic juices flowing and you may even wish you had a bit of their patience and focus.

On the down side, you will find a Saturn stuffy and ponderous and feel deep frustration at them setting the rules whenever they can. You will feel compelled to provoke and tease a Saturn and there may be some devious game playing, with you outwardly confirming while covertly undermining their authority. Generally, you will find the Saturn aura a little too grey for you to want to spend much time around them.

That said, there is the potential for a fruitful professional relationship here, with the Saturn giving overall structure and long-term planning, while you sniff out short cuts and overlooked opportunities. You can deepen a friendship or collaboration with a Saturn with little effort simply by asking them for advice; if you really want to move things along, actually follow their advice and let them know you have benefitted from it.

A Mars

You can relate to the sheer velocity of a Mars, which is similar to your own speed of operation. Their solidity and bluntness is alien to you and you will want to probe and challenge this aspect to see how deep it runs. Occasionally you will benefit from the directness of a Mars reality check, as you know they talk straight when asked.

The potential for conflict here is massive: this is the dynamic that has become shorthand in movies, culture and literature for an evenly-matched compulsive struggle –see Othello and Iago, bullfights and the movie *Terminator 2*. You find yourself baffled by the literal thinking of Mars and may even see them as unintelligent, dogged and plodding. You can't resist teasing them, tricking them and goading their fearsome temper. You just can't leave a Mars alone and vice versa. You find yourself wanting to either wake them up out of their black-or-white view of the world or make them pay for being so bull headed by tripping them up as they march along.

To get the best out of a relationship with a Mars requires you to step back – a long way back – so that your mischievous urges are not triggered and you can gain a more compassionate perspective. Strategies that help to build trust here are for you to recognise the worth of Mars honesty and loyalty and see this: they play an entirely different role in the cosmic drama from you and they play it really well. As a Mercury, you no doubt will want a short cut to building trust with a Mars and here it is to go to them and acknowledge that you have done something wrong; actually use the word 'wrong' and tell them they were right. This may cause you a feeling of nausea, but it will create a bond and a softening in the Mars. Then stop playing tricks on them.

A Jovial

Here is your opposite on the circle of types and the potential for fun, humour, culture and drama. You just love the warmth, generosity and expansive mind of a Jovial; they can keep up with your rapid repartee and match you joke for joke. You will find yourself playing the role of jester in the Jovial royal court. Like a planet orbiting their sun, you keep just close enough to feel the glow and just far enough away to keep the desire strong. This is the formula for a sparkling friendship or a lucrative commercial venture in the arts.

What drives you crazy about a Jovial is their need for approval and validation, which is similar to your own but not as skilfully hidden. You bridle at the sense that they graciously invite you into their circle and then expect something in return which was not made explicit at the outset. Once a Jovial has annoyed you, it is almost impossible to resist the urge to torment them by pricking their vanity and publicly prodding their insecurities.

To bring harmony to this relationship is ludicrously simple: flatter and compliment them as often as possible. Jovials love this. And never, ever criticise them in public.

A Lunar

The unflappable exterior of a Lunar will spark your interest and issue you with an unspoken challenge to get a reaction from them. If you slow down a bit, you will be in awe of their ability to play the long game and find success through persistent application of their talents in a quiet and determined way. As half of a professional partnership, a Lunar can help to ground your frantic ambitions in reality and provide implementation of your schemes, while also alerting you to potential pitfalls. We encounter a darker version of this working partnership in the small print and clauses of large organisations – these are designed to combine Mercurial trickery in laying linguistic traps with the Lunar craft of making these traps watertight and binding. Who do you think puts those pages and pages of legalese above the innocuous-looking tick box on a website?

When this relationship goes sour its usually because you are intolerant of what you see as the pedantic nit-picky stumbling blocks that a Lunar seems compelled to place in your way. As a Mercury, you prefer to bend the rules and get thing done in a hurry, while Lunars love to keep the rules and make sure you do too, all while going at their own more deliberate pace. The potential for conflict and toxicity is huge here, with each type finding the other bewildering and frustrating.

To find peace and harmony with a Lunar requires that you slow down, step back and take a breath. Realise that it's not personal and if you want to really turn on some effective charm, ask a Lunar to explain the small print so you can comply – or at least pretend to comply. We know what you are like!

A Venus

You will find refuge when you are around a Venus. There's no need to perform or impress them and they are happy to listen to your tales of derring-do for hours. You will be soothed by their languid sensuality and may even find yourself slowing down and relaxing for a while – imagine that! A Venus is the type that is most likely to respond to your borderline hypochondria with a cup of herbal tea and a back rub: this is the goddess of healing and nurturing after all. A Venus is also content to let you take centre stage for as long as you wish without competing in any way.

What will agitate you here is the Venus reluctance to stick up for themselves. You see them as a victim and cannot understand their passivity. You would never let someone get one over on you, yet they simply shrug their shoulders and move on when someone exploits them. You may also rebel against the feeling of being in treacle when around a Venus – they are just too slow and you may miss something if you don't move on.

To get the best from a Venus involves you getting interested in them and prodding and poking them a bit. If you view it as a challenge to get a reaction from them, you may be pleasantly surprised at what is bubbling away inside them. The most expedient way for you to get a Venus onside (which is probably the one you are most interested in) is simply to ask them to do something for you and then thank them with your most dazzling smile – yes, that one.

I'm a Saturn: how do I get on with...?

Another Saturn

You will relate to another Saturn in that you both see the rest of the world as disorganised and chaotic and have some great plans to sort it all out. You recognise the paternal outlook, love of justice and decency and sense of structure and procedure that you hold so dear. You will enjoy the polite conversations with attentive listening that will flow quite naturally here.

The irritation comes when subtle competition arises between two Saturns: each of you will believe that you know slightly more than the other and will want to establish that point in a decorous way, like a cerebral martial arts bout. The subtle sense of superiority will raise internal hackles which it would be poor form to show, so this buried conflict can feel like a slow, menacing masked dance. You may even come to view another Saturn as a cold, emotionally-repressed authority figure, who is looking down their nose at you in a mocking manner.

There is a proven short cut to bridging the gap with a Saturn and that is to ask for their advice, as this signals mutual respect and aligns your efforts in a similar direction. Then you can value the altruistic principles and desire to serve the greater good that a Saturn holds so dear.

A Mars

You may secretly wish that you were as straight talking as a Mars and cheer on their determination to take a stand for truth and honesty. Their courage is inspiring to you and you can indulgently smirk at their bawdy humour – it's as if they are challenging you to loosen up a bit with their boldness. You both share a strong sense of justice and both of you will side with the underdog in a conflict. You admire the drive and energy of a Mars and may even yearn to have a bit of it for yourself. As a professional partnership, this is a blueprint for global domination – the Saturns make the plan and the Mars types get on and do the action bit. This was essentially the structure of the British Empire, with the Saturns in London poring over maps and issuing edicts and the Mars troops on the front lines around the world.

A Mars can, of course, rub you the wrong way, as you see them as crude and undisciplined loose cannons who need to be corrected and refined. Their lack of diplomacy will make you cringe and the defiant rebellion of a Mars can undermine your most intricate and purposeful plans in an instant. You will wonder if every negotiation has to be a raucous argument. To avoid conflict in this relationship, you must suspend judgment on a Mars and accept their rough edges.

The short cut to bonding here is for you to invite a Mars to join you in a challenging task or situation, as this evokes their innate loyalty. Be honest, even when you find it uncomfortable, and reward them promptly when they succeed in a task – and lighten up for God's sake!

A Jovial

Even you can't resist lightening up around a Jovial. You relish their personal warmth and support of others and definitely share their love of diplomacy and harmony. You value their tact and respectful approach and you both have an eye for high-quality artworks and furnishings, although with a slightly different slant on quantity – Jovials do tend to fill a space with stuff more than you would. This partnership works well in schools, with a Saturn principal providing purposeful oversight and Jovial teachers awakening and feeding a love of learning in students. You will both find great pleasure in sharing knowledge and you will hold a healthy respect for the eclectic intellect of a Jovial.

Your area of discord is around coaching or mentoring, as you may compete over who provides the best guidance for a third party. You are prone to judging a Jovial as pompous and egotistical, and question the depth of their knowledge (as opposed to the width of their knowledge and their agility in covering up the gaps with humour and charm). From your perspective, a Jovial may well resemble the 'modern Major General' from Gilbert and Sullivan's *The Pirates of Penzance,* because their hearty self-confidence strikes you as shallow bluster

The simplest means to access the good heartedness of a Jovial is to ask for their help or advice. Long-term harmony is achievable when you tone down your judgment and admit that you secretly wish you had a bit of Jovial panache and warmth now and then. Take a step back and recognise that there is often profound depth to the apparent frivolity of Jovial humour and acknowledge that they can deliver real wisdom more effectively with a laugh than you can with a stern lecture.

A Lunar

This is your opposite on the circle of types and the place where stability and calmness creates long-term relationships in romance, friendship and business. You can savour the patience and eye for detail that a Lunar brings. You both prefer fairly Spartan and austere environments that favour quality and functionality over quantity and show (think Scandinavian interior design). Internally, you are both comfortable with a meditative, cool, cerebral approach to life's deeper questions and avoid being intrusive or brash with others.

What you don't like about Lunar people is their stubborn refusal to see things your way and what you see as their annoying habit of tripping up your grand sweeping visions with petty details and procedural objections. You find it tiresome to have to mentally step down from your lofty perch and explain a triviality to a pedantic Lunar. The stage is set for the slow juggernaut of your plan to grate against the rock of Lunar wilfulness and, once you have ground, neither of you will give way.

To find accord with a Lunar means a recalibration of your thinking from big picture to more immediate and intricate. You can best relate to a Lunar by appealing to your own innate sense of justice and treating their view as being equally as valid as yours. This might not be easy, as you have invested in thinking your view through carefully, but the price is worth paying as there is so much inner richness in the harmony you can find with a Lunar.

A Venus

You will savour the unhurried aura of a Venus and be free to unwind in their company. Your sense of fairness and justice for the underdog will be complemented by the Venus caring for those that society tend to discard, and you enjoy seeing the effects of their loving heart upon those they nurture and support. This relationship works well in charitable institutions, with Saturnine definition of purpose being served by Venus caring for those on the sharp end. On a personal level, you will find solace in simply being around a Venus and not having to say or do much.

On the flip side, the lack of self-definition that you see in a Venus will evoke disapproval. You will want them to be getting on with something purposeful and you may find their apparent lack of goals, not just astonishing, but actually offensive to your more Calvinistic side. What you see as the Venus sloth and indolence, coupled with their amoral sensuality can really get your judgement triggered (think Pacific Islanders and Protestant missionaries). You want them on a straight, narrow path to righteousness and they don't seem to want to go anywhere at all!

To tap into the nourishing depths of this relationship, it is essential for you to own your tendency to be judgmental and then suspend it. If there is friction here, it is generally you that initiates it. Resist the temptation to wag your finger; just accept the Venus as they are. Then you can gently coach them to explore their own wishes and desires and offer your wise counsel – but only if they truly want it.

A Mercury

The dynamism and mental acuity of a Mercury will impress you and draw you in to wanting to understand how someone thinks and acts that quickly. The sheer novelty of Mercurial problem-solving and their flexibility in surmounting obstacles may even evoke some envy, when you find your own approach feeling ponderous or plodding. As a professional relationship, a Saturn and Mercury working together make an innovative can-do team, which works especially well in organisations devoted to social causes.

Your paths are likely to separate and there may be prolonged clashes when it comes to the rules: Saturns like to lay down rules and procedures that are just and fair for all parties, and as long as everyone follows the rules then everything works just fine. The Mercury type feels constrained by rules and many genuinely believe that the rules are there for the slower, less creative types. It is thus unfair that their own grand schemes should be restricted by these petty and unnecessary constraints. So as a Saturn you may come to view a Mercury as perfidious or fall into the trap of believing that they simply need to be reminded of the rules and they will then follow them obediently. The stage is set for ever-increasing numbers of regulations being introduced, which simply provide an abundance of loopholes to a Mercury. A clear example is in taxation systems, where dozens of new rules are unveiled and immediately a new Mercurial niche industry springs up, ready to charge people hefty sums to exploit the latest opportunities, a cycle that repeats ad nauseam.

The best way to collaborate with a Mercury is to just give up on trying to figure out the twists and turns of their thinking and allow them to own that territory. Find ways to harness their talents and creativity where the benefit to them is overt from the start, then just relax and enjoy the show.

CHAPTER 10: Frequently Asked Questions

In presenting Reading People to a range of audiences worldwide I am often asked variations around same general cluster of questions that I will address below. If you have a novel question about this book, please feel free to email me at john@readingpeople.biz.

Here are the questions that typically spring to the mind of most listeners or readers:

Q1. Don't you need to test people and not simply look at them?

A1. The idea that what is visible on the outside of us is connected to the inside is somehow unacceptable to some people when they hear it placed in this framework. This objection often comes from those who administer psychometric tests and it goes like this:

I can readily accept there are different types of people which we can recognise but it requires questionnaires to be filled in and scored.

This speaks of the difference between software and hardware mentioned earlier. One's type is the hardware, the vehicle one is born into. The results of one's psychometric test addresses, often with great accuracy, one's software, and sometimes the interaction between hardware and software. Nature and nurture are other terms for this. One's planetary type is purely nature; one's psychometric profile is, broadly speaking, a combination of nature and nurture. Under sufficient duress, one's core attribute, rooted in nature, will emerge as a loud and clear indicator of one's type!

Q2. I can connect some of the types in your system with some of the types in my own system, but not exactly. How can I make them fit better?

A2. You can't, so don't bother. This is a trap which we can easily fall into when we hear new information: a part of us rushes to place it in a familiar mental location so we feel less anxious. This system stands alone; it is focused almost entirely on the hardware of types and is best kept separate from other systems. The parable of 'new wine into old bottles' speaks to this common response to novel ideas.

Q3. Isn't this system negative and deterministic? It's like you are condemned to be a certain type with limited options.

A3. This question stems from the fear that one's type is a lifelong prison from which it is impossible to escape.

The objection is often raised by certain New Age type people (some of whom are found in the chapter called Solar), who tend to believe that people can easily and positively change and develop with little effort beyond a passing desire to be a better person. They often find it hard to accept that some parts of us are fundamental and in many respects the only change we can make is to change our relationship to our mechanistic patterns. Sometimes this objection is also expressed by coaches who successfully assist people in making changes in their lives. Again, according to this system, that change is a change in software; it may be a radical, deep, positive and lasting change, but the fundamental vehicle housing the software remains the same.

Our friend William G Benham, had this to say:

Thus it will seem that there is no greater truth than that we are indeed free agents, planned for a prearranged destiny, but always able to change if we determinedly desire to do so. There is then, no such thing as absolute fatalism, even though we have so strong an indication in that direction from the seven types.

We have, of course, strayed into the ever-unfolding debate over the relative influences of nature and nurture upon our personalities. This system focuses almost exclusively on nature/hardware. I have observed that truly effective change involves recognising and aligning parts of one's software with healthy elements of the core attribute of the individual's type. Attempts to graft non-aligned behaviour onto the core attribute are short lived; it is like watching an organ recipient reject a new organ from an unsuitable donor. It is my repeated observation that under stressful conditions hardware triumphs over software every time. I have personally found knowledge of this system to be tremendously liberating in recognising the difference between the parts of myself I have control over and those parts I do not control.

Reinhold Niebuhr's 'Serenity Prayer', adopted by the 12 step movement, says this rather eloquently:

God grant me the serenity to accept the things I cannot change
The courage to change the things I can
And the wisdom to know the difference.

Q4. Doesn't this system just pigeonhole people?

A4. At a superficial level, this one could hold water, as we are seeking to observe individuals and thereby determine their type and core attribute, so deeper enquiry is worthwhile.

True story: I was asked the following question point blank by a Saturnine senior detective while presenting this system to a roomful of high ranking officers within a large police force: "Aren't you just putting people in boxes here?"

One of the characteristics of my Mars type is a habit called 'mechanical honesty', which is a compulsion to tell the absolute truth when perhaps a little tact would be more appropriate. I was acutely aware that this was a hot topic, as this particular organisation had recently invested heavily in diversity training. Nonetheless I replied with typical candour: "Yes it is, I do it all the time."

This was a memorable moment, marked by an audible intake of breath throughout the room, especially as I had no idea what to say next! So I listened as my seemingly-disembodied mouth and larynx formed the following words: "The reason I put people in boxes is so that I can stop my box from banging into someone else's box and I can then more readily engage with the person inside."

There followed much nodding of heads in the room and a palpable feeling of rapport and understanding. By expressing a healthy aspect of my core attribute (blunt honesty) in response to the very different attribute of the questioner (judgement), we were now engaged in a productive and straightforward discussion. We humans are always automatically judging and assessing other people. By using this system as a way to see the other person's box, while seeing something of our own box, we can have deeper and more open conversations. If we can understand why someone rubs us up the wrong way and recognise their actions as an unchangeable manifestation of their type, plus see our reaction as an automatic manifestation of our particular type, then it is easier to take things less personally.

The heartfelt purpose behind applying this knowledge is that it transforms our relationships as we move from judging to assessing people, to acceptance of them as they are, to compassion and true collaboration. This process can happen within oneself and in relationship to others and is one of the main purposes of this book.

Q5. Could this system be seen as racist?

A5. As discussed in an earlier chapter, this is obviously a highly-charged subject, given the discomfort around the idea of observing physical characteristics, which naturally differ between different races. Let us take a global perspective: each of the six types naturally flourishes in a different environment. So certain types would predominate in specific areas of the planet. Taking motor vehicles as an analogy, Land Rovers are well equipped for harsh off-road conditions but, in contrast with MGs, they are not too nimble at quickly zipping along narrow winding lanes. An aspect of the bigger picture is that there are disproportionate numbers of certain types within races. If this were not the case then within each country, continent or culture exactly one sixth of the population would consist of each of the six types. If this concept raises the spectre of racism, here's how dictionary.com defines racism:

A belief or doctrine that inherent differences among the various human races determine cultural or individual achievement, usually involving the idea that one's own race is superior and has the right to rule others.

I was raised in the UK and the mindset of this society, as well as many others, has changed during my lifetime. In my childhood casual racism was so inherent that it was widely seen as an amusing and acceptable part of mainstream television entertainment. Today, the vast majority of people utterly reject such a notion and we cringe when watching 1970s shows such as *Love Thy Neighbour*. We have progressed to the point where racial prejudice is seen as abnormal and safeguards against discrimination are embedded in civil and employment law.

While the equality of human beings is almost universally accepted as evident, it is impossible to pretend that we are all exactly the same, as some of the more extreme proponents of political correctness would have us do. In this system, recognising and celebrating the differences between races and cultures acts as a deeper and more potent antidote to racial prejudice than legal proscription. By examining human culture through the lens of type, we can gain deeper understanding and appreciation for people whose genetic inheritance is distinct from ours.

So we will be grasping the nettle and exploring 'inherent differences among the various human races' in order to deeply undermine racism. Using this template, we will clearly see that much racist propaganda, from the crudest to the most subtle and insidious, relies on exploiting the unconscious tensions that inherently exist between types. A basic tenet of this system is that no type is any better than any other, so every organisation, nation or business needs the talents of each type in order to flourish and no type can fulfil the natural role of another as effortlessly and elegantly as the appropriate type. By seeing the numerical predominance of a specific type within a specific country, we come to see how the culture of that country reflects the core attribute of that type. We clearly see how this connects to the clichés and stereotypes with which other types label that country. This awareness instantly unravels the dynamic as simply one core attribute fixating on a small slice of the unhealthy elements of another core attribute. The effects of this awakening process can be dramatic and irrevocable. One cannot comfortably return to a state of unawareness and prejudice.

True story: While travelling in West Africa I went to the beach in Limbe, Cameroon for a swim. The local people were astonished that I could simply lie on my back and float in the sea. They tried to copy me and I did my best to help, but they were unable to do this. If they lay horizontally on their backs next to me, my face would be above the surface and theirs would not. Male or female, adult or child, it made no difference; the composition of their bodies was not the same as the composition of my body. We were different. We recognised this difference and had great fun celebrating it, and as far as I know at no point did either party believe 'that one's own race is superior and has the right to rule others'.

It is worth quoting again from William G Benham's Book of Palmistry:

The ancient theory of the seven distinct types of people begins with the idea that the human race was undoubtedly constructed by its Creator under a definite plan. There was no hit-or-miss in shaping and putting together the inhabitants of this globe… Seven distinct types of people were first created. Each of these types represented certain strong qualities, certain strong aptitudes, certain virtues and certain faults, as well as peculiarities of health and character. The reason for the adoption of this plan was that a combination of the qualities represented in these seven types was absolutely necessary to the harmonious operation of the universe. If all humanity was of one type, progress would be stopped, and diversity of talent and thought, with its various methods of expression and operation, would not be present with us today. Take out of existence any one of these types, and it would be like removing one wheel in a watch, the movement would stop. Each type was thus created for a specific sphere in life, and represents some element indispensable to the harmonious operation of the world as a whole.

Q6. This stuff is fascinating, I want to tell everyone, how can I do that?

A6. Good luck! This is not an easy concept to communicate. Many delegates have reported that their excited delivery of the key points of this system to a friend or colleague has been met with bewilderment and even hostility. It is best to start gently and see if there is even any interest in the topic in the first place. Prepare to answer most of the preceding questions. It may be best to keep it to yourself for a while.

Q7. How can I apply this system in my life?

A7. Observe, observe, observe. When you are travelling and there are people passing by, notice the obvious examples of types. Notice which types are in couples. Observe groups of friends. Notice your colleagues and family members. Resist the urge to advise people on how they can 'improve' or change unless they ask you. Above all, observe yourself as if you are an interesting stranger. See how your core attribute runs through your life; notice how you are when you 'lose it' and avoid trying to judge or change yourself. Don't take this too seriously and enjoy the drama between different types as if it is a movie you are watching. Notice characters in movies and how they match their type.

Q8. How can I change my type?

A8. You can't. Focus on the qualities inherent in your type and see the strength of your core attribute when you are 'in flow'. Don't judge yourself when you 'lose it'; it is simply your attribute taking temporary control of your vehicle. See the funny side of it all. Enjoy the ride.

If you have more questions, then please ask me john@readingpeople.biz.

CHAPTER 11: Reports from Early Adopters

Here are a few interviews with people from varying backgrounds who have been successfully applying the knowledge of Reading People in their daily lives for several years. The learning process continues to unfold with time and awareness and the experiences of other people provide useful reference points should you decide to embark on your own journey of discovery.

Phil is the executive director of the UK division of a mobile phone company. He has been using the Reading People information consistently and effectively for more than five years. He is a Lunar-Venus type, with a steady demeanour and a caring and inclusive approach which his team greatly appreciates. Here he is on the effect the system had upon him:

> *I didn't realise at first how much impact it had. I like to be able to categorise and this gave me a process for dealing with people that I never had before. I'm quite rational and fact based and am much more IQ than EQ based. This gave me a template that I can apply to human interactions. I was out to dinner with our CEO, who is a 'nailed on' Saturn; the rest of the board were all Saturn types except for one Mercury type. At the end of the meal, the Mercurial fellow asked me if I was OK because I'd been so quiet. I explained that in a situation like that I'm comfortable to just let things unfold. Since I first recognised my Lunar tendencies in a social situation I don't try to be someone I'm not. I also know that I am far more effective one-on-one with these people, so I'm content to just wait.*

Phil has the typical Lunar approach to networking:

> *I would much rather have one meaningful conversation than lots of superficial ones; I go for quality over quantity. I let the Mercuries run around the room collecting fistfuls of business cards while I enjoy myself having a nice relaxed chat.*

On his fellow Lunars:

> *I frequently deal with a Jovial-Lunar who can be just as stubborn as I can, so I negotiate carefully with him to avoid the two of us getting entrenched in our positions. I know I can be amazingly stubborn over tiny things and I adjust myself to avoid evoking this reaction in other*

Lunars. Prior to having the Reading People knowledge I would have complete stand offs with people to where I could not even bear to open an email from them! I have learned to be more flexible and have a personal conversation rather than getting stuck in a negative pattern.

Phil on Mercuries:

When I first saw the description of the Mercury type I knew someone who fitted the bill exactly. It sounded like you were describing every aspect of our sales director – his dress, actions, thinking and even speech patterns. I realise how Mercuries need a certain style of reassurance for us to collaborate; I need to remind them and be patient and consistent. We are wired very differently; they aren't acting the way they do purely to annoy me – it's just the way they roll.

David is the Global Human Resources Information System Manager of a data collection organisation and has been using the insights he gained from Reading People in his training role. David is Saturn-Mars with a strong emphasis on Mars, ex-military, with the no-nonsense bearing of a soldier and a highly-principled approach to his projects. With a solid background in psychometrics he approached this material in reverse, as it were:

I am used to applying methods which have solid data behind them so came to this system with a rather large dose of scepticism to say the least. I'd say I was at an 8 on a 1 to 10 scale of scepticism, but I was willing to give it a go on my own terms. I was relieved that none of this was to be taken on trust but to be verified by our own observations. So I essentially approached the material from the other end of the spectrum. I observed behaviour first and only then looked at the physical characteristics to see if they matched up. It may sound odd, but instead of observing how people looked I watched what they did and only then considered their type. I did see more and more correlations – even though part of me didn't want to!

I asked David if there was a turning point in his experience:

I had a meeting with a chap called Patrick and although he was actually asking me for a favour he called me into his office as if he was a headmaster and I was a pupil who was in trouble. As soon as I walked in I thought "He's definitely a Saturn". His language was focussed on how he knew what was best for the department and how he could see the road ahead. When Patrick stood up and towered over me his type was confirmed. His managers were reluctant to speak in his presence and the only way I could influence him was to demonstrate my credibility by backing up my position with solid examples. We were able to form an effective working relationship which had parity, rather than him simply giving me orders. Recognising Patrick's type meant that I knew what he needed to hear to respect me.

David told me of his experience with a very different type – in the one dynamic that has the potential for the most misunderstanding and distrust of all the relationships:

I have worked on a project for over a year with a total Mercury called Nate; he has the smile, charm and charisma down pat. As a 90 per cent Mars I know I can have serious friction with a Mercury and my strategy was to find common ground in the passion that we both have for the project. Nate has since moved on within the company and has opened numerous opportunities for me. He really enjoys networking on my behalf because he knows he can trust me to do the job right. This is a mutually beneficial partnership which could have gone in another direction entirely without awareness of our respective types. It is easy to find ways to disagree with someone but what I take from Reading People is that it is my responsibility to make a relationship work – so I just get on with it.

I asked David if he'd been aware of dropping the ball and falling into a conflict of types:

Yes, just a few days ago in fact. I was giving a presentation. I was tired and a delegate asked a question which I assumed was their way of looking good in front of the group. In my irritation I got pretty Mars and just shut down the dialogue and moved on. Immediately I realised I had been unprofessional and the delegate in question was a Jovial. My Destruction had collided with her Vanity and no doubt there will be repercussions. When I make a misstep in a relationship the resulting fallout can generally be plotted (in hindsight) as a reaction of types. Whoops!

David had seen the effects of the Reading People material on his team over an 18-month project:

> *The language of types has stayed with them and entered our culture. The Mars and Mercury tension in the team is continuing but neither side can pretend to be unaware of their part in the drama!*

He ended our conversation with a suitably Mars metaphor:

> *Knowing about types is like seeing where the mines are in a minefield and having more choice about whether to step on them or not.*

Josie is the art psychotherapist who we met in the chapter on Venus. She has used the insights she has gained from Reading People in her professional life:

> *For a long time I did not understand why my boss was not very friendly towards me: she would pick up on little things that I had done and from my perspective make them into bigger issues. For example, she would check my emails for punctuation, which I thought was irrelevant to the core message. However, once I realised that she is a Lunar type I understood her viewpoint. I became more understanding and took her actions less personally. As a Venus type I'm pretty laid back about details, but I can see how she finds details important and especially when communicating with people in the legal profession.*

The above anecdote is a great example of how different types approach similar roles; as a Venus type, Josie just wants to get on with helping her clients and her boss wants to make sure the commas are in place on an email!

> *My manager is a Mars and she wants immediate answers; she seems like a bulldog to me. My boss wants things done properly and my manager wants things done quickly. If I didn't know their types this would create a lot of stress. I now let her impatience wash over me and don't react to every moment of urgency. I feel I have secret knowledge which makes interacting with my colleagues much easier. Sometimes I forget I have this tool and I have to take a breath and remember the dynamics of the type I am dealing with; then things run more smoothly.*

I asked Josie how her awareness of her own type has changed her own life experience:

I'm actually more relaxed about my own relaxedness. I let myself unwind and do things at my own pace rather than be hurried by other people. I'm much better at seeing other people's types and characteristics than seeing my own. [This is of course a classic Venus trait!] People say I'm quite calm and easy to be around so I can recognise that within myself. [When this is pointed out by other people – another Venus trait.]

Josie works with young people and uses Reading People with her clients:

I worked with a six-year-old who rampaged around the room, grabbing the art materials, asking questions and constantly moving. After he left our first session I pondered how best to engage with him in subsequent sessions. It was clear that he was a Mars type and that he needed hands-on activities and consistent messages on what was OK and not OK. It took me a lot of effort to establish clear boundaries, as that goes against the grain for a Venus – I made symbols that said "no hitting" "no throwing things" etc. Once this was in place and understood, he was fine and our work was productive. As a Mars he needed a consistent and fair structure.

One girl would constantly make conditional deals with me and tell me things which were untrue in a convincing manner. She was cheeky and funny and for a five-year-old she was remarkably manipulative. It was obvious that she was Mercury type. Once I knew her type I knew I had to refine the balance of power, otherwise she would be in charge of every session. Every step in our process became a negotiation: if I asked her which of two materials she wanted to use she would inevitably want both! She continually probed for loopholes, exemptions and ways to bend the rules. At the end of one session she asked if she could follow me down the stairs and when I was halfway down she ran back into the room. In recognising her behaviours as manifestations of her type, I was able to accept and play along with them rather than waste time and energy trying to control her creativity. So with two different children I took two very different approaches: consistent rule reinforcement with the Mars boy and a much more flexible strategy with the Mercurial girl. If I'd didn't have the knowledge of types and had done it the other way round it would have guaranteed disaster in both cases.

Will is the CEO of two companies, one makes graphic displays and the other is a global distribution company supplying cooling technology for clothing throughout Europe, Australia and the Middle East. He is close to being a pure Mercury type, with dark eyes and an impish grin. Will has continually applied the Reading People methodology and the language is now second nature to him since first being exposed to it in a half-day training session:

During the first session I was making notes about my head of accounts. We had a terrible relationship at the time. He is clearly a Lunar type and our speed of operation and need for detail are poles apart. I needed instant answers that are light without all the detail he felt was required. He needed time to process the information at depth before he could give me an answer. Once I recognised our relative types I changed my approach and would intentionally give him a day to reply. This transformed our relationship. I realised that he couldn't change any more than I can and we get on far better now. Not only that but I can value the answers he gives me as having been thought through in depth.

I now use the Reading People material daily. My colleagues invite me to help resolve conflicts in the workplace. I usually find that misunderstanding is not based on facts but on personality, so I do my best to look at conflict through the eyes of the other party by recognising their type. So the way I deal with, for example, a dogged Mars type is to go hard up against them to win their respect. When I'm dealing with a Saturn I will appear to bow to their superior knowledge in order to get the result I desire – I am a Mercury after all! – knowing I will never completely win the day with them.

Will has successfully used the techniques in his personal life also:

I'm not a typical school gate father but I went into my daughter's school to smooth over a particular situation with one teacher my daughter was not getting along with. It was immediately obvious that the teacher was a Jovial so I simply told her what a brilliant teacher she was; I basically pampered her and everything was fine with my daughter after that. This was a sticky situation that was quickly and easily resolved. My friends always ask for my insights into their relationships and I'm able to help them by knowing the types of the players involved.

It is refreshing to hear how Will uses his own Mercurial perceptiveness and flexibility to build his businesses; he truly is embracing the qualities of the god of commerce, travel and communication:

I use Reading People to align myself with clients and colleagues on a basis of friendship and respect. In both companies I have pioneered the concept of customer intimacy and use my understanding of types and their interactions to build and maintain this level of trust. One of our areas of rapid growth is the Middle-East and I found it very easy to get past the cultural smokescreen and engage at a deeper level. It seemed to me the Middle-Eastern way of doing business was to project a Mars image which was actually covering up a Venus-Mercury way of doing things. By reading the actual type I could cut to the chase – once I had slipped past their Mercurial defensiveness! I find that in Australia and China the cultural smokescreen is taken away more quickly that in the Middle-East. This information has changed everything around me in my business and personal life.

Russ is the Managing Director of a high-end meat supplier which counts HM the Queen as a patron. Like Will (above) he is almost 100 per cent Mercurial, with an endearing cheeky grin, rapid fire speech and a youthful countenance.

I recognise other Mercuries very easily – when I meet one at a party I just know there's going to be trouble; it's as if we are children of the Devil and are compelled to lead people into mischief! In fact I recently ended a long-term friendship with a Mercury friend because we would just set each other off in the worst way. I used to judge myself because of my capability to manipulate people and situations. I always have an agenda running and I'm unable to stop this reflex. What I can do is use this ability for positive purposes. At a basic level, I can persuade people to get involved in a trip or event and at a personal level I inspire people to face their fears and make better choices for themselves. This is also useful in teaching people. I'm acutely aware of how powerful the Mercurial influence can be over other people's option; it's as if I can reframe their view of themselves and situations without them realising how much I'm steering them.

This facility to alter other people's perception is one of the reasons why so many Mercury types are drawn to practice Neuro-Linguistic Programming, the arch-Mercurial Tony Robbins being the ultimate example, and indeed role model, of many of these practitioners.

Russ finds the knowledge of types to be useful in his family-run business:

My sister and father are both Mars types; in fact my sister looks like she could be on a chariot with her blonde hair flying as she goes to war! My father has always been combative. My Mercury skills don't work on them – I just can't bring them round to my point of view; they are too stubborn. At least now I know why, so I don't take it personally and I waste less time banging my head against a wall. I deal with a lot of chefs and the majority of them are Mars; my strategy with them is to get up and leave when they sit there with their arms folded. This generally brings them around and softens their position; they will get up and come after me and promise to be more open. It's as if they are shocked into seeing that they are being unfair.

Self-acceptance has been one major benefit of Russ recognising his type:

I used to give myself a really hard time for not being as organised as I thought I should be. Now I see that I'm fundamentally not wired that way I can relax and just be myself.

Chapter 12: In Conclusion

This information has a deep and lasting impact on many people. It can get under one's skin and you may start to see types everywhere you look. Airports and train stations become way more interesting as you can observe types passing by and acting according to type. At first you will only be able to spot really obvious examples of types, but with practice and patience your palette will widen and you will be able to place people quite accurately on the circle of types. You may be able to predict the behaviour of someone you have just met and gain deeper understanding for the foibles and quirks of those close to you. You may that find your view of personal and professional relationships changes dramatically.

It may well follow that you find yourself compelled to tell people about this system and 'convert' them. Chances are they will think you are a little unhinged and will not be as receptive as you had hoped. If you observe their resistance, you will notice that the more you push, the more they will resist, using their core attribute. If you observe your frustration at this point you will notice that you are also reacting from your core attribute. It is quite an experience to see these dynamics and be unable to change anything simply by imparting information. In the words of George Gurdjieff, "Trying to change one's chief feature [core attribute] is like trying to lift a plank that you are standing on."

This discomfort is the price of admission. There is no free lunch and the process of deeper learning is filled with confusion and the frustration of seeing something and not being able to fix it. So take a breath and relax, for 'twas ever thus'. Notice that you are noticing your vehicle, your hardware, in action in all of its incompetence and magnificence. Notice that the part of you that is noticing is a little bit removed from this drama. That part may be the more interesting element; it may have a flavour of being, as the Sufis would say 'In the world yet not of it'. We have been focused throughout this book on the vehicle that is the human body and attempting to define different makes and models of vehicle as a means to promote more harmonious relationships.

It is rather easy to forget that you are not your vehicle.

Enjoy the ride.

References

BENHAM, Wm. G. The Benham Book of Palmistry - A practical treatise on the laws of scientific hand reading. Newcastle Publishing Co., Inc.: 1988

BERMAN, Louis. The Glands Regulating Personality - A study of the glands of internal secretion in relation to the types of human nature. Columbia: Dodo Press, 1922

CARTLEDGE, Tony. Planetary Types. Dublin, Ireland: Bardic Press: 2009

COLLIN, Rodney. The Theory of Celestial Influence. Boulder, Colorado: Shambhala Publications, Inc.:1984

EASLEY, Thomas M. On the Elephant's Knee. South Lake Tahoe, CA: Triple "e" Productions: 1998

FRIEDLANDER, Joel. Body Types - The Enneagram of Essence Types. Yorktown, NY: Joel Friedlander, publisher: 1986

ZANNOS, Susan. Human types essence and the enneagram. York Beach, ME: Samuel Weiser, Inc.: 1997

Illustrations

The Planets represented as planetary deities
Collaert, Jan the Younger (c1561-c1620) after Straet, Jan van der (Giovanni Stradano, Johannes Stradanus) (1523-1605)
New Hollstein Collaert 6, p. 30, H. 1306.I; New Hollstein Stradanus 3, p. 94, H. 390.I
Courtesy of The Warburg Institute's Iconographic Library

Mars
Collaert, Jan the Younger (c1561-c1620) after Straet, Jan van der (Giovanni Stradano, Johannes Stradanus) (1523-1605)
Courtesy of The Warburg Institute's Iconographic Library

Jupiter
Collaert, Jan the Younger (c1561-c1620) after Straet, Jan van der (Giovanni Stradano, Johannes Stradanus) (1523-1605)
New Hollstein Collaert 6, p. 30, H. 1308.I; New Hollstein Stradanus 3, p. 94, H. 392.I
Courtesy of The Warburg Institute's Iconographic Library

Diana Luna
Collaert, Jan the Younger (c1561-c1620) after Straet, Jan van der (Giovanni Stradano, Johannes Stradanus) (1523-1605)
New Hollstein Collaert 6, p. 32, H. 1312.I; New Hollstein Stradanus 3, p. 95, H. 397.I
Courtesy of The Warburg Institute's Iconographic Library

Venus
Collaert, Jan the Younger (c1561-c1620) after Straet, Jan van der (Giovanni Stradano, Johannes Stradanus) (1523-1605)
New Hollstein Collaert 6, p. 31, H. 1311.I; New Hollstein Stradanus 3, p. 95, H. 395.I
Courtesy of The Warburg Institute's Iconographic Library

Mercury
Collaert, Jan the Younger (c1561-c1620) after Straet, Jan van der (Giovanni Stradano, Johannes Stradanus) (1523-1605)
New Hollstein Collaert 6, p. 32, H. 1312.I; New Hollstein Stradanus 3, p. 96, H. 396.I
Courtesy of The Warburg Institute's Iconographic Library

Saturn
Collaert, Jan the Younger (c1561-c1620) after Straet, Jan van der (Giovanni Stradano, Johannes Stradanus) (1523-1605)
New Hollstein Collaert 6, p. 30, H. 1307.I; New Hollstein Stradanus 3, p. 94, H. 391.I
Courtesy of The Warburg Institute's Iconographic Library

Apollo
Collaert, Jan the Younger (c1561-c1620) after Straet, Jan van der (Giovanni Stradano, Johannes Stradanus) (1523-1605)
New Hollstein Collaert 6, p. 31, H. 1310.II; New Hollstein Stradanus 3, p. 95 H. 394.II
Courtesy of The Warburg Institute's Iconographic Library

With special thanks to Berthold Kress at The Warburg Institute for his gracious assistance.

To find out more and see more examples of relevant iconography visit www.readingpeople.biz